914

D1393855

This

THE BORDER COUNTIES

being the fourth volume in the series

THE QUEEN'S SCOTLAND

Edited by **Theo Lang**

Nearly 100 years have passed since any full-scale attempt was made to describe the whole of Scotland in one comprehensive series of books. THE QUEEN'S SCOTLAND—entirely new and thoroughly up-to-date—is triumphantly succeeding in that task.

THE QUEEN'S SCOTLAND collects all the pictures and all the stories of notable scenes and famous people of Scotland into a *complete library*. There is no other modern work comparable with it.

Every town and village, every loch and every glen has been visited in the preparation of this vast survey of the northern kingdom. This volume, THE BORDER COUNTIES, is the fourth in the series, and its publication completes THE QUEEN'S SCOTLAND story of the southern half of Scotland.

THE QUEEN'S SCOTLAND

The four volumes now published are:

EDINBURGH AND THE LOTHIANS

"There has never been in this century a work which deals so faithfully and excitingly with Scotland's capital." That was the greeting given to this book by one of Scotland's most eminent historians. (Incidentally the book is one of the only two modern books recommended every year for visitors to the Edinburgh International Festival.)

The Edinburgh section of this volume is indeed unsurpassed, and the book includes also a comprehensive description of the three Lothian counties—Midlothian, West Lothian and East Lothian. There are stories and pictures of such famous towns as Linlithgow, Dunbar and Haddington, and of all the villages and castles and places of interest along the shores of the Firth of Forth and inland to the Borders.

GLASGOW, KYLE AND GALLOWAY

This volume, a major triumph in the great series, is particularly outstanding for its courageous treatment of Glasgow. Scots at home and overseas have hailed Theo Lang's inspired approach to a city too often and quite unfairly condemned as ugly. His brilliantly readable "Glasgow" reveals the dynamic nature of the city and uncovers its latent beauties and fascinating history. The book also includes the whole south-west of Scotland, from Glasgow to the Mull of Galloway. Thus you will find in it stories and pictures of all the towns and villages of Lanarkshire, Renfrewshire, Ayrshire, and of the two lovely Galloway counties—Wigtownshire and the Stewartry of Kirkcudbright.

THE KINGDOM OF FIFE

This volume, devoted to the neighbour counties of Fife and Kinross, describes in enchanting "close-up" the varied beauties and interests of that richly historic territory between Tay and Forth which has often been called "the birthplace of Scotland".

THE BORDER COUNTIES

This is the volume now in your hands. It surveys the counties of Peeblesshire, Berwickshire, Selkirkshire, Roxburghshire and Dumfriesshire. The merest glance at it will reveal to you its wealth of detail and story.

★

The great work goes on! To present THE QUEEN'S SCOTLAND in a form most convenient to all readers the series is planned in eight sections. Each section is devoted to an area of Scotland which, by geography and history, has a self-contained interest not only for the native Scot but also for the visiting tourist.

Peebles   **Neidpath Castle**

THE QUEEN'S SCOTLAND

THE BORDER COUNTIES

EDITED BY
THEO LANG

TWEEDDALE, MERSE and TEVIOTDALE
—The stories and pictures of all the places of
interest in PEEBLESSHIRE, BERWICK-
SHIRE, SELKIRKSHIRE, ROXBURGH-
SHIRE and DUMFRIESSHIRE

LONDON
HODDER AND STOUGHTON

First printed 1957

Printed in Great Britain for Hodder and Stoughton, Limited
by Richard Clay and Company, Ltd., Bungay, Suffolk

THE QUEEN'S SCOTLAND

This great series presents an entirely new and comprehensive survey of Scotland. Here, in word and picture, is the Scottish scene: mountain and loch, city and village, castle, church, monument and cottage. Here also are the men and women of Scotland, their history and their romance.

Throughout the preparation of the work we have borne in mind three kinds of reader by whom the books will be used and enjoyed. First, the Scot who—at his own fireside in some far-away corner of the world—wants to look upon the scene he loves and read the stories of his kinsfolk. Secondly, the visitor to Scotland who—seeking something more than dates and names and measurements—wants to know something of the tragedy or comedy behind the carved worn stone, something of the spirit and scene before him, and of the lives and loves of the men and women who walked these Scottish streets and climbed these Scottish hills. And thirdly that reader who—although no Scot and never having seen Scotland—has heard, like so many others, the call of this lovely and romantic land and would know more about it.

How to Use this Book

The arrangement of The Queen's Scotland *is so simple as to be self-explanatory. Each volume covers one well-defined separate area. Within the volume there are no confusing routes to follow; each place of interest is treated as a separate subject, given a chapter headed by the name of the place, and appears in the volume in alphabetical order. As an added aid the names of places so treated are printed in* **black type** *wherever the name will help the reader to refer immediately and easily to the separate chapter devoted to the place mentioned.*

MASTER INDEX: *In addition, each* Queen's Scotland *volume is provided with a "master index". Here are given all the names of places, people and things mentioned in the book. Also in this index subjects of particularised interest are grouped under headings—such as castles, monuments, notable antiquities and the like.*

PICTURES: *On page ix is a separate index to all the pictures in the volume.*

MAPS: *Each volume of* The Queen's Scotland *contains maps of the area covered by that volume. Map references of places are given in the index, so that there is no need for the reader to refer to any other map or book when he wishes to locate any place of interest. The Maps in this volume are on pages 222 and 223.*

In every town and village described in this volume there is one person—and often many more than one—who has helped in the work, with advice, with information and with general assistance that has often involved him in laborious research and correspondence. Among helpers are ministers of the Border parishes, many of whom spent hours correcting proofs, and the Town Clerks and other public officials who also helped. The editor wishes to thank all these people and expresses his regret that it is impossible to mention them all by name.

Special mention must be made, again in this series, of Mrs Beatrice Sawyer, from whose energetic pen comes practically all the material on the Berwickshire parishes, and who has again assisted by proof-reading and compiling that "master-index" which is a particular feature of the series.

Of the many helpers, the editor would like particularly to mention:

Mr E. A. Hogan, *Registrar General of Scotland*;
Dr James S. Richardson, *formerly Inspector of Ancient Monuments of Scotland*;
Mr W. A. Nicholson, *of the Scottish Tourist Board*;
Mr W. M. Ballantine and Mr A. G. Christie, *of the Scottish Information Office*;
The National Trust for Scotland;
The Scottish Headquarters of the Ministry of Works;
Mr Colin McWilliam, *of the Scottish National Buildings Record*;
Mrs Patricia Maxwell-Scott, *of Abbotsford*;
Mr F. Maxwell-Stuart, *of Traquair*;
Mr George Fraser, *of Hawick*;
Mr T. M. Hardie, *of Hawick*;
The Rev. Thomas Anderson, *of Lochmaben*;
The Rev. John A. Hall, *of Selkirk*;
The Rev. George L. Heatley, *of Annan*;
The Rev. James McKenzie, *of Lilliesleaf*;
The Rev. John R. Spence, *of Southdean*;
The Rev. John C. Steen, *of Lockerbie*;
The Rev. Sydney H. B. Warnes, *of Thornhill*;
The Rev. Frederick Warren, *of Dunscore*.

For Contributions:

Mrs Beatrice Sawyer and Mr Jeremy Bruce-Watt.

For the Maps:

Mr A. Spark

For Editorial Assistance:

Mrs Anne Dooley, Mr Duncan Crighton and Mr Jeremy Bruce-Watt.

PICTURES OF THE BORDER COUNTIES

(Small figures refer to the list of photographers on Page xi)

ix

PICTURES OF THE BORDER COUNTIES

KEY TO ACKNOWLEDGEMENTS

[1] G. Douglas Bolton
[2] Theo Lang
[3] Alasdair Alpin MacGregor
[4] Ministry of Works, Crown Copyright
[5] Scottish Tourist Board
[6] H. J. Smith
[7] Fred G. Sykes
[8] Valentine
[9] Reece Winstone

THE BORDER COUNTIES

Crossing the Border! In all Britain there is no more exhilarating adventure than this.

The loveliest route for the northward crossing is the road that climbs over the Cheviots by way of Carter Bar. As you travel through the last strip of England the counties of Cumberland and Northumberland give you a mild foretaste of the country you will see north of the Border. Then, at Carter Bar, suddenly Scotland lies before you. You stand at the gateway of the northern kingdom, and you know that for countless travellers through all the ages of our island story this has been the first sight of Scotland.

No moment of travel anywhere in England can compare with this one moment on the Border. England has, admittedly, regions of beautiful country. But they are only patches, and always as we travel across them we are accompanied by the melancholy possibility that the next hill might lift us into sight of industrial chimneys or the next bend in the road might lead us back into a straggle of suburbia or the tricked-up tawdriness of a holiday resort.

Here on the Border we leave such fears behind. Before us now lies a whole country of varied beauty through which—if we choose our route—the narrow belt of industrial Scotland will interrupt for only a few hours days and days of travel through scenes of mounting beauty all the way from this Cheviot height to the farthest north.

From the Cheviots we can see the hills of all the five Border Counties described in this volume. Across the grassy brows of Roxburghshire we can glimpse the Eildons. Further north are the Moorfoots, and—a shaded ripple on the far horizon—the Lammermuirs at the northern tip of Berwickshire. To the west are the summits of Tweedsmuir, the massy boundary between Peeblesshire, Selkirkshire and Dumfriesshire.

Indeed, at this first glance the whole Border country seems to be nothing more than a sea of billowing hills, high and clean and windswept, sparkling with the brittle light of bracken and shadowed with deep-cut wooded valleys. It is not until we resume our journey north and leave these Cheviot heights that we discover the wealth and wonder hidden between the enfolding hills.

Our first discoveries will be the Border towns. They are towns of a particularly strongly defined character. Each one is a little metropolis for its own kingdom of satellite villages. Each one glories in its Border history and keeps alive, amid the humdrum bustle of the 20th century, some customs of its antique past. But the joy of those towns for such travellers as ourselves is the way each one is tightly grouped beside its river banks with hardly any despoiling offshoots or suburban building.

Even the two Border towns that are most heavily industrialised, Galashiels and Hawick—neither of them very lovely to look at—have sweeping open country at their very doorstep, and within a few steps from their high streets you can be within the solitude of the hills or beside tree-fringed waters. Their neighbour Jedburgh also has its mills, but Jedburgh also possesses a magnificent Abbey ruin—and we have ventured to describe it as the loveliest town in this volume. It is our personal choice, and we are prepared to see it hotly contested.

Others will vote for Peebles, enchantingly sited on the banks of the Tweed. Or Selkirk, sitting on a kind of grandstand of high hill. Or Kelso, which Scott thought the "loveliest village" of the Borders, and which possesses not only a beautiful Abbey but also one of the finest cobbled squares to be seen in Britain.

Westward, in Annandale, is Moffat, lying exquisitely in a great bowl of grassy hills and preserving to this day some of the elegance it wore when it was a fashionable 18th-century spa. Southward lies Dumfries, a bustling untidy town and an intensely lovable one, with its jolly Mid-Steeple and an ancient buttressed bridge making a glorious river-scape of the wide Nith.

Our next discoveries will be the Borders' four great Abbeys— Kelso, Jedburgh, Melrose and Dryburgh. All four of them were begun within a mere forty years of the 12th century, a fact which conjures up an exciting vision of that great age of Scotland's awaking and building. All four were sacked and burned by Eng-

2

lish invaders and are now in ruins. But do not think that they are the kind of ruins giving pleasure only to learned historians or archaeologists. We declare that anyone, even the least informed, will find infinite joy and excitement in visiting them.

We again venture into opinion when we say that we find Kelso the loveliest and most moving of the Abbeys, Jedburgh the most impressive, Melrose the most enchanting for its prodigal wealth of carving, and Dryburgh most notable for the sheer beauty of its setting in a horseshoe bend of the Tweed. But, again, readers will dispute these categories.

The Abbeys are all so near to each other that you could visit all four within a day. They are all so rich in interest that you could still be finding joy in them after a year at each one.

Our next discoveries might be the great houses of the Borders. We declare the most beautiful of these is the rare and gentle Traquair. Grandest is Drumlanrig, near Dumfries, seat of the Dukes of Buccleuch, who have in this Border country the other seat of Bowhill beside the Yarrow. Most princely is the turreted pile of Floors, at Kelso, seat of the Duke of Roxburgh. Mellerstain, magnificent castellated mansion, is a masterpiece begun by William Adam and gloriously adorned by his son Robert. Bemersyde is famous as the home of the Haigs. And then, of course, there is Abbotsford, an architectural monstrosity, but the home of the most lovable Scot who ever breathed. To this list of these few of the great Border mansions we must certainly add the lesser house of Maxwelton in Nithsdale, if only because of Annie Laurie.

Mention of Abbotsford brings us to the recognition that the Border country is undeniably the country of Sir Walter Scott. Throughout this volume his name appears with a regularity which, we confess, might almost amount to monotonous regularity. That was impossible to avoid. From these valleys he mined the raw material for his romances, and even if we had tried to avoid mentioning too often the books he wrote each mention of famous Border folk must necessarily lead to some reference to the man who wove them into his work.

But other great writers come into our Border story, among them the greatest of them all, Robert Burns, who wrote some of his finest work at his Ellisland farm in Dumfriesshire and died in Dumfries. In the same parish, the parish of Dunscore, lived Thomas Carlyle. One of the loveliest scenes in the Border, St Mary's Loch, has a monument to James Hogg, the Ettrick Shepherd. Hugh MacDiarmid, Scotland's great modern, is a Border man.

Constantly in our Border travels we shall see the formidable remnants of Scotland's embattled past, those great Border fortresses which are for many of us more fascinating places to visit than towns or mansions or literary shrines or even abbeys. Of the castles of the Borders we choose only two for passing mention in this introduction; Caerlaverock, because of its sheer size and enormous dignity, and Hermitage, because of its grim history and savage appearance.

This volume of *The Queen's Scotland* marks an important stage in the progress of our descriptive census of all Scotland. It completes, with its three preceding volumes, the census of the whole southern half of Scotland.

In this volume we have held fast to our firm belief that what people most love to read in such a book is the story of the men and women who have lived and died in these towns and villages, these mansions and castles and cottages which we can see today. And in writing this book it has been our greatest delight to tell the stories of such lives, stories of loves and hates, ambitious enterprises and radiant successes, tragedies and failures, joys and deaths. Having completed the task, we feel now that surely no other region in all Britain can lay claim to a richer variety of such stories than this Border region, which, when we first see it from Carter Bar, we see as no more than a mere roll of grassy bracken-tufted hills.

ABBEY ST BATHANS   *A Lady and Her Dog*

Within a recess in the east wall of the parish church of Abbey St Bathans lies the worn stone figure of a woman. Her hands are joined in prayer, a kirtle falls in heavy folds to her feet, a wimple and two veils shroud her head and neck. And lying across her ankles—faithful companion through all the centuries she has lain there—is her little dog.

She is, it seems, a Prioress, and almost certainly she lived at the time when Geoffrey Chaucer was writing of his Prioress in her seemly wimple, who rode with grace and dignity on her way to Canterbury. You will recall that Chaucer's Prioress had small dogs *"that she fed, with roasted flesh or milk and wastel bread. But sorely wepte she if one of them was dead"*.

The placid centuries-old figure at St Bathans is an appropriate custodian for a place so ancient and so peaceful. The dreaming hamlet—a few houses grouped around the church and all within ear-shot of Whiteadder's chuckling waters—lies in a tree-clothed glen. Its road curves between shadowing rhododendrons and sky-pointing firs. It is one of the quietest and loveliest retreats in all the Lammer-moors, and perhaps the liveliest incident that has ever happened here is the suspension of the minister. He had—to the great scandal of his neighbours—actually held a Penny Wedding in his manse.

The old stones in the church's east wall—where the Prioress sleeps with her dog at her feet—are all that is left of the Cistercian Priory founded in the 12th century by Ada, Countess of Dunbar and daughter of William the Lion. There must have been an earlier church even before her day—possibly a 7th-century one founded by Bothan, Prior of Old Melrose. Andrew Lang has written wrathfully of the "dull brutish ignorance" which allowed the remains of the Priory and chapel to be torn apart in the 19th century to build some wall or repair a drain.

Not far from the church, in the grounds of the mansion-house, is St Bathans Well, the Holy Well. Once it was said that its water would heal all manner of sicknesses, and to this day the superstitious declare that it remains always at the same temperature. A nearby path still bears the name of Pilgrim Path.

The motorist leaving this delightful spot will be momentarily surprised when—as he drives along the sinuous road beside the

Whiteadder—he sees a signpost bearing the strangely unScottish name of "Toot". Only when he has swept too quickly round the sharp corner does he realise that the sign was a command and not a place-name!

ABBOTSFORD *Walter Scott's Greatest Story*

Clarty Hole! That, in Scots, means Dirty Hole. And that was the name people around here once gave to the place where Abbotsford now stands. They were calling it that when Walter Scott bought it in 1811. Its real name was Cartleyhole; the way in which the locals had twisted that name showed what they thought of the place—a little farm house and steading, and 100 acres sprawling, sour and neglected, in a hollow beside the river.

But the river was the Tweed, and Walter Scott loved the Tweed. He loved too the **Eildons,** whose peaks formed the gracious horizon of the place. The territory had been dear to him since boyhood days, when his father brought him to see the site of the last clan battle fought between his Scott forbears and the Kers in 1526. And, what was more, the despised Clarty Hole was haunted by a presence from the romantic past. Here Huntly Burn ran through Rhymer's Glen, reputed haunt of Thomas of Ercildoune, that mysterious figure, half history, half legend, who, 600 years before Scott's day, had done what Scott was now doing: had woven into verse the legends and histories of his land, before returning with the Fairy Queen to Elfland.

So Walter Scott bought Clarty Hole. He wrote: "It consists of a bank and a haugh as poor and bare as Sir John Falstaff's regiment," but he could not disguise his joy at having taken possession of it, and that joy is revealed by the quotation he added: "It is a poor thing, but mine own."

And any one of us who has loved a thing for a long time—particularly a coveted home—and then acquired it, will appreciate Scott's feelings when Clarty Hole became his own. For each one of us in Britain is notoriously sentimental and enthusiastic about his home; whether it is one of that group of stately houses that are the wonder of the world and the envy of our neighbours, or whether it is just a mediocre "semi"—a poor thing, but our own.

That is why the story of Scott and his Abbotsford so strongly appeals to us. It is the story of the creating of a home—with all the joys and annoyances, all the excitements and wearinesses which cast light and shadow over the path of this intensely human enterprise.

Abbotsford is, in fact, the greatest story Scott has left us. All the romances of this master, thronged with characters, resounding with clangorous incident and gaudy with colour though they are, seem almost pallid when compared with the personal story which tells how, beside the Tweed, he raised the grandiose and grotesque edifice of Abbotsford—most embattled and illustrative of all his works.

When Walter Scott came to Clarty Hole in 1811 he was 40. He was at the dawntide of his fortunes. Three more years were to pass before he turned his talents, with tempestuous magnificence, to the writing of novels and, in so doing, transformed the whole landscape of fiction. But for the moment he was more feverishly concerned in the task of transforming contemptible "Dirty Hole" into memorable Abbotsford.

Ford of the Abbots

He began, of course, by blowing clean away the stigma of that contemptuous name. He renamed the place. In grand romantic Walter Scott manner he coined for it the name "Abbotsford". For he delighted in the knowledge that here had been an abbots' ford: across those shallows of the Tweed—where the Braw Lads of Gala now ride every year in honour of Walter Scott—the Abbots of nearby **Melrose** had driven their cattle centuries before.

After changing the name he set about building the modest home he planned for himself as his Border retreat. Within a year the cottage was ready, and the Scotts flitted from **Ashiestiel**—the old country house near **Clovenfords** which they had rented since 1804.

> The neighbours have been much delighted with the procession of my furniture, in which old swords, bows, targets and lances made a very conspicuous show. A family of turkeys was accommodated within the helmet of some preux chevalier of ancient Border fame; and the very cows, for aught I know, were bearing banners and muskets. . . . This caravan, attended by a dozen or so ragged rosy peasant children, carrying fishing rods and spears, and leading ponies, greyhounds and spaniels would, as it crossed the Tweed, have furnished no bad subject for the pencil.
>
> My present intention is to have only two spare rooms, with dressing rooms, each of which at a pinch will have a couch bed.

When the dear inveterate romancer wrote those words he might perhaps have believed that this was all it was to be. Yet he had—

cannot we so clearly see it?—a premonition of what might happen.
For he goes on:

> But I cannot relinquish my Border principle of accommodating
> all the cousins and duniwastles who will rather sleep on the floor and
> in the hay-loft than be absent when folks are gathered together.

Yes, he glimpsed even then what he might do at Abbotsford. If only
he had time and energy and wealth enough to do it.

He had all three. Time? Ahead of him were thirteen years for
building and planting and furnishing his house, and eight more years
—the saddening latter years—for living in it. Energy? That he
poured out prodigally, driving himself on mercilessly to ill-health:
this lovably generous man was more reckless in the expending of his
vigour and his self than he was even with his money. And he had
the wealth. Wealth that he earned, abundantly, with his immense
talents. When moments came, as often they did, when he could
not lay his hand on a pile of guineas, well, then he could mortgage
the next few weeks of his writing life, selling some as yet unborn
child of his genius, and thus raise money for the immediate purchase of what he desired at the moment—a score more acres, or
some suits of armour, or some ornamental curtain-poles with brass
rings.

Washington Irving, who visited Scott at the time when Abbotsford's square tower was being built, tells how happy his host was at
his recent acquisition of Cauldshiels Loch. To acquire this "desolate
and naked mountain mere" was, says Lockhart, a project so dear to
Scott that hardly any sacrifice would appear too much. In May,
1813, when Scott was looking forward to the purchase of the loch
with "the deepest anxiety"—and, incidentally, inquiring at the same
time about "that splendid lot of ancient armour advertised by
Winstanley", the celebrated London auctioneer—he was trying to
raise money on a poem that was then not even written. He offered
Constable the whole copyright of that work for £15,000. He would
call it, he said, "The Nameless Glen". Just think what he could do
at Abbotsford with £15,000!

Planting his Estate

Three years after that—when he had been at Abbotsford only five
years—the one-time 100-acre estate of Clarty Hole had become the
1,000-acre estate of Abbotsford.

I have been banking, securing and dyking against the river, and planting willows and aspens and weeping birches around my old well . . . and have now only to beg a few years to see how my colours will come out on the canvas.

That communiqué from the field of operations gives one the merest glimpse at only one aspect of Scott's work at Abbotsford—the actual physical toil he engaged in, often only on week-ends, for he was still working five days a week in Edinburgh.

He loved the painting of that canvas of hills around his home. And he suffered the setbacks of a planter with good grace. The Marchioness of Stafford sent a supply of acorns from Trentham and the plantation was hopefully named "Sutherland bower", but the "field-mice, in the course of the ensuing winter, contrived to root up and devour the whole of her ladyship's goodly benefaction". An admirer in Seville offered to send some Spanish chestnuts. Delighted with the idea, Scott enclosed a plot for them and prepared the soil for planting. But when the chestnuts arrived "it turned out they had been boiled"!

Well, the joy of all this is, that he did live to see his "colours come out".

I look back to the time when there was not a tree here, only bare heath. I look round and see thousands of trees growing up, all of which—I may say almost each of which—have received my personal attention.

This joy in the creation of a home inspirited him to the building and planting of Abbotsford, just as passionate and tireless love of the legends and history of his land drove him on in the creating of his romances. The estate swelled out over meadows, pastures, woods and hills; the country cottage puffed itself up into a castellated mansion. Just as one of his own notebook ideas, jotted on a scrap of paper on his desk, could flourish into a poem, or into a romance, or, if it came to that, into a whole library-shelf of novels, so the writer's humble retreat blossomed into this Abbotsford we now see— a bewildering conglomeration of crow-stepped gables and Gothic windows, hanging turrets, towers, stone parapets, carved stone, cast iron, antique doorways and ancient gateways, and the whole lot— furnished with suits of armour, sabres, guns, spears and historic bric-à-brac—costing its prodigal builder £76,000.

By every artistic and architectural standard Abbotsford is a monstrosity, one of the many like it that sprouted elsewhere on

Scotland's soil in that age of deplorable building. Quite a lot of the same kind of thing that Scott did at Abbotsford in the way of building was repeated—with grander and regal vulgarity—later by our Sovereign when she allowed the pompous glower of Balmoral to affront the Dee and added adornments of which tartan furnishings are one outrageous example.

But we have not come to Abbotsford to judge architecture or to study good or bad building. We have come here to try and see something of the great and good and generous soul who built this big house.

And when you go into the room where he worked and you stand beside his desk and worn leather chair, do not be ashamed or frightened to admit the truth—for truth it most probably is—that you are one of the thousands of his fellow countrymen who troop annually to this place and yet have never, since the days you turned his pages so unwillingly at school, read a word he wrote. Walter Scott would not mind. And certainly he would be delighted in the knowledge that Abbotsford—the thing he laboured over for thirteen years—is more of a "best-seller" today than any one of those novels he sometimes tossed off in as many weeks. He was as proud of the thing he built as he was of anything he wrote: he probably loved it more. He himself declared: "I have seen much, but nothing like my own house." No one else has either.

He made of it a veritable museum of Scottish lore. Outside we see the door brought from Edinburgh's Tolbooth and the porch copied from Linlithgow Palace. The entrance hall is floored with a mosaic of black-and-white marble from the Hebrides, walled with carved oak panels from Dunfermline Kirk, emblazoned with the shields of Border families, and in the arches of the roof are the escutcheons of the house of Scott.

In the Armoury are such things as Scott collected avidly: Rob Roy's sword, dagger, gem and sporran; a pocket-book worked by Flora Macdonald; Queen Mary's crucifix; Montrose's sword; the pistols of Claverhouse, "Bonnie Dundee"; Prince Charles Edward's hunting-knives; a sword and cuirasses from Waterloo; Napoleon's pistols, and the blotter and pen taken from his carriage after his defeat; a lock of Nelson's hair and the keys of Loch Leven Castle.

In the drawing-room, clothed still in its original hand-painted Chinese wallpaper, are Portuguese ebony chairs presented by George IV, and in the library—where 20,000 volumes are housed below a roof of carved cedar-wood copied from Roslin Chapel—is Chantrey's bust of Scott, claimed to be the best likeness of Scott ever achieved.

The Master's Study

But all these grandeurs sink to the level of paltry knick-knacks when we step into the austere little room where the Master worked. This small plain room is the fount and power-house of all the magnificence and glory of the name of Scott. Here is the desk, and here the worn leather chair. Here, on one tragic day, ill and ageing beyond his years, he sat, facing a disaster which would have overwhelmed utterly any lesser man. In his journal he wrote his determination to wipe out, with his own devoted industry, the gigantic debt that had tumbled upon him.

> I shall not yield without a fight for it. . . . My own right hand shall do it. . . . O invention rouse thyself!

Now he was driven on by a new goad, one determined by his own honourable soul. Between the ages of 55 and his too early death at 61 he had paid off £86,000 of that mountain of galling debt.

Almost up to the eve of his death Scott tried to carry on the great task he had set himself. Lockhart has described the poignant scene when the dear romancer last tried to write.

> On Monday he remained in bed, and seemed extremely feeble; but after breakfast on Tuesday the 17th he appeared revived somewhat, and was again wheeled about on the turf. Presently he fell asleep in his chair, and after dozing for perhaps half an hour, started awake, and shaking the plaids we had put about him from off his shoulders, said, "This is sad idleness. I shall forget what I have been thinking of, if I don't set it down now. Take me into my own room and fetch the keys of my desk." He repeated this so earnestly that we could not refuse; his daughters went into his study, opened his writing-desk, and laid paper and pens in the usual order, and I then moved him through the hall and into the spot where he had always been accustomed to work. When the chair was placed at the desk, and he found himself in the old position, he smiled and thanked us, and said, "Now give me my pen, and leave me for a while to myself." Sophia put the pen into his hand, and he endeavoured to close his fingers upon it, but they refused their office—it dropped on the paper. He sank back among his pillows, silent tears rolling down his cheeks; but composing himself, by and by, motioned to me to wheel him out of doors again. Laidlaw met us at the porch, and took his turn of the chair. When he was awaking, Laidlaw said to me, "Sir Walter has had a little repose."

"No, Willie," said he, "no repose for Sir Walter but in the grave."
The tears again rushed from his eyes. "Friends," said he, "don't let
me expose myself—get me to bed—that's the only place."

That then is the story of Abbotsford; a story whose tragic grandeur
stifles at their illmannered birth smug criticisms of the place and the
man who built it.

If we can imagine some more than usually hurried tourist, someone who would see during his life all those places in the world that
hold great memories, and someone who has allowed himself time in
Scotland for only two pilgrimages, then those two are easily chosen.
They are the birthplace of Robert Burns at Alloway and the home of
Walter Scott at Abbotsford. Those are the two most notable
shrines of Scotland's greatness.

Scott was not a great artist in the sense that Burns was a great
artist. His work does not belong, as Burns' assuredly does, to the
blazing heights of almost immeasurable genius. But as a human
being, as one we could know and love, he is, beyond all question, the
greater man. The greatest of men, a lovable man, a giant of his day.
And, above all, a good man.

Opened now to the public is the dining-room at Abbotsford, a
room most poignantly associated with Scott; for here on an autumn
day in 1832, he died, having been brought from his bedroom so that
in his last hours he could see his beloved Tweed. Among the portraits in the room is one of his dark-haired French wife; and one of his
daughter Anne, who nursed him here through his last illness and
died herself in the following year.

As he lay dying in this room Walter Scott uttered the words that
are his own glorious and imperishable epitaph. Grasping Lockhart's
hand he said:

> I may have but a moment to speak to you. My dear, be a good
> man . . . be virtuous . . . be religious . . . be a good man. Nothing
> else will give you any comfort when you come to lie here.

But this room, despite such sombre memories, is haunted by a
happier shade—the vigorous, lovable, good-hearted, sanguine Laird
of Abbotsford, and he, genial soul, would have us remember merrier
things. Look at the dining table. He had oak brought from Drumlanrig Castle and then had a London craftsman make it into this
dining table. Then he himself made it the most famous festive board
in the world. Here as his guests, each one full of joy and honour to

be there, sat such folk as Wordsworth, Irving, Hogg, Fergusson, Thomas Moore and Maria Edgeworth. And scores upon scores of others too: good friends and neighbours and casual visitors and all of them among the vast company who enjoyed the friendship and the meat of the grandest host man could ever know.

Three Great Events

He never turned away a guest. Throughout the whole twelve-month he entertained freely and lavishly, but four particular events in the hospitable year at Abbotsford must be recalled.

One was the "Boldside Festival", the salmon-fishing jaunt which culminated in boiling, roasting and grilling the catch beneath a great ash adjoining Charles Purdie's cottage at Boldside, a mile up the Tweed from the big house.

Another was the annual "Abbotsford Hunt" held on the 28th October to celebrate the birthday of his eldest son. This, Lockhart tells us, was a coursing-field on a large scale, including—with as many of the young gentry as pleased to attend—all Scott's personal favourites among the yeomen and farmers of the surrounding country. Rarely under thirty and sometimes over forty neighbours used to sit down to dine, drink and sing the night through at Abbotsford.

> The feast was such as suited the occasion—a baron of beef, roasted, at the foot of the table, a salted round at the head, while tureens of hare-soup, hotchpotch and cockeyleekie extended down the centre, and such light articles as geese, turkeys, entire sucking-pigs, a singed sheep's head, and the unfailing haggis, were set forth by way of side-dishes. Blackcock and moorfowl, bushels of snipe, black puddings, white puddings and pyramids of pancakes, formed the second course. Ale was the favourite beverage during dinner, but there was plenty of port and sherry for those whose stomachs they suited. The quaighs of Glenlivet were filled brimful, and tossed off as if they held water. The wine decanters made a few rounds of the table, but the hints for hot punch and toddy soon became clamorous. Two or three bowls were introduced and placed under the supervision of experienced manufacturers—one of these being usually the Ettrick Shepherd—and then the business of the evening commenced in good earnest. . . .

Little wonder that one farmer told his wife after such an evening: "I wish I could sleep for a towmont, for there's only ae thing in this warld worth living for, and that's the Abbotsford hunt!"

Then every November, before quitting the country for Edinburgh, Scott gave a *harvest-home* to all the peasantry on his estate, their friends and kindred, and as many poor neighbours beside as his barn could hold. Old and young danced from sunset to sunrise to the music of John of Skye's bagpipe and the violin of some "Wandering Willie", while the tubs of whisky-punch were emptied.

The other big event of the year was, of course, Hogmanay, when Scott sat at the head of the table, handing out cakes and pennies to the bands of children who trooped in from the neighbouring estates and farms, and then, with his neighbours gathered convivial around him, welcomed the New Year with traditional toasts and jollity.

This dining-room, too, saw its joyful gatherings celebrating the progress of Abbotsford. There was the dinner given in the autumn of 1818. Lockhart writes:

> I had never seen Scott in such buoyant spirits as he showed that evening, and I never saw him in higher afterwards. When we rose from the table he proposed that we should all ascend his western tower to enjoy a moonlight view of the valley. The stairs were dark, narrow and steep, but the sheriff piloted the way, and at length there were as many on the top as it could well afford footing for. Nothing could be more lovely than the panorama; all the harsher and more naked features being lost in the delicious moonlight. Scott, leaning on his battlement, seemed to hang over the beautiful vision as if he had never seen it before. "If I live," he exclaimed, "I will build me a higher tower, with a more spacious platform and a staircase better fitted for an old fellow's scrambling."

Ah, that dinner was to celebrate "the completion of Abbotsford". But within three years grander extensions were in hand, and not until Christmas of 1824 was Abbotsford complete. At last all was finished.

> Abbotsford is all I can make it, so I resolve on no more building and no purchases of land till times are safe again.

Walter Scott had built, during his own lifetime, a memorial more true of him, more richly true, than anything anyone has ever raised in his honour since. In all its incongruous stone—and each fault of it is doubly endearing because of him—it is, indeed, the greatest story he has left us.

AE   *The Newest Village*

From Queensberry Hill to the River Kinnel runs a turbulent burn with the shortest name in Scotland. In its 16-mile course it gathers into itself the waters of streams which bear such descriptive names as

Deer, Bran, Capel, Windyhill, Goukstane, Black Linn and Garrel. Then, having swallowed them all up, the burn reduces the whole prodigious lot to one syllable, to one exclamatory diphthong . . . Ae.

That name has now become famous as that also of Dumfriesshire's newest village. The village, some nine miles from **Dumfries,** founded in 1947 to house workers in the Forestry Commission's Forest of Ae, begun 30 years ago, was the first of the Forestry's self-contained villages; complete with shop, social centre and recreation field.

The Forest, covering 10,733 acres of the hills beside the Ae, will, when fully developed, yield 67,000 tons of timber a year.

The Ae rises on Queensberry Hill, southern outpost of the Lowther Hills on which the Blue Cairn marks the site of a Wallace victory, and joins the Kinnel near Lochmaben.

AMISFIELD   *Fortress Becomes a Home*

Half-a-mile from the little village of Amisfield—a cluster of houses on the banks of the head stream of Lochar Water in the Dumfriesshire parish of Tinwald—is one of Scotland's most interesting old towers.

The lower half of Amisfield Tower is a solid bare structure in the ancient style; the baronial fortalice of the Anglo-Norman family of Charteris who held this land from the 12th century. But the upper half is a flourish of gables and turrets and elaborate garrets of freestone.

Here is a text-book example of the transition from fortress to house. When, in the 16th century, the upper parts of castle walls became of less military importance, the inhabitants of castles began to realise that the upper storeys of the old square fortresses were domestically the most pleasant. This led to the kind of development we see here; what is in effect a whole self-contained house built at the top of a tower.

The Charteris family have figured prominently in Scottish history since the time Sir Thomas was Alexander III's Lord High Chancellor in 1280. A Sir John Charteris, Warden of the West Marches under James V, was personally punished by that monarch for wrong-doing to a widow! Another Sir John took arms in the Stuart cause during the Great Rebellion when Cromwell marched on Scotland in 1650, and Sir John's brother, Captain Alex, was beheaded in Edinburgh that year for his Royalist sympathies.

Two miles south of Amisfield is the hamlet of Locharbriggs, adjoining a knoll where, according to a tradition of long standing,

15

witches met to dance and perform their devilish rites. Midway between the two villages is the parish church of Tinwald, with its nearby manse. The church was rebuilt in 1763, on an ancient foundation. In the churchyard is an interesting Martyrs' monument.

Eastwards, on the far side of a ridge of rising ground is the farm of Skipmire. Here, in 1658, was born William Paterson, founder of the Bank of England, projector of the Darien colony, and author, among many other things, of a pamphlet in favour of the Union of England and Scotland signed "Lewis Medway". The Darien failure deprived him for a time of his sanity: the Union secured him a recommendation to Queen Anne. His grand-nephew, Dr James Mounsay, also born at Skipmire, was one of the many Scottish doctors who tended generations of Russian Rulers.

ANCRUM   *Brave "Maid of Teviotdale"*

Ancrum village stands on a bold sharp curve of the River Ale, and near the village runs the main road from **Jedburgh** to **Melrose**. It suffered harshly for lying thus by a northward route: Ancrum, and the now extinct neighbouring Over Ancrum, were burned to the ground by the Earl of Hertford when he marched back to England in 1544.

The Scots were bloodily revenged a year later when English invaders under Sir Ralph Evers and Sir Bryan Latoun were overtaken on Ancrum Muir by a force led by the Earl of Angus and Scott of Buccleuch. The English were routed; Evers and Latoun were slain. On the village green is the reputed shaft of the village's 12th-century Cross.

A ridge of high ground at the scene of the battle is known as Lilliard's Edge, in memory of a heroine of the battle, Lilliard, the Maid of Teviotdale, who, when she saw her lover killed, seized a weapon and rushed into battle and fought to the death. A monument was erected on the summit, crudely but succinctly telling her story:

> *Fair Maiden Lilliard lies under this stane;*
> *Little was her stature, but great was her fame;*
> *Upon the English loons she laid mony thumps,*
> *And when her legs were cuttid off, she fought upon her stumps.*

South of Ancrum is the village of Bonjedward, where the Romans built and maintained a military station of considerable strength.

ANNAN

At Nisbet, a village on the right bank of the Teviot on the road three miles east of Ancrum, was born Samuel Rutherford, the fiery preacher and leader of the forces of the National Covenant during the "Killing Times" of the 17th century.

ANNAN   *The Red Border Town*

Come into this ancient Border town on a summer evening as the sun sinks over the Solway estuary and you see it all ruddy and warm, its solid sandstone face glowing a quite rose-coloured welcome. On such occasions you can understand why it reminded Dorothy Wordsworth of towns she had seen in France and Germany.

Annan is centuries old, but it has few antiquities to show: it lay too near the Border to enjoy peace, and again and again the onslaughts of war plucked away its treasures and levelled its edifices. In 1317, it is recorded, "the vale of Annan lay so wasted and burned that neither man nor beast was left".

But two relics of its proud embattled past have survived—an ancient parchment, inscribed in Latin, testifying to the courage of the sons of Annan, and the Brus Stone.

The document—the Charter of Novodamus granted to the town by James V in 1538—declares that although the town had been repeatedly burned and destroyed "by our ancient enemies of England", the men of Annan had never hesitated to risk all in defence of the frontiers of their country "and have always been faithful and just to our Crown of Scotland".

The other relic, the Brus Stone, is a carved tablet believed to have belonged to the castle built on or near the Mote of Annan by the Brus lords. It is a rectangular inscribed stone, boldly and regularly lettered—with fine straight antique dignity—somewhat like the legionary tablets of the Romans. The inscription on it refers either to the Robert de Brus who died in 1304 or perhaps to Scotland's warrior King.

In the 19th century the Stone suffered an adventure reminiscent—in reverse—of that suffered by Scotland's Stone of Destiny in 1950. It appears that the English—even after they had renounced aggression against the territory of their northern neighbour—still coveted her antiquities, especially Stones, and the Brus Stone disappeared from the township in mysterious circumstances. For a century its loss was mourned by the townsfolk. Then, in 1916, the late Dr George Neilson of Glasgow caused a stir among a Dumfries audience when he read a paper revealing its whereabouts. It was in North Devon, in the possession of a Miss Halliday, maiden aunt of a Liverpool professor.

How the relic ever got so far south as Devon has never been explained, but Miss Halliday generously agreed to hand it back to Annan, and in July, 1925, it came back. Its journey was a prosaic one: it travelled north in the car of Mr Thomas Dykes, antiquarian and provost of Annan.

The Brus Stone, now housed in the Town Hall, is built into the wall of the Court Room, whose windows are decorated with the coats of arms of Dumfriesshire families—the flying heart of the Marquis of Queensberry, the stag's head of the Mackenzies of Newbie, and the four stars and a cross of the Jardines of Castlemilk, whose motto is the ominous *Cave Adsum*—Beware, I am here!

The broad curve of Annan's High Street is dominated by the 19th-century baronial Town Hall tower, and terminated by the wedding-cake tiers of the tower of Annan Old Church.

Not far from the Town Hall is Annan Academy, rebuilt in 1820. Thomas Carlyle was a pupil here from 1803 to 1810. He declared that during those seven years under Old Adam Hope he led "a doleful and hateful life". Nevertheless, in 1814 he was back at the Academy, coming there as mathematics master and frugally saving a few pounds out of his salary of some £60 a year.

While he was a pupil at Annan, Carlyle met Edward Irving, the famous preacher, who became his lifelong friend. The fearless religious unorthodoxy of this son of Annan aroused the anger of the Presbytery. But by 1892—fifty-eight years after Irving's death—the burgesses of Annan considered Irving worthy of honour and subscribed for the erection of his statue in the town square. It stands now in the churchyard of Annan Old Church—the building in which he was baptised, ordained and deposed.

The Blind Poet

The Academy's roll contains the names of other distinguished pupils. One was the blind poet, Dr Thomas Blacklock, born in an Annan bricklayer's cottage, who lost his sight before he was six months old as a result of smallpox. Blacklock's poems, first published when he was 25, were popular enough to lift him out of his humble homelife at Annan and take him to Edinburgh, where he studied divinity. He became a revered figure and an acknowledged

Abbotsford   Walter Scott's Greatest Romance

Abbotsford   The Study

Annan   **Scene of Border Battles**

Brydekirk   **By Annan's Banks**

Bowhill   **A Duke's Home**

friend of literature. "There was, perhaps, never one among all mankind," wrote Heron, "whom you might more truly have called an angel upon earth."

But undoubtedly his greatest gift to Scottish letters was the part he played in the life of Robert Burns. He was an early admirer of the poet's work. He was immediately confident that Burns was a formidable genius. Of the Kilmarnock edition he wrote: "I think I shall never open the book without feeling my astonishment renewed and increased", and he it was who first suggested to Burns that he should abandon his plan of emigrating and come to Edinburgh.

> I had taken the last farewell of my few friends; my chest was on the road to Greenock; I had composed the last song I should ever measure in Caledonia, *The gloomy night is gathering fast*, when a letter from Dr Blacklock to a friend of mine overthrew all my schemes. . . .

For Burns realised that Blacklock's praise was a tremendous prize. He admitted that "the doctor belonged to a set of critics for whose applause I had not even dared to hope".

Annan has another link with Burns. The poet came there as visiting exciseman, and it was while he was lodging in Annan that he is reputed to have composed that song for smugglers and their sympathisers, *The Deil's awa wi' th' Exciseman*. The house, which was in High Street, no longer stands.

Another Academy boy was Hugh Clapperton, who ran away from home—and Academy—at the age of 13 and went to sea. He became one of the world's foremost explorers. In August 1825 he set out on an expedition from the Bight of Benin to determine the course of the Niger. All but one member of the expedition perished in the attempt, Clapperton being the last to die at Changary, near Sokoto.

In common with other Border towns, Annan still celebrates with colourful pageantry each July an ancient and formerly necessary custom—the Riding of the Marches. At Annan Riding the Marches of the royalty constituted a duty incumbent on each citizen under penalty of fine for omission. Indeed a Burgh Record dated the 30th October, 1682, ordains every inhabitant:

> To wait upon the Magistrates and Town Council the morrow, on their best horses and in their best apparel, and that before sunrising, for the Riding of the Town Marches and that under the pain of Forty Pounds, Scots money, to be paid each person inhabitant in case of failure.

The colourful pageantry of mounted horsemen and horsewomen in hunting pink still exists, with applauding townsfolk in holiday apparel, but the actual Riding of the Marches has been thoughtfully retarded to eight o'clock in the morning and no one pays £40 Scots if he does not go.

The merry week which precedes the Ride starts with a Church Parade on the Sunday, and the programme includes the presentation of Sashes to the Cornet and Cornet's Lass in front of the Town Hall, the coronation of the Queen of the Border and the popular Cornet's Ball.

On the Saturday the customary riding of the boundaries is halted at Creca, where refreshments of beer, mineral waters, biscuits and cheese are provided. At Landheads a boy is put through the hole in the hedge and the burgh snuff-box is duly handed round by the Provost. At the conclusion the riders congregate on the Holm, where the lively Cornet's Chase takes place. The afternoon passes with a town procession, followed by a gymkhana and sports. And just for good measure a dance in the evening winds up the time-honoured programme which so graciously and appropriately links past and present-day Annan.

ASHIESTIEL   *"Seven Miles from Market"*

In 1804, after a reminder from the then Lord-Lieutenant of Selkirkshire that Sheriffs must reside at least four months each year in the area of their jurisdiction, Selkirk's most famous and most popular Sheriff, the young Walter Scott, moved from Lasswade to the "decent farm-house" of Ashiestiel "overhanging the Tweed and situated in a wild pastoral country".

Although Scott described the "flitting" from Lasswade as a tribulation "which, of all bores under the cope of Heaven is bore the most tremendous", he zestfully scoured brokers' shops and other "hospitals for incurable furniture" and by August he was writing happily from his hill-surrounded refuge:

> We are seven miles from kirk and market. We rectify the last inconvenience by killing our own mutton and poultry; and as to the former, finding there was some chance of my family turning pagans, I have adopted the goodly practice of reading prayers every Sunday, to the great edification of my household.

Scott's eight years at Ashiestiel—his first Border home—were among the happiest of his life and it is possible that had he been able

Bemersyde   **Home of The Haigs**

Eyemouth   **The Smugglers' Harbour**

Ayton Castle   **"Built without Plans"**

Carlops   **Beside the Pentlands**

Cockburnspath   **Cove Harbour**

to purchase the property from his cousin, the young laird of Ashiestiel, the later ambitious project of Abbotsford might never have been realised.

Lockhart records that when Scott first examined Ashiestiel he contemplated employing James Hogg to superintend the sheep-farm and keep watch over the house during winter. This proposal fell to the ground, but Scott had hardly been a week in possession of his new tenancy when he met Thomas Purdie, the man who was his faithful servant and devoted friend until death.

Tom had been hauled before the "Shirra" on a charge of poaching but described the triple cause of his misdemeanour—work scarce, family and grouse abundant—with such pathos and original humour that at the end of it he found himself in the job Scott had recently proposed James Hogg should accept.

Among Scott's many guests at Ashiestiel was James Skene of Rubislaw who gives this account of Scott's day at Ashiestiel:

> Previously it had been his custom, whenever professional business or social engagements occupied the middle part of his day, to seize some hours for study after he was supposed to have retired to bed. His physician suggested that this was very likely to aggravate his nervous headaches, the only malady he was subject to in the prime of his manhood; and, contemplating with steady eye a course not only of unremitting but of increasing industry, he resolved to reverse his plan, and carried his purpose into execution with unflinching energy.
>
> He rose by five o'clock, lit his own fire when the season required one, and shaved and dressed with great deliberation. Arrayed in his shooting-jacket, or whatever dress he meant to use till dinner time, he was seated at his desk by six o'clock, all his papers arranged before him in the most accurate order, and his books of reference marshalled around him on the floor, while at least one favourite dog lay watching his eye, just beyond the line of circumvallation. Thus, by the time the family assembled for breakfast between nine and ten, he had done enough (in his own language) "to break the neck of the day's work".
>
> After breakfast, a couple of hours more were given to his solitary tasks, and by noon he was, as he used to say, "his own man". When the weather was bad, he would labour incessantly all the morning; but the general rule was to be out by 1 o'clock at the latest; while, if any more distant excursion had been proposed overnight, he was ready to start by ten; his occasional rainy days of unintermitted study forming, as he said, a fund in his favour, out of which he was entitled to draw for accommodation whenever the sun shone with special brightness.

Much of *Marmion* was penned from the Shirra's Knowe, a wooded knoll overlooking the Peel and Glenkinnon Burns, and the river walk towards Elibank Tower was Scott's own favourite Sunday walk. At Elibank, ancient seat of the Murrays, young Scott of Harden is said to have married "Muckle Mou'd Meg".

Ashiestiel is now the home of Admiral Abel Smith, commander of the Royal yacht *Britannia*.

ASHKIRK   *By "Palace Walls"*

This little village, on the banks of the Ale Water five miles south of **Selkirk,** was once the country haunt of Archbishops of Glasgow, that was maintained for them by the See of Glasgow, and local people still refer to the site as "Palace Walls". West of the parish church is St Ninian's Well where early Christians were baptised.

AUCHENCRAW   *Haunt of the "Witches"*

Auchencraw, eight miles from **Duns,** lives in Berwickshire lore as a haunt of witches. The Witches of Edincraw—so the name is still locally pronounced—figure in many Berwickshire rhymes, and in this district women who were probably only demented innocents suffered the frightful operation of "scoring above the breath": gouging a cross on the brow as a protection against the suspected witch's cantrips.

One local Laird dealt this way with a woman because his crops had been destroyed by the storm she raised. This Laird's mother herself made Auchencraw notorious early in the 18th century by being one of a party who viciously mutilated a man they disliked, stifling the screams wrung from him during the torture by thrusting his head into a barrel of feathers.

AYTON   *Legend of a Castle*

The pleasant village of Ayton suns itself on each side of one long street sloping southward to the Water of Eye. On one side crimson couchant lions mark the yard before a hostelry; on the other an imposing gateway leads to Ayton Castle, a huge red stone building which, so the story goes, developed from its foundations without an architect and without a plan. Every day the owner would cross the river and contemplate the progress made, returning to convey to the builders his ideas for the next day's work. Not even the existence of James Gillespie Graham's plans has killed local belief in this legend.

A broad and gracious bridge takes the road across the Water of Eye; and to the east of the present parish church, built in 1864, stands the ruined ivy-covered remains of the pre-Reformation Kirk of Ayton, where the emissaries of Scots and English Kings often met to arrange their short-lived truces. Still to be traced among the ivy are the shapes of the door by which they entered and the mullioned three-light window through which the sun would witness their signatures.

Thick as the ivy itself have burgeoned the tombs of bygone Aytonians. They cling like rock-plants to every available crevice. Tombstones stand up flat against the outside walls, storied urns are set back deep into hollowed-out niches in the nave, marble plaques have been plastered inside, while the whole of the south transept is lined with memorial stones marking the graves of the Fordyce family, one-time owners of Ayton Castle.

The Church Lodge at the south-west entrance to the churchyard was a Toll House on the Berwick–Edinburgh post-road until Parliament abolished such things in 1883.

The parish of Ayton includes the village of Burnmouth, on the Great North Road, together with the hamlets of Partanhall and Lower Burnmouth, at the foot of steep cliffs at the sea's edge. Much of it has been rebuilt in recent times to house a small population engaged on crab and lobster fishing.

BEMERSYDE *Home of the Haigs*

The old house of Bemersyde, near **Melrose,** is a famous one in Border lore and is rarely mentioned without mention being also made of the prophecy made by Thomas the Rhymer. This prophecy —quoted in many differing versions—is:

> *'Tide, 'tide, whate'er betide,*
> *There'll aye be Haigs of Bemersyde.*

Even in the Rhymer's day, it seems, the descendants of the Norman baron, Petrus de Haga—in 1162 the first chronicled Laird of Bemersyde—had become firmly entrenched. The prophecy has held good until this day. It was in danger in 1854 when the twenty-fifth Laird died unmarried, but the house was left to Colonel Balfour Haig and then, after the 1914–18 War, it was bought by the nation and presented as a tribute to Field-Marshal Earl Haig.

This gift not only preserves, in this age of change, one of the oldest

Border traditions, but also continues the warrior tradition of the Haigs of Bemersyde. Haigs of Bemersyde fought under Wallace and Bruce. The eleventh Laird fell at Flodden. And now in the writing-room in the old part of the house, the great square tower, are relics of the 1914–18 War, including Earl Haig's big map of the Western Front.

The old tower is the most striking feature of the solid, dignified mansion of Bemersyde. It was built in 1535, by order of the Act of Parliament calling for defence of the Borders. In 1690, when marauding English were considered no longer a danger, Anthony Haig enlarged the tower. In the 18th century Bemersyde grew again, sprouting more wings. But the peel tower beautifully remains.

All who visit the house—which is open to the public—take the opportunity of pausing on the road that winds grandly up Bemersyde Hill to enjoy "Sir Walter's view". This magnificent vista of Border country was always much beloved by Walter Scott. From here he could look down upon the wooded valley of the Tweed, scan all its majestic sweep from his own **Abbotsford** down to the Cheviots. He was certainly not wrong when he described it as the "grandest and most extensive panorama in the Borderland". In 1956 the Automobile Association provided this famous viewpoint with a "roadside map" to point out and identify features of Scott's view.

Here on his rides Scott always halted his horse for several minutes while he sat and enjoyed the view; and here the horses halted for several minutes when his funeral cortege climbed the hill on its way to **Dryburgh.**

BIRGHAM   *The Frontier Village*

"Go to Birgham!" they say hereabouts, and that is equivalent to saying "Go to Jericho!" or any other where. It is an apt dismissal, for that command sends you to the very limits, to a place which is a kind of last shred of Scotland's soil.

Birgham is the frontier village of Scotland's history, lying near the "ancient enemy" and facing across the Tweed the English place of Carham where, in 1018, Malcolm II of the Scots carved up an English army, won the fat lands of Lothian for his nation, and made the blow for the independence of Scotland that was to be utterly and unmistakably ratified in this very village of Birgham nearly 300 years later.

From that time Birgham became the venue for "talks at the highest level", the "Yalta" or "Geneva" of Anglo-Scottish relations.

Birgham was, for instance, chosen in 1188 for the meeting when William the Lion argued with the Bishop of Durham and Henry II's envoys against the English claim to supremacy over the Scottish Church. A hundred years later a convention of the Scottish Estates met here to consider the proposed marriage of Princess Margaret of Scotland, the Maid of Norway, with Edward Prince of Wales. The Treaty of Birgham which established in detail the national independence of Scotland was signed here on 18th July, 1290.

BLACKHOUSE TOWER *Murder of Lady Margaret*

Here is something to remind us that at times the history of Scottish families is dyed to an almost Corsican bloodiness. The forbidding ruins of Blackhouse Tower—three miles up the "gloomy glen" of Douglas Burn amid the wild Blackhouse mountains behind **St Mary's Loch**—perpetuate the memory of a vendetta murder.

We can read the sad history of the lovely Lady Margaret Douglas in the ballad known as *The Douglas Tragedy*. This tower was her home, and from here she eloped with a noble lover detested by her seven brothers. The fleeing lovers were pursued, and soon overtaken. Lady Margaret's lover stood to do battle. One by one he slew the brothers. Seven large stones near the tower were once pointed out as marking the spots where each of the seven died. But in the fighting the lover was wounded, and Lady Margaret herself was injured. They died that night.

> *Lord William was buried in St Marie's kirk,*
> *Lady Marg'ret in St Marie's quire;*
> *Out o' the lady's grave grew a red rose,*
> *And out o' the knight's a brier.*
> *And they twa met and they twa plat,*
> *As if full fain they would be near;*
> *Sae that a' the world might ken right weel*
> *That they grew frae twa lovers dear.*
> *But bye and rade the Black Douglas,*
> *And wow but he was rough;*
> *For he pulled up the bonny brier*
> *And flung't in St Mary's Loch.*

The tower stands, it is believed, on the site of an earlier building used by Sir James Douglas, friend of Robert Bruce.

At nearby Blackhouse Farm James Hogg was employed from 1790 to 1800 by the father of Walter Scott's steward and close friend, William Laidlaw.

BOWHILL   *The Buccleuch Treasures*

A century ago Bowhill, then only a small shooting lodge designed by William Burn, was enlarged, by Sir Charles Barry, to a mansion in the Italian style to serve as summer Forest residence of the Duke of Buccleuch. Lodged on the face of a finely wooded hill it has become the favourite house of the family and was the home of H.R.H. the Duchess of Gloucester.

Here is a priceless collection of paintings, tapestries, china, furniture, silverware and books. Among the portraits is the first Raeburn of Sir Walter Scott, friend of the fourth Duke of Buccleuch and frequent visitor to "sweet Bowhill".

In the dining-room are two famous Reynolds of the Earl of Dalkeith and his sister, Lady Caroline Scott. The story is told that when Sir Joshua was painting the boy Earl with his dog—a picture which later became known as *The Pink Boy* in contrast to Gainsborough's *Blue Boy*—his three-year-old sister stole into the room to watch the artist at work. The artist was so enchanted with her appearance in large black hat and enveloping cloak that he asked her father to let him paint her in this costume. This picture, *Winter*, is considered to rank among his finest work.

Bowhill has many mementoes of the Duke of Monmouth, who married Anna, daughter of the second Earl of Buccleuch. Among these are French furniture given to Monmouth by Charles II as a wedding present, Monmouth's saddle-leathers, and an iron fireplace with marble mantel built for Lady Anna at Dalkeith Palace.

The magnificent collection of china and silverware includes a massive silver wine-cistern weighing a hundredweight and bearing Queen Anne's coat-of-arms, and a set of china that belonged to Madame du Barry adorned with her monogram.

From the front of the house a succession of terraces drop down to a small artificial lake stocked with trout that have the mixed reputation of being easy to catch but poor to eat.

Higher up the **Yarrow** in the grounds of Bowhill there stands on the crest of a low hill fine old Newark Castle where Anna, Duchess of

Buccleuch and Monmouth, lived during her widowhood. Scott rode to this castle many times with Lord and Lady Dalkeith, and it was on one of these visits that the Countess suggested he should write a ballad on *Gilpin Horner*. The castle is famous as the scene for the opening of *The Lay of the Last Minstrel*, whose success on publication decided Scott to make writing his main purpose in life.

Within sight of Newark's impressive ruins is the estate of Broad-meadows which Scott, in those days, long hoped to buy, a dream which must have been in his mind when, in *The Lay*, he wrote

> ... *close beneath proud Newark's tower*
> *Arose the Minstrel's humble bower.*

This was a long time before his first purchase at Abbotsford, and Lockhart, commenting on Scott's dream of settling down at Broad-meadows, says:

> I consider it as, in one point of view, the greatest misfortune of his life that this vision was not realised; but the success of the poem itself changed "the spirit of his dream".

(See also Yarrow chapter.)

BRANXHOLM CASTLE   *"Nine-and-twenty Knights"*

From its mound above the Teviot, three miles up river from **Hawick**, Branxholm Castle commands a far view up and down the valley.

It is an old house, but not so ancient as the grim, enormously strong tower would make it seem. Most of it dates from the 1570's, when the then Sir Walter Scott and, later, his widow, rebuilt it. The Earl of Surrey had blasted it apart with gunpowder in 1570; not long before that—in 1532—the Earl of Northumberland had set it ablaze.

Invaders were always having a crack at Branxholm, for it was a stronghold on the road and, as master-fort commanding the all-important valley between the Tweed basin and the English march, it was the gathering place of Scots planning expeditions over the Border. It combined with this strategic purpose a reputation as a centre of baronial hospitality, opening its gates throughout the year to retinues of Border lords.

Walter Scott gave a romantic picture of Branxholm as it was in its feudal heyday in *The Lay of the Last Minstrel* when he wrote of the "nine-and-twenty knights of fame" who "hung their shields in Branksome Hall".

> *Ten of them were sheathed in steel,*
> *With belted sword and spur on heel;*
> *They quitted not their harness bright*
> *Neither by day nor yet by night.*
> *Ten squires, ten yeomen, mail-clad men*
> *Waited the beck of the warders ten.*
> *Thirty steeds both fleet and wight,*
> *Stood saddled in stable day and night.*

Branxholm appears in the verse of Allan Ramsay in *The Bonnie Lass of Branksome.*

> *As I cam' in by Teviotside,*
> *And by the braes of Branksome,*
> *There first I saw my blooming bride,*
> *Young, smiling, sweet, and handsome.*

BROUGHTON — *Gold in the Hills*

This pleasant cross-roads village on the road from Dumfries to Edinburgh is a jumping-off place for travellers from the south-west on their way to the Tweed, for it stands, as it were, on the threshold of that lovely valley. Westward from it runs a narrow winding road, climbing through the hills towards Biggar, passing the wild and deserted lands of Kilbucho. The former manse of Kilbucho, hidden in a fold in these hills beside the ruined church, is an enchanting old house whose courtyard, shadowed by two round towers, stares on to a wall of steep pastureland.

Beyond, higher up the rolling moorland, there is in the side of a hill above the farm of Thriepland a large hole in which Scots kings mined lead and gold. This hole is honoured by a local verse, supposedly written by a tramp who had failed to get charity anywhere in this countryside.

> *Glenkirk an' Glenkotho,*
> *The Main of Kilbucho,*
> *Blendewan and the Raw,*
> *Mitchelhill and the Shaw,*
> *The hole ayont Thriepland*
> *Wad haud them a'.*

CAERLAVEROCK

At Broughton House lived the "Apostate" Sir John Murray, secretary of Prince Charles Edward during the '45, and one of the persons most responsible for encouraging the exile to embark upon that high-flown and ill-fated adventure. On its site now stands Broughton Place, a castellated mansion with gardens famous for their beauty.

CAERLAVEROCK   The "Shield of Scotland"

Three thousand English troops with that brilliant general King Edward I in personal command! Yet it took them two days to overcome the mere sixty Scots who held the castle of Caerlaverock in July 1300. That shows how immensely powerful this castle was.

In Edward's train was a Franciscan friar, and in the British Museum there is a chronicle of the siege written by him in rhymed Norman–English. Let him describe the castle.

> Caerlaverock was so strong a castle that it did not fear a siege. Therefore, the king came himself, because it would not consent to surrender.
>
> Its shape was like that of a shield, for it had only three sides, all round, with a tower on each angle. But one of them was a double one, so high, so long, and so large that under it was the gate, with a drawbridge well made and strong, and a sufficiency of other defences. And it had good walls and good ditches filled to the edge with water.

Shaped like a shield! What a beautifully apt description that is. Like a shield it was—in shape as well as in purpose. Twice it was destroyed and rebuilt; these ruins we see today preserving an air of fortress strength are the remains of a later castle than the one Edward besieged; but the shape of the shield persisted through the centuries.

That triangular shape is not the result of any attempt at architectural originality; it is determined by its site. The island of rock on which it stands amid sea and swamp is triangular.

Caerlaverock's position in the expanse of low-lying ground between the sandy estuary of the Nith and the sinuous meanderings of Lochar Water increased its strength. It stood only a few feet above high watermark, and anyone who sought to attack it had to seek amid a maze of lakes and bogs the only one sure path—a thin spine of firm ground which ran between the impassable Lochar Moss and the Nith.

The local saying "The poor of Caerlaverock are the lairds of

Colvend" owes its existence to one of Caerlaverock's distinguished natives, John Hutton: Hutton who began his working life as herd-boy to the minister at Caerlaverock and studied medicine. When in Holland he happened to be the nearest doctor at hand when Princess Mary of Orange fell from her horse. This won him the gratitude of Prince William who, when he became King of England, made the former herd-boy his first physician. Hutton never forgot his native Caerlaverock. In 1708 he built a new manse and bequeathed £1,000 to the parish. To that bequest the minister added £200 and bought up Rockcliffe, Kipford and Colvend. The income from the Hutton bequest, £1,200 per annum, is used for education, relief of the poor and upkeep of the kirk and manse. Hence the local saying.

As a ruin Caerlaverock is one of the most romantic.

The grim and cavernous maw of its entrance is flanked by massive round towers, and the round tower at the western point of the Caerlaverock triangle is known as Murdoch's Tower, for in 1425 this tower—soon after Caerlaverock's second rebuilding—was the prison of Murdoch, Duke of Albany. Murdoch was one of the great nobles liquidated by James I when, ransomed from England by his people, he began his task of cleaning up Scotland, breaking the power of the great warring families, and settling his kingdom.

"If God grants me life," the king declared, "I will make the key keep the castle, and the bracken-bush the cow." Murdoch, Duke of Albany, two of his sons and the Earl of Lennox, his father-in-law, were executed on the Heading Hill at Stirling.

A Hidden Gem

This great crag of a fortress holds a rich surprise for the visitor. Its outer aspect is all huge and grim and powerfully forbidding, but if you pierce through this rough rind you find within it all sweet beauty, for within the courtyard is one of the loveliest bits of old building in all Scotland—the Renaissance façade built by Robert, first Earl of Nithsdale, when, in 1638, he restored and enlarged the castle.

This work, embraced in the craggy arms of the ancient fortress, belongs to that fascinating period of transition when Scotland was emerging from centuries of battle into what it believed would be centuries of peaceful and gracious living. The three-storeyed façade, with its tapestried array of exquisitely sculptured doors and windows, is a bequest from the Renaissance, illustrating the influence of the Auld Alliance and a gentler mood in Scotland's building. The days of battlements and spear-guarded slits were gone: now wide-eyed windows—opening on to a courtyard with flowers and shrubs— would make a peaceful frame for ladies sitting at their embroidery. This gentle façade, locked like a treasure within the stern casket of the shield-shaped fortress, puts us in mind of the north façade in the courtyard of Linlithgow Palace: less sumptuous it is, but not less beautiful.

Caerlaverock parish includes the village of **Glencaple**, once a ship-building centre on the Nith; and Bankend, where Robert Paterson—Scott's Old Mortality—died. Paterson was buried in the churchyard of Caerlaverock Church, but his name is carved on the family stone at Balmaclellan in Galloway.

CANONBIE   *The Border Gorge*

Liddel Water, boundary of Canonbie parish, south of **Langholm,** flows along the Border frontier. The little burn puts on a spectacular scenic show three miles from its meeting with the Esk when it swirls around the foot of rocky precipices rising sheer from the water on the Scottish side, and Penton Linns is one of the most picturesque waterfalls in the Border country.

From his stronghold, Gilnockie Tower, on the banks of the Esk just north of Canonbie, Johnnie Armstrong rode to meet his king and his doom at Caerlanrig. No walls remain of Gilnockie: its last stones were pulled away in the 19th century to make room for a footbridge, but foundations can still be traced.

In ancient disused Sark churchyard are reputed to rest the re- mains of Kinmount Willie who lived at Sark Tower of which no trace remains.

CARLOPS   *The Witch's Leap*

This little village—a string of cottages laid along the verge of the Edinburgh–Biggar road—is chiefly remarkable to the passerby for the peculiar outcrop of rock, a grotesque tower perpetrated by Nature, which rears its threatening brows above the roofs at the northern end of the village.

One could believe that this freak could surely be the witch's leap— the "Carline's Loup", from which, according to some accounts, comes the name Carlops. But tradition has it that the famous witch of Carlops lived just west of the village at the foot of Carlops Hill, in a dell between two conical rocks "from the opposite points of which she was often observed at night bounding and frisking on her broom".

The village, founded in 1784 for weavers, lies close to the Pentland Hills and in easy reach of such gentle beauty spots as Ramsay's Habbie's Howe.

CARTER BAR   *Gateway to Scotland*

The road from England climbs in a great snaking curve up the eastern shoulder of Carter Fell, one of the Cheviot summits, and here, at Carter Bar, high between the English valley of the Tyne and the Scottish valley of the Jed, we stand at the gateway of Scotland with all the northern kingdom ahead of us.

This is the lofty entrance to Scotland; and certainly the most glorious gateway of the Borders, giving us—as we descend the sweeping roads to **Hawick** or **Jedburgh**—an unforgettable vista of Teviotdale and Tweeddale and the billowing hills of the Border countries. (See Jedburgh chapter.)

CATRAIL   *The Mysterious Ditch*

If you want to enjoy the fascinating game of plotting the course of the Catrail, it will lead you across some of the wildest and much of the finest Border country, and if you have time and patience and skill enough to stay the course, you are likely to end up at Peel Fell in Northumberland. At the end of this exhilarating journey you are qualified to join in the controversy that has been popular for generations and give your answer to the question "Why does the Catrail exist?"

The Catrail has been a subject of involved and obstinate contention among antiquarians for years. During the last century eminent investigators believed it to be an ancient earthwork whose course extended from Tordwoodlee, near **Galashiels,** to Peel Fell, and to have taken the form of a deep wide ditch between two walls, at some points achieving a breadth of over 24 feet, flanked on each side by ramparts between six and seven feet high, each of them 10 or 12 feet thick.

In his *History of Scotland* Dr Hill Burton, 19th-century antiquary, gave a fascinating account of how he had followed the course of the supposed Catrail. His tour of discovery led him across such well-known Border territory as **Yarrow,** Deloraine Burn, **Melrose,** Liddisdale and **Hermitage Castle.**

CATRAIL

The historian Gordon argued that a clue to the Catrail's age was the moss which at one place had thickened until it was level with the top of walls whose sides could only be exposed by digging. This, he said, proved that the earthwork must be of great antiquity—possibly pre-Roman. He also tells us: "There are several hill-forts on the line of this rampart, so disposed as to leave little doubt that they are elements of the system of fortification connected with the walls and ditch."

In 1880, however, shortly after publication of Volume One of Gordon's painstaking *History*, his deductions were challenged in a lengthy newspaper correspondence published in the *Scotsman*, where the view was put forward that the Catrail, far from being intended as a fortification, had been erected merely as a mutual boundary line between friendly, neighbouring tribes. In support of this theory it was argued that the ditch was not continuous, while in places, e.g. on Woodburn farm, the ditch was only three feet deep, the rampart only three feet high and the breadth did not exceed seven feet.

Modern scholarship, however, has ruthlessly condemned this romantic conception of the Catrail as a myth. In the whole supposed course only two lengths have been accepted as ancient works—the true Catrail and the Picts' Work Ditch. The Catrail is 13½ miles long and runs from Robert's Linn, eight miles south of **Hawick,** to beyond the course of Borthwick Water, eight miles west of Hawick. The Picts' Work Ditch, 4¼ miles long, runs from Linglie Hill, near Philiphaugh, two miles north-west of **Selkirk** to Mossilee, near **Galashiels.**

Walter Scott records an inconsequential and entirely feminine view of this ditch. In a letter to George Ellis, he writes:

I showed Charlotte yesterday the Catrail, and told her that to inspect that venerable monument was one main object of your intended journey to Scotland. She is of opinion that ditches must be more scarce in the neighbourhood of Windsor Forest than she had hitherto had the least idea of.

But Scott himself, always predisposed to the romantic version of things, naturally favoured a more colourful approach to the mystery. He describes it:

From Selkirkshire to Cumberland, we have a ditch and bulwark of great strength, called the Catrail, running north and south, and obviously calculated to defend the western side of the island against the inhabitants of the eastern half. Within this bulwark, at **Drumelzier,** near **Peebles,** we find the grave of Merlin.

33

This ancient earthwork played a sad part in Scott's life. It was the scene of the fall which ended forever the furious joy he had found in his favourite sport of hunting. Lockhart tells the story:

> Towards the close of a hard run on his neighbour's, Mr Scott of Gala's ground, he adventured to leap the Catrail. . . . He was severely bruised and shattered; and never afterwards recovered the feeling of confidence without which there can be no pleasure in horsemanship. He often talked of this accident with a somewhat superstitious mournfulness.

CAVERS   *"Hotspur's" Gauntlets*

A pair of gauntlets with a lion embroidered upon them in seed pearls. These relics, nearly 600 years old, souvenirs of the Battle of Otterburn in 1388, were treasured at the mansionhouse of Cavers. They were won at Otterburn from "Hotspur" Percy, Earl of Northumberland; the lion is the Percy lion. More precious still to the family at Cavers was the pennon borne in the battle by the Earl of Douglas who fell at Otterburn.

The old mansion, now a ruin, was a huge rectangular building in baronial style. The oldest part of it is the square tower built by Sir Archibald Douglas, younger son of the Earl, and it stands on the site of a castle which belonged to the Baliol family in the 12th and 13th centuries.

Cavers parish is a stretch of magnificent hill country. Around the village of **Denholm,** where we find farms such as Caversknowes and Caversmains, the land lies low, only 300 feet above sea-level, and hills encircle it in bold 1,000-foot ramparts. "Dark Ruberslaw" in the south-west is 1,392 feet.

In the lee of Ruberslaw was the house of Henlawshiel, to which the family of John Leyden came from Denholm, but the building was long ago demolished. The old parish church of Cavers is a long unadorned building with traces of Norman architecture. The present church was built in 1822.

CESSFORD   *Seat of the Kers*

Cessford Castle, three miles from **Morebattle,** which crumbles into ruin above its dismal dungeon, will always be remembered, if for nothing else, by the strangely ambiguous remark made about it by the Earl of Surrey, who successfully besieged it in 1545. Said the

Earl: "It might never have been taken had the assailed been able to go on defending."

Its age is uncertain, but it is known that from around 1466 it was the seat of the Kers of Cessford. In 1606 Sir Robert Ker—better known as Habbie Ker—was made warden of the Scottish Middle Marches and raised to the peerage as Lord Roxburghe. From him the Dukes of Roxburghe are descended.

A large artificial cavern on the steep bank of Cessford Burn, half-a-mile north of the Castle, was always known as Habbie Ker's Cave.

CHANNELKIRK *The Shepherd Saint*

Thirteen hundred years ago a shepherd-boy, tending his flocks by night on the hills above Leader Water, saw a vision in the skies overhead. In the morning he made his way to Old Melrose, leaned his shepherd's crook on the wall by the Priory door, and told the Prior he would be a shepherd no longer, but would give up his life to God.

St Cuthbert, that great and good man who was chief missionary to the violent Borderland, now lies buried in Durham Cathedral. But it was Lauderdale that bore him and watched him grow: it was in Lauderdale, by the Well of the Holy Water Cleugh, that he proved himself "not disobedient to the heavenly vision". And Lauderdale's first church was built at Channelkirk—either by St Cuthbert himself to mark and commemorate the spot, or by later Christians who recognised the sanctity of the ground where the shepherd-boy walked with his God.

The name Channelkirk has appeared through the centuries in many forms, and suggested derivations range from *Childreschirche*, church of the children of Bethlehem (or Holy Innocents), to *Chingilkirk*, as in the local ryhme

> *Jinglekirk bell*
> *Rings now and ever shall.*

The modern church of Channelkirk, one mile to the north of Oxton, principal village in the parish, possesses an old mortsafe, the ugly iron contraption that was laid over new-made graves to foil body-snatchers collecting their "goods" for sale in Edinburgh only 20 miles away.

An ancient roadway, the Girthgate, runs through the parish some four miles west of the main Edinburgh–Lauder road. This "sanctuary-road" which may once have come all the way from

Melrose is now a broad green path on which, they say, the heather never grows. On this road, at a point due west of Channelkirk church, stand the remains of Restlaw Hall, which tradition maintains was the resting-place for monks and pilgrims making that journey between Melrose and Edinburgh.

Within the parish of Channelkirk is the old coaching-stage of Carfraemill, once a day's march from Edinburgh for Prince Charles Edward and his Jacobite followers, by Dalkeith and Soutra and Channelkirk, and on next day towards Carlisle.

CHIRNSIDE   *The Wife who Came Back*

The despoiling of a grave, the attempt to rob a corpse, and the uncanny outcome of the crime compose the strange story of Chirnside churchyard.

A Rev. Henry Erskine, minister of Chirnside, had married in 1674, as his second wife, Margaret Halcrow, an Orcadian. A few months after the marriage she died and she was buried in the churchyard with a valuable ring still on her finger.

The village sexton, who had purposely filled in the grave but lightly, returned after dark, opened the coffin and tried to pull off the ring. As it would not come, he tried to cut off the finger; whereupon the minister's wife sat up in her coffin and screamed, leaped out of her grave and returned to the Manse. At the door she knocked loudly, and her sorrowing husband heard her familiar voice calling: "Open the door, for I'm fair clemmed wi' the cauld".

Some years later this wife who returned from the dead became the mother of Ralph and Ebenezer Erskine, who were to be founders of the Original Secession Church.

Chirnside is beautifully situated on the grandstand of Chirnside hill gazing on a widespread view of the rich plains of Berwickshire, from Berwick Bay to Teviotdale, unrolling grandly to the south beyond Blackadder and Whiteadder and Tweed to the distant tumbled blue-grey Cheviots. But the builders of Chirnside have made woefully poor use of Nature's munificence. Some Georgian town-and-country-planner might have made an artist's dream of a country town, but matters were not ordered thus. Instead, an architect's apprentice in a hurry seems to have leaned his T-square upright against the southern slope of the hill, drawn a hasty pencil round its outer edges, and cried "There's your Chirnside for you".

East to west runs the one long irregular street, each house separate

36

and shouldering away its neighbours. From the middle of it the dull leg of the T stretches southward. At the junction there is an open space called the Crosshill, where once on every last Thursday of November a fair was held chiefly for the sale of sackcloth. The ashes, perhaps, would be supplied free.

But even in this unpromising place is an antique and lovely treasure. At the western end of the south wall of the church, protected now by a much later and projecting porch, is a 12th-century Norman doorway which seems, in its serene and rounded beauty, to reflect the spirit of the moulded outlines of the distant Cheviots. Embedded in a wall inside the church is a square tablet bearing the date 1572 and the words "Helpe The Pur".

A church has stood here since at least 1100, possibly much longer. The last alterations to its fabric were made early this century by the Marjoribanks family, who lived at one time in the estate of Ninewells. Earlier Ninewells was the home of David Hume, historian, philosopher and sceptic. This estate possesses the remarkable Rock House, built into the hillside. The back of it is hewn out of the solid rock; its frontage of door and two pointed windows, ivy-clad, faces direct on to the busy Berwick–Duns road.

A Mysterious Bridge

At the junction of the Whiteadder and the Billy Burn is a bridge across the Whiteadder. A pack man left money for the building of this bridge and stipulated this as its site. His wishes were disobeyed, and the bridge was built at Hindhaugh, a little above the Mansion House of Ninewells. Whereupon a voice was heard, prophesying:

> *Hyndhaugh brig shall never stand,*
> *For breaking o' the dead's command,*
> *But lift it up to Billy-burn-fit,*
> *And there it will stand for ages yet,*
> *And there it will stand as firm's the Bass,*
> *Till owre it a thousand years shall pass.*

Two bridges were built in the wrong place. Both were swept away by floodwater. In 1782 this bridge was built in the right place, at Billyburnfoot. And there it stands to this day.

By the side of Edington market-garden stands an ancient dovecote with tiled roof and crowstep gables, and the scanty remains of Edington Castle. Here at the farm some 200 years ago dwelt Mr and Mrs Paterson, who attempted one morning to murder a pack-man who had spent the night with them. Sidney, the wife, grasped his shirt-tail as he struggled to leap through the window; and the husband cried out:

> Haud fast, Sidney, by the sark-tail,
> And I'll gully-mudge him without fail.

Hence comes the local by-word, still in use: "Haud fast, Sidney!"

CLOVENFORDS   *A Sheriff's Days Off*

The village of Clovenfords, on Caddon Water and three miles from **Galashiels,** profits to this day from the distinction of being the spot chosen by Walter Scott for his halts when he travelled from his home, then at Lasswade, to Selkirk to fulfil his duties as Sheriff. For him the inn at Clovenfords was an ideal halting-place, for it lies close to the vales of Yarrow and Ettrick.

The famous Tweed Vineyards were established at Clovenfords in 1868 by William Thomson, then the Duke of Buccleuch's head gardener, and are still carried on by members of the Thomson family.

In 1792 John Leyden was schoolmaster at Clovenfords, and just beyond the village is a monument inscribed: "Site of the Luggie where John Leyden taught 1792. A Lamp Too Early Quenched—Scott."

One mile south of Clovenfords, on the banks of the Tweed, is Caddonfoot. Its church prettily situated on a hill has memorial windows to Sir Walter Scott and the Earl of Inchcape.

From Caddonfoot the road follows the Tweed into its gorge at Yair.

> From Yair—which hills so closely bind,
> Scarce can the Tweed his passage find.

In the turret of the old Manor House of Fairnilee, opposite Yair House, Alison Rutherford composed her version of *The Flowers of the Forest.*

COCKBURNSPATH   *Best of All Worlds*

Apart even from the distinction it holds of once selling its sausages by length—the foot or the yard—instead of by weight, the parish of Cockburnspath seems to comprise within its bounds the best of all possible worlds. The wonderful sandy bathing-beach at Pease Bay is populous all summer through with day-trips and outings and

Sunday-school picnics. Westward from Pease Bay an excitingly cliffy coastline runs to Cove Harbour, built in 1831 by Sir John Hall, where are all the delights of an old-fashioned fishing-port: rugged pier with bollards to leap-frog over, mooring-rings to trip over, irregular steps to clamber down precariously to the sea's edge, boats and nets and ropes and tar. To crown all, real smugglers' caves run deep into the hillside above the harbour, and there is, of course, the usual tale of underground passage leading to some distant building inland—always stoutly postulated, but never through the years discovered. A century ago the curing-house dealt with white fish and herring, and made cod-liver oil; but crab and lobster are now the only catch, and the one-time fisher houses round Cove harbour are week-end cottages for city-dwellers. There was fishing once from Bilsdean, Old Cambus and Redheugh too, but that also has ceased.

But to return to our list of Cockburnspath's varied charms. The southern section of the parish is a broad mass of healthy hill-land, the eastern end of the Lammermoor range. From these hills a handful of streams make their exuberant way northwards to the sea, through deep denes and leaping falls.

Then there is the great satisfying stretch of forest, Aikieside and Penmanshiel, acres and acres of glorious timber that has served Scotland well through the centuries. Here Robert Bruce got the wood he needed to build catapults for the siege of Berwick in 1318. In World War One the great oaks fell again. They were replaced by larch and fir, which took their share in winning Hitler's War, and now once more the hillside is dark with the regular rows of Scots fir, splashed here and there with patches of the lighter larch.

Finally, surrounded by fine farms, stands the friendly little village itself—Co'path to the natives—with its good old-fashioned Square, and its thistle-crowned mercat cross in the middle, set up perhaps in 1612, when James VI created Co'path a free Burgh of Barony, with market rights and harbourage and a yearly fair.

The church on the south side of the Square has a most remarkable feature: a 30-foot-high round tower let into the middle of the west gable. Surprisingly, its walls are a mere 18 inches thick, but the wheel-staircase of stone inside has the effect of binding the tower together and giving it strength and solidity. The sun-dial which forms the terminal of the south-west buttress has sloping dials. The projecting stone lug seems to form the gnomon of a supplementary evening dial, telling the hours from 3 p.m. onwards. At the south end of the village is the old Manor House, known locally as Sparrow Castle.

Two miles east of this church, close to the sea-shore, stands the ancient church of Auldcambus, St Helen's Kirk; a Norman building of great simplicity, probably pre-1200. It is dedicated to Helena, mother of Constantine the Great, daughter—it is reputed—of Old King Cole. There is a tradition that St Abb, St Helen and St Bey, the three beautiful daughters of the King of Northumbria, all renounced the world and devoted their dowries to the building of churches, thus:

> *St Abb, St Helen and St Bey,*
> *They a' built kirks, whilk to be nearest the sea;*
> *St Abb's upon the nabs,*
> *St Helen's on the lea,*
> *St Bey's upon Dunbar's sands*
> *Stands nearest to the sea.*

No matter which of the sisters won the contest, St Helena certainly had the artist's vision to set her pointed gables just where they focus the eye, dominant on the lonely green-brown headland, silhouetted against the sea.

COLDINGHAM   *An Antique Treasure*

Coldingham Moor, that wide wide stretch of changing colour, of heath and rock and cropped grass, purple in the sun, blue-grey in the mist, deep dark brown in a November rain-storm, has captured men's imagination and got into their blood, so that continually it crops up, in books, in proverbs, in local saws of unknown antiquity. For instance, "my heart was as desolate as Coldingham Moor on a misty day", says a character in an old book. And again, an unscrupulous man has a conscience "as wide as Coldingham Common". That desolate vastness is dramatically matched by the North Sea, which, from where the moor so abruptly breaks off, leads similarly on and on across wide wastes.

This was the setting chosen for the Priory founded in 1098 by Edgar, King of Scots, for the Benedictines of Durham. Of that building remain what are locally known as "Edgar's Wa's", and part of the 13th-century Priory Church now forms the northern wall and eastern gable of Coldingham Parish Church.

In 1214 King John of England set the Priory ablaze. In 1544

raiding English again set a brand to it, but luckily at the wrong end for the direction of the wind, so that time it escaped. In 1648 Cromwell blasted it. The pieces remaining, though but a fragment of the once glorious whole, are exquisite enough to repay a long long pilgrimage. The chevron enrichment on the arcading of the east wall and the Transitional mouldings are among the most beautiful 13th-century stonework to be seen in this country.

In 1854 the heritors undertook a partial restoration. An Ayton mason rebuilt the west wall in 13th-century style, in keeping with the north and east walls. The effect was spoiled by a long plain south wall, entirely out of keeping with the original walls. The roof was renewed, and a ceiling of polished stained wood installed. The pulpit was placed at the centre of the south wall, with pews facing it and at either side—an awkward and unbeautiful arrangement to be found, alas, only too often in 19th-century Scottish kirks.

But a recent restoration has brought it back to the beauty that befits one of the oldest churches in Scotland where public worship is still observed. A new chancel was built at the east end of the church, with Communion Table, pulpit, baptismal font, elder's pews and reading-desk. The pews were turned to face the sanctuary and a pipe-organ was installed. An appeal for funds for this work had as its patrons the Earl of Haddington, the Earl of Home and Earl Haig of Bemersyde.

Coldingham Priory had the right of sanctuary for law-breakers, and the bounds of that sanctuary were marked by crosses whose position appears in the present-day place-names Whitecross, Cairn-cross, Crosslaw, Friarcross and Applin Cross. The last of these, between Coldingham and the shore, recalls the tale of the vessel from Leith which drifted into the harbour without a living soul on board. All had died of plague on the passage down the Forth; and ere long all the inhabitants of Northfield Farm were smitten with the same dread disease. And it was at Applin Cross—Appealing Cross—that the kindly but terrified villagers of Coldingham deposited food and medicine for the sufferers. They did not need such things for long. They were buried together in a common grave, which was turned up not so very long ago, to prove the story true.

COLDSTREAM   *Gateway of Valour*

A famous name this, one that for nearly 300 years has been the very name of valour. Only a little burgh at the gateway of Scotland, yet its name known, and sometimes feared, in the far corners of the earth, carried there by the Guards.

The Coldstream Guards, second oldest of our British regiments, were not—as is so often wrongly claimed—raised here. The Guards owe the name to the fact that their first Commander, General George Monk, established his headquarters here on 8th December, 1659. His soldiers had by then already been with him for some ten years. They were chiefly Borderers, tried and hardy men who cared little for the cause of either King or Commons, but loved and trusted their leader. They had followed him for a decade with blind and obstinate obedience through all his changes of opinion and fortune, and now that he called on them to march into England they would not think of questioning the wisdom of that command.

At the head of 6,000 foot and 1,800 horse Monk crossed the Tweed into England on 2nd January, 1660. It was a lightning advance. Newcastle surrendered on sight. The Cromwellian armies melted away. The Commonwealth collapsed.

When Charles II arrived in London, Monk reviewed the men who had marched with him from Coldstream, ordered them to ground arms and consider themselves disbanded . . . no longer soldiers of the Commonwealth. Then he commanded them to take up their arms again as soldiers of the Crown. They were known as My Lord General's Regiment of Foot Guards and later as the 2nd Foot Guards, but the historic significance of the march from Coldstream had given them a nickname which eventually became their fine-sounding official title.

In the Market Square—not far from where an elegant fountain stands, handsomely and conscientiously supported by four stout and scaly fishes with gaping mouths and predatory teeth—is an unobtrusive building with a plaque above the door. This is the head-quarters of the Coldstream Guards, oldest but one of our British regiments. . . . "A small company of men whom God made the instruments of great things."

Coldstream is a real river-town; so clean, so spacious, with everywhere wide sweeps of water to be seen, clean gravelly stretches running along the banks, dark clumps of woodland and the shimmering of rose bay willow-herb resting the eye between bright river and bright sky. Every lane, every street, broad or narrow, level or abrupt, seems to bring the wanderer face to face with a river-view of moving beauty. Any of the cobbled wynds that join the main street to Nuns' Walk give glimpses of Tweed's cool black depths.

But Coldstream has not only one river. There is the Leet as well, coming briskly from the north, bustling under the shining new metal bridge which carries the main road on to Kelso, and flinging itself into the Tweed just by the famous ford which has so very often run red with the blood of Scots and English. Though nowadays trailer caravans cluster there, and Scots play rounders on the grass with the English, mingling their accents.

This caravan plot is the Lees Haugh, where the Scots camped on their way to Flodden, and which very much later was associated with the family of Marjoribanks of Lees. One of them—Charles Marjoribanks, Esq., Member of Parliament for the County of Berwick— stands perched, Nelson-like, on his fluted column at the other end of Coldstream, a frock-coated Victorian gentleman with the notes of his speech in his hand, eternally addressing his constituents with a lightning-conductor sticking up out of the back of his neck.

Coldstream is sited at the first ford of any consequence west of Berwick. The Cistercian Priory founded here by Gospatrick of Dunbar in 1165 stood for four centuries just near to that ford where Leet and Tweed unite. The lane leading down to it from the main street is still called Abbey Road, but of the Priory itself there is no trace, so thoroughly did Hertford's men carry out his dreadful orders of demolition in 1545. Last century, in 1834, a stone coffin and many human bones were dug up in its long-disused burial-ground, and of these some had doubtless been brought in carts from the waesome field of Flodden, as the Lady Abbess is known to have given orders for the dead flower of nobility to be conveyed thither for consecrated burial.

Flodden Field

Flodden! There's a sad memory close to this town. Few battles— even greater and more disastrous ones—have been so long remembered and with so much grief.

Flodden Field lies over in England, five miles across the Border from Coldstream and there—near the church at Branxton in Northumberland—is a memorial to "the brave of both sides" who

died more than 400 years ago. The memorial stands on the spot where
James IV King of Scots was killed. His loss—in such a foolish chival-
rous contest—was a grievous one, for he was a lovable, gifted, for-
ward-looking monarch. But even the loss of such a sovereign was but
a little drop in an ocean of disaster that day. The blood not only of a
king, but of thirteen earls, twelve lords, an archbishop, a bishop, two
abbots, three Highland chiefs and thousands of young Scots ran on
Flodden Field. And their bodies were piled on carts to be brought to
the Lady Abbess of St Mary's at Coldstream. There was hardly a
nobleman's family of note in the whole land that did not mourn
someone dead at Flodden, and it is indeed difficult even today to
assess the full loss and the effect still felt from the disaster of Flodden
and that other slicing away of the nobility of the nation which
followed only two centuries later.

Three chapels belonged to Coldstream Priory: one at Herissille,
or The Hirsel, now the Earl of Home's beautiful home; one at Bassendean, now in the parish of **Westruther**; and the third at Lennel,
which last was the ancient name of the whole parish until 1716.

There are lighter more rollicking pages in Coldstream's history.
From 1766, until an Act of Parliament ended the practice, it was a
common sight to see post-chaises from the south flying across the
bridge to the Old Toll-house at the Scottish end, where blacksmiths
or " priests " were always in attendance to perform a hurried
marriage ceremony . . . and no questions asked. Among the couples
who eloped to Scotland for these runaway marriages were no fewer
than three Lord Chancellors of England . . . Lords Eildon, Erskine
and Broughton.

It was at the other end of the bridge that Robert Burns first set
his foot upon English soil. The entry in his diary for 7th May, 1787
reads: "Coldstream—went over to England—Cornhill—glorious
river Tweed—clear and majestic—fine bridge."

The bridge bears a tablet recording the first entry of Scotland's
poet into the land of the auld enemy.

That day Burns was given tea and a flattering reception at Lennel
House by Mr Patrick Brydone, son of the Manse of Coldingham,
author of *Tour through Sicily and Malta*. Lennel House, long, low,
pillared and set deep among trees, was for some time a seat of the
Earls of Haddington.

Half a mile beyond it on the road to Berwick stands all that is
left of Lennel Church. "One frail arch", Walter Scott called it, and

had his Marmion rest in its shadows on the eve of Flodden. Surrounded by ancient graves and by modern ones too—for this is still Coldstream's burying-ground—the western gable of the old church alone remains, its pointed masonry closely imitated by a dark and lonely firtree, while far below it, down a precipitous bank, lie the dark waters of the Tweed.

CRANSHAWS   *A King's Reminder*

It is a parish of hills, wave after wave of them, with a road turning and twisting through them along the valley of the Whiteadder, and every mile or so another Water hurrying from the hillside to join in the light-hearted scramble towards the Tweed and Berwick and the wide North Sea. Kell and Faseny and Killmade there are; Bothwell and Hall and Watch and Dye, and many more.

Once there were six castles, too, guarding the passes over the Lammermoors. Six castles on the few miles of Whiteadder between its source on Clints Dod and its joining with Dye Water. But of these only Cranshaws remains; a miniature Borthwick Castle, still lived in, beautifully preserved, 50 feet high, and set in an exquisite garden with a flourishing farm around it.

The Swintons, oldest family in Berwickshire, owned Cranshaws from 1400 to 1702, and it was a Swinton—the Rev. Alexander—who once had to be reminded of his duties by a king. That was on a day when James VI rode across the hills from Yester to attend service at Cranshaws Kirk.

The minister, flustered no doubt by the unexpected visitor, omitted to pray for the King's Majesty. The King made sure this would never happen again. He had the Royal Arms of Scotland carved upon stone and had this royal reminder fixed to the wall opposite the pulpit.

That old church, 200 yards south-west of Cranshaws Tower, is a ruin, but the King's tablet was transferred to the new church, and can be seen inside above the north door.

That this church ministered to a sheep-farming community is proved by the local saying: "It's like Cranshaws Kirk—there's as mony dogs as folk", which reminds us of the old days when every shepherd in his pew had his sheepdog beside him in the aisle, silent, obedient and devoted.

CUMMERTREES   *Grandstand for the Solway*

The Solway Firth, notorious for its racing treacherous tides, is one of the most unusual firths in the whole world, and the village of Cummertrees, some four miles west of **Annan,** is an ideal place for making its acquaintance.

Cummertrees, on Pow Water, is less than a mile inland, and—at the end of a smugglers' road still known as the "Brandy Loaning"— the hamlet of Powfoot stands on the very edge of Solway's shore. Powfoot is the grandstand from which you can see—and hear—the awesome performance of the Solway and its fabulous Spring tides. "He that dreams on the bed of the Solway may wake in the next world," said Redgauntlet.

The wonders and dangers of the Solway tides have perhaps never been more colourfully recorded than by Francis H. Groome, who described the Solway as

> alternately a surging brown sea, tinctured with silt and oscillating with the tide, and a naked flat unrelieved expanse of sand, a wilderness of desolation, a miniature Sahara, strangely interposing its dark dreary projection between the blooming slopes of Cumberland and the fertile lands of Scotland.
>
> All its tides are rapid [he continues]. A spring tide is heard by the people along the shore more than 20 miles before it reaches them, and approaches with a hoarse loud roar, with a tumult far more sublime than if the wide sandy waste were scoured by the fleetest host of invading cavalry. Before the first wave can be descried from the shore, a long cloud of spray is seen, as if swirling on an axis, zoned with mimic rainbows, sweeping onwards with the speed of a strong steady breeze. Then follows a long curved white and flowing surf. And then suddenly appears the majestic van of the tide, a deeply dimpled body of waters, from three to six feet high, rolling impetuously forward, and bringing closely in its rear a tumbling mass of sea, glittering and gorgeous all over with the most fitful play of the prismatic colours.
>
> The rivers which traverse the bed of the firth being easily fordable, strong inducement is offered by the shortness of the path to cross the sands to England during the recess of the tide. But Scotchmen, even when well mounted, have, in numerous instances, been overtaken and drowned, while returning from the Cumberland fairs. Even persons best acquainted with the locality are liable to mistake the time when the tide will approach; and, when they are halfway across, may hear the appalling sound of the watery invasion so near and menacing, that a clear atmosphere, a good steed, much self-collectedness, and a steady remembrance of the direction of the path, may all be necessary for their preservation.

Dense fogs frequently arise, and so bewilder experienced guides that they can proceed in safety only with the aid of the compass; and quicksands are occasionally formed, and fitfully shift their localities, to the imminent peril of every intruder.

Not far from Powfoot, beyond Brandy Loaning at the farm of Broom, is a field known as Bruce's Acres, where Robert Bruce is said to have suffered a severe repulse from the English.

Mansion Without Wood

North of the village is one of the fabulous houses of Scotland—a mansion that was built without one scrap of woodwork in its whole frame. This is the great mansion of Kinmount, sited in magnificent parkland. William Douglas, first Earl of Queensberry, friend and often the host of James VI, bought the estate in 1633. The house built there by the Queensberrys in the 18th century was burnt to the ground with a tragic loss of life, and when Kinmount was built again orders were given that no wood whatever should be used in it. Many of the original stone floors remain, but the ban on wood has been broken, and within recent years one room has been panelled with oak from the estate.

Repentance Tower

Further still to the north, in the valley of the Annan, are two famous ancient buildings, near neighbours and both in Cummertrees Parish, but more easily reached from **Ecclefechan** than from Cummertrees village.

The square, squat, 25-foot-high block of Repentance Tower stands 350 feet above sea level on the crest of a hill which was the site of one of the chain of beacons sounding the "alert" to the West Marches.

The tower and its name recall the story of a man who became a traitor because he was crossed in love: the 16th-century John Maxwell. The Earl of Arran, Regent of Scotland, refused to give Maxwell permission to wed Agnes, heiress of the lands of Hoddam. In pique Maxwell placed his 2,000-strong cavalry at the disposal of the English. But at the eleventh hour he was offered the hand of Agnes, repented of his treason, took arms against the English and defeated them. The English revenged themselves by butchering the Scottish hostages they held. The contrite Maxwell built the tower to

47

expiate his crime, to help the defences of the country he had betrayed and to proclaim his own repentance.

> *Repentance, signal of my bale,*
> *Built of the lasting stane,*
> *Ye lang shall tell the bluidy tale,*
> *When I am deid and gane.*
> *How Hoddam's lord ye lang shall tell,*
> *By conscience stricken sair,*
> *In life sustained the pains of Hell,*
> *And perished in despair.*

At the foot of Repentance Hill is Hoddam Castle, commanding lovely views of the valley of the Annan.

DALGARNOCK   *Old Mortality Memorials*

Thornhill's Dalgarnock Place perpetuates the name of this oldest village in Dumfriesshire, and we find the ancient churchyard of Dalgarnock a mile from **Thornhill.** Shaded by immemorial beech-trees are Covenanters' tombs of unusual interest, some of them the work of Walter Scott's Old Mortality, Robert Paterson, who was tenant and sculptor at the quarry of **Gatelawbridge.**

The cross raised to the memory of the Nithsdale martyrs bears names that are still common family names in the valley of the Nith, and also in Australia, for the Australian descendants of these martyrs have honoured the memory of their Covenanting forbears by erecting a stone at the foot of the cross.

Time has completely obliterated the village which once clustered around this churchyard and was the scene of a famous market tryst alluded to by Burns:

> *But a' the next week, as I fretted wi' care,*
> *I gaed to the tryst o' Dalgarnock;*
> *And wha but my fine fickle lover was there!*
> *I glowr'd as I'd seen a warlock, a warlock;*
> *I glowr'd as I'd seen a warlock.*

DARNICK TOWER   *"Duke Walter's" Home*

Here is a castle that has been home for one family for more than 500 years. But centuries of habitation have not domesticated Darnick. Nothing could subdue the warlike aspect of the massive tower, battlements and steeply peaked roof. The castle stands amid its flower-beds and tree-shaded gardens as grandly and incongruously as a Spanish galleon stranded in a tiny harbour.

It is a lovely building. We can see at a glance why Walter Scott coveted it so sorely that he earned from his friends the nickname "Duke of Darnick".

Darnick, built in 1425 and rebuilt again in fierce pride in 1569, after it was destroyed by Hertford, is an architectural treasure of the Border country, but the armoury which once held the axes and steel and leather caps of its many warrior owners, one of whom fell at Flodden and another at Bothwell Bridge, is now stripped of such warlike things and is a bedroom.

The ancient entrance has an outer yett, an inner door of nail-studded oak and an old tirling pin still serving as a knocker. Above the lintel are the date "1569" and the initials of Andrew Heiton and his wife Kate Fisher.

A mile to the west of Darnick the Huntly Burn runs down from Cauldshiels Loch on **Abbotsford** estate through Rhymer's Glen.

DENHOLM   *The Cotter's Son*

The placid little village of Denholm on the road from **Jedburgh** to **Hawick** seems hardly big enough to embrace its village green—so large and open a plot, such a remarkable expanse for so few buildings.

On the green is the obelisk erected in 1861 to the memory of Denholm's famous scholar, John Leyden, born in 1775 in the low-roofed cottage, whitewashed and thatched, which still stands on the north side of the village.

Leyden's is a remarkable story. Entirely self-educated, he had—before he was 19—confounded the learned men of Edinburgh with his knowledge in almost every department of learning. All he asked of life was bread and water to keep himself alive and access to books and lectures. Thus equipped he conquered science after science. He was seen in the little Edinburgh bookshop where Archibald Constable began business, "a daily visitant of barbarous aspect and gestures". But he had not come to buy books, but to study them, "often balanced for hours on a ladder with a folio in his hand".

Scott, hearing of this, sought him out and discovered that

young Leyden was the "J. L." whose translations of Greek and Latin verse in the *Edinburgh Magazine* had previously excited his curiosity.

Fired with an ambition to go to the East, Leyden got the chance of a job. But it was one for which he must pass examinations in medicine, and he had only six months in which to become a doctor. He succeeded. In six months he conquered a completely new science, sat for his examination, took his degree and sailed to India. There within seven years he won a reputation as the most marvellous of Orientalists. Then, at the peak of his brilliance, he died, aged 36.

Another famous scholar son of Denholm was Sir James Augustus Henry Murray, whose name will be forever associated with that monumental labour, the *New Oxford English Dictionary*. He was the creator of this work and editor of A-D, H-K, O, P, and T. Yet another Denholm-born scholar was John Scott, the botanist.

Denholm has later, and less erudite, claims to fame. The local saddler makes stirrup straps for Grand National horses. One tall house elbowing its way among the cottages around the green was built by Dr Haddon, a local eccentric, and is known as "The Text House" because its walls are adorned with such exhortations as "All was Others', All will be Others' ", and "The sleep of the labourer is sweet whether he eats much or little".

Denholm is in Cavers parish, and under **Cavers** we have described the hill of Ruberslaw which dominates the landscape here. In days gone by many Denholm folk must have climbed up there when William Peden—well-known preacher of the Killing Times and the days of the National Covenant—addressed the faithful from a crag still known as "Peden's Pulpit".

DORNOCK   *Scene of Ancient Battles*

This little village near Solway's shores three miles from **Annan** is unexpectedly rich in antiquities. There are the remains of an ancient stone circle, traces of a Roman military road, and two old towers.

Among tombstones in the churchyard are three locally associated with the battle of Annan Moor in 1297, but obviously older. Swordwellrig—north-west of the village—is claimed to be the scene of the victory over the English in the 15th century, when Sir William Broun of Coalstoun slew Sir Marmaduke Langdale and Lord

Crosby, and the victorious Scots washed the blood from their
dripping swords in "Swordwell Burn".

DRUMELZIER   *Merlin's Grave*

A burn, once called the Powsail Burn, runs through the village of
Drumelzier, and at the side of this water, a little below the churchyard, Merlin lies buried.

We can, in these surroundings, believe such things. For this is a
land of enchantment. It is the quietest of villages, the most dreamy
shadowy place, shrouded with heavy trees and ringed with big brown
hills.

In one of his prophecies Thomas the Rhymer declared:

> *When Tweed and Powsail meet at Merlin's grave;*
> *England and Scotland shall one monarch have.*

One day the Powsail Burn, we are told, overflowed violently.
It left its course and poured into the Tweed beside the resting-place
of Merlin. That happened to be the day when Queen Elizabeth of
England died and James VI of the Scots became also James I of
England.

Ruined Drumelzier Castle, on the bank of the Tweed, was once the
stronghold of the Tweedie family, who levied an illegal toll on every
person who passed under those frowning walls. Until one day King
James V came ambling along in one of his customary Gudeman dis-
guises, and, when challenged for his toll, declared himself and put an
end to the nefarious practice. On the top of a conical hill, north-east
of the church, is the more ancient Tinnies Castle. James VI ordered
it to be destroyed as a punishment to its owner, James Stewart,
for the part he played in the Gowrie conspiracy.

Dawyck House is known to gardeners throughout the world, for
one of its proprietors, Sir John Nasmyth, was a pupil and later host
of the great Linnaeus. Here are trees and shrubs from almost every
part of the world, and in the grounds were planted the first larch
trees introduced into Scotland.

Across the Tweed from Drumelzier are the wild hilly lands of
Glenholm. This is covenanting land. In June 1681—six weeks
before he died for his beliefs in Edinburgh's Grassmarket—Donald
Cargill held a conventicle on Glenholm Common.

DRUMLANRIG   *Castle for a Night*

The reckless eccentricity of the Queensberrys has left no lovelier thing than Drumlanrig.

This Renaissance palace, on the crest of a low hill beside the Nith, three miles from **Thornhill,** one of the grandest homes in Scotland, was built by Sir William Bruce for the first Duke of Queensberry. He began it in 1679, and it was not until 1689 that this sumptuous quadrangular building with a wealth of turrets and fortune of windows was ready for His Grace.

The Duke moved in. He was unwell that day. And, we suppose, in a vile temper, enjoying a fine fit of Douglas petulance. Around him was the vastly beautiful result of ten years of immense spending, his new luxurious home. But he found no joy in that. What he needed was a doctor, and the nearest one was miles away.

We can imagine him fretting there, sitting in a fine chair below a magnificent ceiling, and grumbling like the devil. The great house awaited his inspection. It lay all richly about him craving ducal approbation. The servants were putting into place the last pieces, sliding an unnecessary duster over new wood, straightening an untrodden rug, rehearsing once again the domestic routine of this great palace which was now their charge, learning their way about the stairs and corridors and softly giggling when they got lost.

And upstairs, not even deigning to look through the tall windows at the sleek new-planted parkland in the rich Nith valley, His Grace, nagging and fretting over a bowl of gruel—or a glass of port—and awaiting the arrival of the rural doctor, a doctor who would certainly be incompetent and unlearned, a doctor who would be ignorant of ducal ailments, or unsympathetic to them.

In His Grace's dressing-room the valet was unpacking His Grace's coats, laying the ducal breeches and linen in the handsome new presses, setting out in the accustomed pattern the pomades and powders and scents and brushes.

Next morning the servant is taking them all out and packing them in the trunks again. His Grace is leaving. "Leaving so soon!" thinks the man, and, because he has to know how much to pack, dares to ask, "For how long, Your Grace?"

Forever. His Grace has had enough of his wondrous palace. In Edinburgh's Canongate is Queensberry House, built in 1681 by the third Earl of Lauderdale and bought by the builder of Drumlanrig.

Dalveen Pass   **In the Southern Highlands**

Craigenputtock   **Carlyle's House**

Dryburgh
North Transept Chapels

James I Memorial

Walter Scott's Tomb

Dryburgh   **The Tweed and Eildons**

Dumfries   **The Auld Brig**

Dumfries   **Mid Steeple in High Street**

There he could have at instant petulant command the best doctors in the world.

Ten years to build a palace for a one-night stay! The story beats all the legends and fables of oriental princes and caliphs.

Of course the Duke had still to pay the builders' bills. He paid them. But one day—perhaps on a day when he had signed another fat order to his bankers—he turned his pen viciously to the Drumlanrig accounts and scrawled across them, "The Deil pike out his een wha looks herein".

Though, of course, such a curse would not deter his successors from looking in and *living* in. After all, Douglases are inured to cursing. Each one of them has been suckled on horrific stories and dire prophecies.

One of this first Duke's descendants was the reprobate "Old Q". When Drumlanrig fell into his hands its woods and 18th-century lime avenue were the glories of Nithsdale, but "Old Q", notorious as a spoiler of woods and celebrated as a patron of the turf, wrought havoc here as he had done at Neidpath. So that when Wordsworth came here in 1803—looking for the woods Burns had loved to wander in when he visited Drumlanrig's chamberlain, John McMurdo—he found the hills naked.

On the death of "Old Q" the Dukes of Buccleuch inherited Drumlanrig and the great house moved into kinder hands.

Even in this 20th century—which would look askance on such extravagant adventures as that of the first Duke—the Duke of Buccleuch is sometimes in residence in the castle of Drumlanrig. Though, in accordance with the age, he lives most of the time at the more modest **Bowhill,** near Selkirk, and has around him there the choicest of the paintings which once made Drumlanrig a treasure-house.

Scotland is rich in great houses, but Drumlanrig is like none of its compatriots. Yet it does bear a striking resemblance to one Scottish building, Heriot's Hospital, the most beautiful building in Edinburgh, which was begun in 1628, more than 50 years before Duke William began. Those who know Heriot's have some idea of Drumlanrig if they imagine Heriot's transplanted, magnified a little, its visage adorned, and beautifully so, with a curved moustache of Renaissance stair, and set in the heart of grand parkland with a broad and noble avenue for our approach.

Like Heriot's, Drumlanrig is built around a tower-guarded quadrangle. Like Heriot's, it has a whole pageant of towers and a prodigality of windows. The architraves of windows and doors are profusely adorned with the armorial hearts and stars of the Douglases, owners of the barony of Drumlanrig certainly from 1356 and possibly even earlier.

Drumlanrig still houses the "wounded" portrait of William III, its canvas pierced with claymores of Highland soldiers who spent a night in the castle during their retreat from Derby in 1745.

Walter Scott, who visited Drumlanrig as guest of his beloved patron, Charles, fourth Duke of Buccleuch, provides a splendid illustration of the changing fortunes of Drumlanrig from Queensberry to Buccleuch days. In September 1813 he writes:

> It is really a most magnificent pile, and when embosomed amid the wild forest scenery, of which I have an infantine recollection, must have been very romantic. But old Q made wide devastation among the noble trees. . . . The indoor work does not please me so well, though I am aware that, to those who are to inhabit an old castle, it becomes often a matter of necessity to make alterations. . . . Thus a noble gallery, which ran the whole length of the front, is converted into bedrooms—very comfortable, indeed, but not quite so magnificent; and as grim a dungeon as ever knave or honest man was confined in, is in some danger of being humbled into a wine-cellar.

Thirteen years later he revisited the castle:

> The exterior is much improved since I first knew it. It was then in the state of dilapidation to which it had been abandoned by the celebrated old Q—and was indeed scarce wind and water tight. Then the whole wood had been felled, and the outraged castle stood in the midst of waste and desolation, excepting a few scattered old stumps, not judged worth the cutting. Now the whole has been, ten or twelve years since, completely replanted and the scattered seniors look as graceful as fathers surrounded by their children.

DRYBURGH   *Building an Abbey*

From Melrose, five miles away, where the Cistercians were building an Abbey, there had been much coming and going of monastic officials and architects during the early weeks of 1140. The Cistercians had been at work for some years at Melrose, and they naturally had a fellow feeling for the black-robed, white-coped brethren of the Premonstratensian Order who were planning to build a monastery at Dryburgh, on a horse-shoe of land encircled by the Tweed.

One of the monks who, like most of his fellows, was an expert in farming and gardening, reported that this land was fertile and that

the pasturage was rich. The river, said another monk who had made
a few sorties with his line, was wonderfully rich in trout. In the
season there was "a prodigious plenty of salmon".

The architects thoughtfully paced the proposed site, which sloped
down gradually towards the south, and pondered as they walked
how best they could use that pleasant providentially southern aspect.

All in all—with a ford nearby to link it to the road to its Cistercian
neighbour at Melrose—this would be an ideal setting for a religious
house. So, at last, the decision was made, and on a day in 1140 the
Canons Regular of the Order chose this place for their first home in
Scotland.

They scored the ground out with a plan very much like that of
their parent home at Alnwick, and Dryburgh's southern aspect was
used to grand advantage, for the whole establishment was built
down the slope in three great steps of buildings, with the Abbey
church, highest of all, overlooking the cloister, and then the cloister
overlooking the chapter-house and kitchen and living quarters.

The stone for the building—that clean, warm-tinted Dryburgh
stone—was cut from freestone quarries north of the Abbey, and
across the river the masons worked, chipping the blocks into shafts
and bosses and groinings according to the architect's drawings. For
beams oaks were felled in the woods nearby. Lime was carted from
Kelso. During the work the monks and the masons from Alnwick
lived in wooden huts on the banks of the Tweed. On rare occasions,
when they had time off, they would go along to see how Melrose
was getting on. But most times they were hard at it, English and
Scots working happily side by side, building great church and wide
cloister, chapter-house and refectory, guest-house and dormitory,
bake-house and brew-house and warming-house and kitchen.

On 13th December, 1152, 12 years after the choosing of the site,
the Dryburgh monks moved into residence. By the standards of
those days it was not an overwhelmingly grand Abbey. Nor was it
immensely rich. But Dryburgh was a lovely building. Most
assuredly it was that. That much we can see from the fragments
idiot time has left us. It suffered, as did Melrose and Kelso and
Jedburgh, in the savage warfare of the Border.

For when the English came again to Dryburgh they were not
carrying mason's chisels and mortar-trowels. This time they had
axes and burning brands in their hands. The retreating army of
Edward II set the place ablaze, King Robert the Bruce gave liberally

for its restoration, but in 1385 Richard II's men were making a bonfire again. At last in 1545 Hertford left it a smoking ruin. Centuries of neglect completed the destruction, and now we have but a few ravaged fragments—a skeleton of a plan which we can clothe only in imagination and with difficu ty with the flesh of ancient Dryburgh.

Yet, visit it on a windless day in high summer, when walls and arches etch midnight shadows across the silent lawns, and you will occasionally be brought to a halt, gazing spellbound at some vista which will give you momentarily a vision of what this place must have looked like in its completed wonder.

That glimpse, for instance, through the doorway at the corner of the cloister—the east processional doorway where you look upward over the falling flow of steps towards the arches in the church beyond. There is a sight as lovely as anything you could hope to see in a building so desperately ruined. Or when, in the vestry and the chapter-house, you examine the treasured patches of mural decoration, and find in them a whispered reminder of the colour that lit the walls of Dryburgh 800 years ago.

Graves of Scott and Haig

Very little is left of the Abbey church, but the ruins of the transepts help us to judge its size; low walls and pillars show us its plan. In the north transept, St Mary's Aisle, is the grave of Sir Walter Scott, who lies there by right of his ancestors, the Haliburtons. Nearby is the burial vault of the Haigs of Bemersyde, whose founder, Petrus de Haga, gave gifts to the Abbey. There now lies Field-Marshal Earl Haig.

Of the monastic buildings there are more extensive remains, and we can still see the kitchens, wine-cellars and store-rooms below the refectory.

In the cloister, near to the east processional doorway, is an aumbrie —a wall-press—once fitted with doors and shelves for the books used in the cloister. The door to the right of this leads into what is known as "St Modan's Chapel", which was the library and vestry.

The west gable of the refectory is enriched with a wheel window like the one in the west façade of Jedburgh. Over the doorway leading from the cloister walk to the kitchen is a 16th-century carving of the arms of John Stewart, second son of the Earl of Lennox.

Another doorway in the cloister leads into the barrel-vaulted parlour, the only place in the Abbey where the canons were allowed to talk. A third leads to the chapter-house, used daily for a reading of a chapter from the Rule of the Order. Here is preserved a stone basin, carved in relief on all four sides with bird-like creatures. When unearthed over 100 years ago near the refectory entrance part of the lead overflow pipe was still attached to it.

The warming-house—where the canons were allowed the comfort of a fire—had a hooded fireplace with carved corbels built in the centre of the west wall. Two hundred years ago, when the warming-house was used as a byre, the vaults were intact.

The principal feature in the west wall of the cloister is the arched recess, situated near the entrance of the refectory. Here, conveniently situated, was a lead-lined trough in which the monks could wash their hands as they went in for meals.

Upon such remains—the battered but still soaring arches of the church and the domestic furniture of the monastery—we build our picture of Dryburgh and recall some of the personages in its history.

Roger, first Abbot, to whom was granted by Papal bull a great privilege: "Permission to hold divine service in such time as the country lay under interdict, provided that it was celebrated behind closed doors, without ringing of bells and excluding all interdicted and excommunicate persons."

Hot-tempered Marcus, a canon whose suspension is recorded by a 14th-century commission from Avignon. His sin: striking down the Abbot with his fist.

The melancholy Nun of Dryburgh, who made her home in a vault in the 18th-century ruins of the Abbey, and was never again seen by man or woman in the light of the sun, because, says Walter Scott, "she had made a vow that, during the absence of the man to whom she was attached, she would never look upon the sun. Her lover never returned. He fell during the civil war of 1745–6."

In the grounds stands a quaint and appealing memorial built in 1794 by David, Earl of Buchan, in honour of his ancestors. Recessed into one side of an obelisk is a nearly life-size statue of James I with drawn sword and wearing a plumed hat. On the other side is his successor to the Scottish throne wearing 16th-century armour.

DRYHOPE TOWER   *Mary Scott's Marriage*

The unknown writer of an old Scottish ballad declares he wishes he had never set eyes on the tower set amid loch and encircling hills that shelter "Yarrow's fairest flower".

"Happy the love that meets return, but mine meets only slight and scorn", complains this poet. His fair one was Mary Scott, born around 1550 in Dryhope Tower, a mile away from the foot of St Mary's Loch.

Mary—whose legendary beauty was later lauded by a more famous poet, Allan Ramsay—married Walter Scott of Harden. Her marriage was the occasion of a strange contract, witnessed by five local barons who pledged themselves to see that the bargain was carried out. None of the parties or the witnesses could write, so the notary had to sign for the lot. Under the terms of the contract Mary's father agreed to furnish Wat with "man's and horse meat for a year and a day" at Dryhope, in return for the profits of the first Michaelmas moon.

Wat's depredations won him a notoriety almost equal to the fame of his wife's beauty. In July 1592 James VI issued a Peebles warrant ordering that Dryhope be demolished in punishment for the treason perpetrated by its owner, "Walter Scott of Harden". Walter Scott was proud to claim descent "from that ancient chieftain whose name I have made to ring in many a ditty, and from his fair dame, the Flower of Yarrow".

Commanding a superb view of **Yarrow** and the Loch of the Lowes, this ancient tower, though now in ruins, convinces us of its claim to have been one of the strongest peel towers in Ettrick Forest.

DUMFRIES   *Capital of the South-west*

Here is one of the most lively and lovable towns in all Scotland. It seems, in many ways, to be more Scottish than most. Perhaps that is because it lies so beautifully off the main streams of commerce— just a few valuable miles from the overburdened highways linking Glasgow and Edinburgh with England—and thus remains untainted, as it were, with too much traffic with the outer world.

Certainly it sits magnificently and powerfully in the south-west, lording it over the whole of that territory in the guise of a capital city in its own right.

Admirers of the Royal Burgh call it "Queen of the South", and Robert Burns, who lived in it and loved it and was eventually laid to rest in it, wrote of Dumfries as "Maggie by the banks of Nith, a dame wi' pride eneuch".

We come to it across the wide green valley of the Nith, where gardens, woods and pasture-land grow as lush and luxuriantly as anywhere in the Border lowlands, and we find it a town of sturdy Scottish buildings grouped with rakish charm along the banks of the river.

The Auld Brig

Four town bridges span the Nith. Chief of these is the narrow and massively buttressed Auld Brig, once the only gateway west into Galloway, built by the people of the district in 1432. It is referred to as the Devorgilla bridge, being ascribed by tradition to Lady Devorgilla, third daughter of Allan, Earl of Galloway, and mother to John Balliol, Scotland's sorry puppet king. The bridge was wrecked by a flood early in the 17th century and now has six arches, although originally it had more—one authority says nine, and another thirteen. Its west arch is believed to be of the original 15th-century structure.

Below the Auld Brig the water foams over the cauld (weir) built to provide water for the old Town Mills. This is a well-known landmark within the Burgh, and in all photographs taken from the air it shows up like a giant white feather fan stuck on the bed of the river. Above the cauld, where the water runs slow and deep, mirroring the old houses, fishermen once cast their nets in circles from the backs of their cobles, and hauled the gleaming salmon inboard. Below the cauld, still right in the middle of the town, a dry spell splits the river into streams; and in season the rod-and-line fraternity drop their flies to lure the wily herling (salmon trout).

There are of course times in every year when the river thunders down in spate from the hills to the north, obliterates the cauld and pours into the houses on its banks. Angry brown water drives through the arches of Auld Brig close to the keystones; and yet they stand.

The New Bridge, or Buccleuch Street Bridge, is also of stone. It was built in 1793 and widened a century later. Below it is the Suspension Bridge, erected in 1875. Below that another modern road bridge completes rather unhappily the company. The widening of the Upper Bridge deprived it of its character, but not of the splendid view of its centre, both up river and down.

Buccleuch Street joins High Street at what reminds one quite irresistibly of a *place* in a French town. On the north side stands Greyfriars Church, and in front of the church is a sentimental, much-photographed white marble statue of Robert Burns, showing him resting against the stump of a tree with a posy of daisies in his hand. At his feet lies his dog, placidly accompanied by two field mice. The people of Dumfries had this £1,000 statue—the work of Mrs D. O. Hill—erected in April 1882, "as a loving tribute to their fellow-townsman, the National Poet of Scotland".

Burns' Pubs

The poet's favourite haunts in the town are both in High Street. They are The Globe Tavern, close by the County Hotel, and The Hole in the Wa', and retain relics of the poet. At The Globe—whose "hearty gay and lavish Scottish barmaid", Anna Park, bore a Burns child—are his chair, punch-bowl, jug and ladle, and on the pane of an upstairs window are scratched—reputedly by Burns himself with a diamond ring—the quatrain in praise of *Lovely Polly Stewart* and a new version of *Coming Through the Rye*. The early 17th-century Hole in the Wa' has many Burns manuscripts.

Burns moved to Dumfries from **Ellisland** in December, 1791, to take up his job as an excise officer, and during his four-and-a-half years in the town he wrote nearly 100 of his most popular songs, including *Auld Lang Syne, Scots Wha Hae, A Man's a Man For A' That, My Love is Like a Red, Red Rose*, and *Ye Banks and Braes o' Bonny Doon*.

In a two-storey house in the Mill Vennel (now Burns Street), he died on 21st July, 1796. Alan Cunningham has described that day:

> Dumfries was like a besieged place. It was known he was dying, and the anxiety, not of the rich and learned only but of the mechanics and peasants, exceeded all belief. Wherever two or three people stood together, their talk was of Burns and of him alone.

His widow, "Bonnie Jean Armour", lived there until her death in 1834. In 1850 the house was bought by the poet's son, Lt.-Col. William Nicol Burns. Today the house contains relics of the poet, including manuscripts presented by Sir James Barrie. Adjoining the poet's bedroom is the tiny room in which he wrote those immortal pieces, and a signature, reputedly his, is scribbled on the window-pane.

He was buried first in the northern corner of the cemetery of St Michael's and honoured with nothing more than a plain stone slab provided by his widow. But, after a distinct pause, the conscience of the nation was awakened and a subscription was begun for a memorial more illustrative of the regard the great poet deserved.

At last a mausoleum in the form of a Grecian temple rose in another part of the graveyard. The mausoleum was designed by Thomas F. Hunt, of London, and cost £1,450. At the back of the mausoleum a sculptured group depicts the Muse of Poetry discovering Burns at the plough.

The poet's body was transferred to its new resting-place at midnight on 19th September, 1815. Here also rest Jean Armour, and their five sons.

Also in the cemetery are mass graves of victims of Dumfries' two plagues of Asiatic cholera, and a memorial to the memory of three Covenanters, two executed in 1667 and one in 1685.

Not far from Greyfriars Church are the buildings of Dumfries Academy, which J. M. Barrie attended. (On the banks of the Nith—behind Moatbrae Nursing Home—is the garden where Barrie used to play, now labelled "The Garden of Peter Pan".) The older portion of the Academy buildings has a handsome portico and turret.

In a side street nearby is the Ewart Public Library. It was William Ewart, M.P. for Dumfries Burghs, who introduced the Public Libraries Act which gave burgh councils the right to raise rates for public libraries.

The Murder of Comyn

Greyfriars Church stands partly on the site of the Maxwells' Castle, which was once bounded by the monastery of the Greyfriars, founded by the Lady Devorgilla. The name of present-day Friars Vennel is all that survives of the monastery, yet the monastery was the scene of a decisive event in Scotland's history, the stage for one of those deeds which in one moment of violence change the destinies of men and the whole fate of nations. Here in 1306 Robert the Bruce and John Comyn, Lord of Badenoch, the "Red Comyn", met and quarrelled.

The quarrel ended bloodily. Bruce lost his temper and struck the Comyn with his dagger. Horrified by what he had done, Bruce rushed out of the church to his escorts and told them, "I doubt I have slain the Red Comyn".

The Scots, who love putting a pawky twist to their history, have lightened this scene by adding to it the legend that Roger

Kirkpatrick one of Bruce's men, replied: "You doubt! Then I'll mak siccar!" Drawing his sword, he rushed in with another of Bruce's men and, to the horror of the monks, stabbed the Comyn to death at the Altar.

The stabbing to death is certainly borne out by evidence: the remark is doubtful, for its phraseology belongs to a much later date. Those near-Norman barons were more accustomed to Norman–English than to broad Lowland Scots. But this dark event undoubtedly gave a savage quickening wrench to the wheel of history, and spurred Bruce on to that irrevocable deed of assuming the Crown of Scots and, as their King, leading them to the victory of Bannockburn, the first great milestone in their march to national independence.

In 1951 a bronze plaque was unveiled on the wall of a shop in Castle Street marking the supposed spot where the Comyn was slaughtered.

Immediately after the death of the Red Comyn, Bruce and his men stormed the castle on the Castledykes. On 10th February, 1906, the sex-centenary of the capture, Dumfries Town Council erected a memorial stone on the Castledykes. The inscription reads:

> King Robert the Bruce, on 10th February, 1306, captured the Castle of Dumfries, which occupied this site, and so began the War which vindicated Scotland's Independence.

During the war between England and an awakening Scotland, the English King, Edward I, halted at Dumfries on some of his sorties.

Once he paused to put to death for treachery the brother-in-law of Bruce, Christopher Seton. The execution took place on the gallows hill, more recently known as Christy's Mount, to the east of the town. Here Seton's widow erected a chapel, dedicated to St Christopher, to commemorate her husband's memory, but no sign of it now remains.

Dumfries Castle passed from one side to the other with exasperating frequency. Edward I seized and garrisoned it after the fall of John Balliol. Bruce re-took it when the Comyn died. By 1312 it was again in English hands, and in that year Bruce captured it again. The moat surrounding the castle is still remembered in the name Castledykes (Castle-ditches) given to a part of Kingsholm.

The line of the moat can be seen clearly, and a section of the castle wall and the chapel wall are now exposed and visible to visitors.

The Mid Steeple

High Street is divided by the Mid Steeple—a narrow rectangular block of mellow and genial red stone, with a broad outside stair and surmounted by a shuttered steeple.

The Steeple was first known as the "Tron Steeple" and saw service until 1867 as courthouse, Town House, prison and storehouse for the burgh's ammunition at the time of Napoleon's threatened invasion. It is now occupied only by shops. The Burgh Arms, the Royal Arms of Scotland, and the old Scots ell wand of 38 inches are sculptured on the south face of the building. The work of Tobias Bachup, of Alloa, it is one of Scotland's finest 17th-century buildings of its class.

Further on we come to where the High Street suddenly expands into the Plainstones, looked upon by the whole of south-west Scotland as their own "Piccadilly Circus".

Nearby stood a Doric column designed by Robert Adam and erected to the memory of Charles, Duke of Queensberry. For 150 years it was the hub of busy Queensberry Square, but it became necessary to remove it to a quieter spot. The County Council offered a site outside the County Buildings in English Street, where it now stands.

St Michael's Church, with its bold 130-foot-high steeple, stands on the Dumfries side of the bridge of the same name. The steeple was built in 1744, and the following year the men of Prince Charlie's army saw work in progress on the rest of the building. They showed their respect by stripping the roof of the new lead, which they used to make bullets. St Michael's was renovated in 1869 and 1881.

Inside the present building, the pulpit stands on the spot occupied by the altar of the pre-Reformation church. On the walls there are memorials to Allan Cunningham, sculptor and poet, and to Thomas Aird, poet and journalist. A small brass plate on one of the pillars near the door marks the pew Robert Burns used.

On the south wall, the most eloquent of all its memorials reads:

In Gratitude. When the Germans invaded our country, we Norwegians found in Scotland a home, and in this House of God peace and strength. "I was a stranger and you took me in." 1940.

The County Hotel—formerly the Commercial Hotel—was Prince Charles Edward's headquarters on his broken-hearted retreat from Derby. The beautifully panelled upstairs room, still known as "Prince Charlie's Room", was the scene of a council of war.

As the burgh had not been over-friendly to Prince Charles on his southward march (indeed, citizens had impudently annexed a section of the Prince's baggage train), he treated it with severity on his return. He demanded 1,000 pairs of shoes for his army and £2,000 sterling. Hearing, however, that the Duke of Cumberland was marching on him from England, the Prince had time to collect only £1,195 of the levy before he had to hurry off, taking ex-Provost Crosbie and Mr Walter Riddell of Glenriddel with him as security for the remainder. The Government later reimbursed Dumfries for the loss, giving £2,848 5s. 11d. for the money paid and for 225 pairs of shoes. Which indicates that somehow Dumfries did rather good business out of it, after all.

"Disorderly Maxwelltown"

Over the bridges from Dumfries lies Maxwelltown (not to be confused with **Maxwelton,** whose braes are bonny, and which lies 16 miles away on the road to **Moniaive**). A chronicle of last century describes this now pleasant suburb in this robust fashion: "This is one of the most disorderly villages in the kingdom, without any proper local government, and serving as a refuge to the delinquents of Dumfries". Maybe that is why one can still hear Dumfries citizens referring to Maxwelltown with unjust contempt by its old name of simply "The Brig En' ". The community's lawless days were ended in 1810, when it was elected into a free burgh of barony, under the name of Maxwelltown, in honour of Mr Maxwell of Nithsdale, its superior. Placed under the iron rule of a provost, two bailies and four councillors, it "speedily underwent a very remarkable improvement". Today it is as douce and law-abiding as anywhere else in Scotland, although in 1929 it lost its independence as a municipality and became part of Dumfries—geographically it is still in Galloway.

Conspicuous in the Maxwelltown skyline is the tower of the Observatory, once a windmill, and now the Burgh Museum. Here can be seen much Burns material and such objects as Paul Jones' *Euclid*; Old Mortality's pocket-book; a replica of the world's first pedal-propelled bicycle, built by Kilpatrick Macmillan, the Keir blacksmith; and the "Siller Gun" presented to the seven incorporated trades of Dumfries in 1617 by James VI to be shot for on Kingholm Merse. The winding stair up the shaft of the old windmill leads to a camera obscura affording fascinating peeps at the surrounding district. In the grounds are a familiar sculptured group representing Old Mortality with his inseparable pony companion.

A mile out of Maxwelltown, at the junction of the Cluden and the Nith, is Lincluden Abbey.*

Like every other Border town, Dumfries has her common-riding ceremony. The Cornet, Cornet's Lass and Pursuivant make their gay ride in June, on Guid Nychburris Day. Guid Nychburris Week takes its name from the old custom whereby quarrelsome citizens would be haled before a magistrate and compelled to take an oath to keep Gude Nychborhude. During this week of good fellowship and celebration, the Marches are ridden, a pageant of local history enacted, and during a ceremony at the Mid Steeple a Pursuivant (King's Messenger) hands over the Charter of Freedom granted by William the Lion, the Burgh Seal and the Burgh Flag and seisin of stone, earth and water to the Provost, who then delivers the Burgh Flag into the safekeeping of the Cornet.

Another colourful ceremony in the Dumfries calendar is the crowning of the Queen of the South at the Mid Steeple.

During the last week of September the tree-lined thoroughfare, Whitesands, along the left bank of the River Nith, is the scene of the Rood Fair, believed to date from the time of William the Lion. In a charter dated 30th September, 1592, granted by King James VI, it is stated that "Our Burgh of Dumfries has but one Fair yearly . . . being at harvest time; but, as the people have worked so well at this harvest, they will be allowed to have another Fair at Candlemas".

The motto of Dumfries is "A Lore Burne"—evolved from that significant phrase "All at the Lore Burn". This rallying cry of terrible urgency was shouted through the streets in times of imminent peril, and they were many. At Dumfries the mustering ground was to the east—the side nearest the Border—and a street in the vicinity of the original course of Lowerburn still bears the name Loreburn Street.

The yells of "Lorburn!" are known to have rung out in 1607,

* Fully described in the *Glasgow, Kyle and Galloway* volume of *Queen's Scotland*.

when a Government officer with a small party of horse was driven from Dumfries, but local tradition claims that the cry was used also in 1715 when the Viscount Kenmure camped on the heights of Tinwald with the intention of leading his army on the town. But so fearsome were the war-cries and other preparatory noises coming from the town that he removed himself and his army to Annan.

DUNS
Duns Dings A'

One of the days we visited Duns was a market-day, when the cars and vans and jeeps of many farmers jostled one another in the central square. We could not but note that the buildings in Duns were very like those vehicles—set at odd angles just where their owners had seen fit, some large, some small, some short, some tall, some pushing well forward, others shouldered into the row behind and turning half sideways to peer past their neighbours.

Dominating all this company of Scottish buildings—quite a few of them have typical and attractive Scots visages—is the Town Hall. Bang into the heart of the spacious square of Berwickshire's County Town strides this piece of Victorian Gothic—genial, full-breasted, self-important. A high square tower topped with four finials proclaims its civic pomp; a white clock-face blandly counts the prosperous busy hours.

The square lacks only one thing to complete the utter Scottishness of it all—a mercat cross. Duns has one, a slender and gracefully proportioned one, but it was pensioned off from market square duties some 60 years ago, and now lives in flower-bedded idleness in Duns grand public park.

The parish church is not so intrusive as the Town Hall. It and its graveyard have to be sought out, and reached through an opening between shops and offices. And when we arrive there, we are, architecturally speaking, too late. For the minister of Duns, as late as 1874, insanely pulled down the original chancel of a Norman church, "to improve the churchyard". The only vestige is a lintel stone from the Wedderburn aisle, inscribed *Death cannot sinder . . . 1608.*

To this church on Sunday morning, 6th May, 1787, Farmer Ainslie of Berrywell and his son Robert and his daughter Rachel went for morning service. With them was Mr Ainslie's guest, Robert Burns.

Doctor Bowmaker, the minister, preached about sin, and like the bishop in Calvin Coolidge's story he was against it. The charming Miss Rachel thumbed through her Bible, but she could not find the text. Burns took the Bible from her and wrote on the end-paper:

> *Fair maid, you need not take the hint,*
> *Nor idle texts pursue:*
> *'Twas guilty sinners that he meant,*
> *Not* Angels *such as you.*

Over the next two weeks Miss Ainslie appeared frequently in the poet's Journal. The last entry, on 23rd May, is: "Charming Rachel; may thy bosom never be wrung by the evils of this life of sorrows, or by the villainy of this world's sons." Charming Rachel died nearly forty years later . . . unmarried.

Of the origin of the town's pugnacious motto—"Duns Dings A' "—the most likeable story is the one about the townspeople of Duns driving away the Earl of Northumberland's army on a night in 1377. All they used were a few home-made rattles—dry skins stretched over a frame and filled with small stones. These appliances were in use to frighten deer away from crops: "dinged" at night around the camp they set horses and English in a panic, and those soldiers who didn't run fast enough to get out of reach were butchered on the banks of the "Bluidy Burn".

Duns Castle

Duns Castle, elegant and Gothic, the work of James Gillespie Graham, stands in a wooded estate less than a mile north-west of the town. At the east end of it, and incorporated into it, is an ancient tower, much modernised, reputed to have been built for Randolph, Earl of Moray, in 1320, as a gift from his uncle, Robert the Bruce.

General Leslie is said to have had his G.H.Q. in this castle in 1639 when he brought Scottish troops from Kelso and from Dunglass, and encamped on Duns Law, while the English army under Charles I waited at Horncliffe, south of the Tweed. This has been named The Prayerful Encampment. Before every captain's tent stood a standard proclaiming in golden letters *For Christ's Crown and Covenant*. This Covenanting Army, with its "superfluity of ministers", witnessed a remarkable landslide in which part of the hill fell away and disclosed to view "innumerable stones, round in shape and perfectly spherical . . . like ball of all sizes". Many interpreted this free issue of ammunition as a direct sign from God. But no battle took place. A Pacification was arranged, and the Scottish army was disbanded. On Duns Law is still to be seen a stone where the standard of the Covenant is alleged to have flown.

A distinguished native of Duns was John Duns Scotus, the "angelic doctor". The Franciscan friar, born in a house near the Castle, lectured at Merton College, Oxford, went to Paris in 1304 and to Cologne in 1308. He died in Cologne and was buried in the Cathedral there. Renowned for his learning and his originality, he divided the allegiance of the Schoolmen with the Dominican Thomas Aquinas, and for centuries the name of Scotists was applied to half the medieval theologians of Christendom.

A second illustrious and well-loved theologian born in Duns was Thomas Boston (1676–1732), author of *The Fourfold State*, which for long ranked second only to the Bible in every pious Scottish household. He ministered for eight years at Simprin in Swinton and spent the last twenty-five years of his saintly life at Ettrick.

Visitors to Duns through the ages make a noble and historically illustrative pageant. Bruce himself is believed to have lain here with his army in 1318, immediately before his successful assault on Berwick. King James IV met his nobles in Parliament Close, in South Castle Street. King James VI came to Duns in 1602 and "gart hang many Border thieves". Mary Queen of Scots rode through on 14th November, 1566, on her way from Langton to Wedderburn Castle.

Broch of Edinshall

Away up in the glorious moorland country, on the north-eastern slope of Cockburn Law, still in Duns parish though very much nearer to Abbey St Bathans, stands the Broch of Edinshall. The view from the Broch over the curving waters of the Whiteadder must be one of the loveliest—and, incidentally, the least-known—landscapes in our island. But it is not for the view that we have climbed pantingly to the summit of the Law. We have come to see a strange dwelling-house of our forbears.

The actual broch is built in the interior of a fine fort, probably of earlier date, oval in shape, 500 feet long by 300 broad, with double ramparts, and further walls and mounds within. Thus, elaborately protected, this remarkable specimen of an ancient dwelling—a type found only in Scotland—survives sufficiently to give a clear idea of its prehistoric architecture. Narrow chambers are set in the thickness of the walls around a central paved courtyard 55 feet across. The surrounding ring of dry-stone masonry is 15 to 20 feet thick. Let into it, at the four points of the compass, are four quite separate "flats", approached by a narrow passage from the courtyard, giving access to left and right into cells nine or 10 feet long. The un-mortared stonework, mostly of whinstone, interlocks most cunningly by means of grooves and projections.

It is an amazing work—one that seems to bring us close to those remote ancestors of ours. Picture them huddled together in their dark and smoky houses, with Fear always one of the company: fear of enemies, fear of illness and loss, fear of death, fear of the unknown in an age when so much was unknown. Before we go down the hill-side to our waiting car, we salute those forbears, those men and women who lived through and surmounted those fears, who wrought with skill and foresight to outwit their enemies and to protect and nurture their children. They handed on no mean heritage to us, their descendants, with our "higher standards of living", but perhaps no higher standards of fortitude and love and patience.

DUNSCORE   *Ellisland and Craigenputtock*

What a parish is this Dunscore between the Nith and Cairn Water! Could any other 11 miles of quiet countryside contain such rich and contrasting associations? Robert Burns and Thomas Carlyle in the same landscape, with Grierson of Lag to add a bitter salt to the tale.

In the history of any nation's letters it would be difficult to find two more dissimilar in character and art than those two giants of Scotland's literature—Burns and Carlyle. And yet here in this one parish we find, only 11 miles apart, the homes they chose and to which they brought their wives.

Burns' Happiest Home

Some five miles east of the village of Dunscore, on the banks of the Nith, is the farm of Ellisland, which Burns—making "a poet's choice but not a farmer's"—rented from Patrick Miller of Dalswinton. The farmhouse we see today—equipped in 1955 with electric light—is a long, low building, the home he built for Jean Armour and their children. A stony uphill road leads to it and we find it a modest place, though not so modest as it was when Burns lived here. Yet its gentle pastoral setting and the walks along the river banks of the Nith remain as he knew and loved them.

It was here towards the end of November 1788, that the poet welcomed Jean to her new home in the song "I ha'e a wife o' my ain, I'll partake wi' naebody". It was the first time he had enjoyed a roof of his own with his young family, and often in later years he described his first winter at Ellisland as the happiest of his life. Happiness indeed is reflected in the work he did there. His love for Jean comes singing out of another lovely song he wrote soon after she had arrived at Ellisland, *O were I on Parnassus Hill*.

> *Then come, sweet Muse, inspire my lay;*
> *For, a' the lee-lang simmer's day,*
> *I couldna sing, I couldna say,*
> *How much, how dear I love thee.*

And here, too, he wrote one of the greatest works in all literature—the magnificent *Tam O' Shanter*, a poem sadly too often mouthed and murdered for haggis-swollen audiences at Burns Night suppers, and sadly too seldom given the study and attention a mighty masterpiece deserves. Such richness of imagery, such eloquence of metaphor is rarely seen outside Shakespeare; had Burns written but this one poem and no other he would still be worthy of his place at the summit. For having been the ground that saw its creation, Ellisland is forever hallowed.

Carlyle's Home

A poet's choice led Burns to the pastoral acres on the gentle eastern side of the parish. Carlyle's choice was more austere, and took him to a very contrasting eyrie. West of Dunscore lie Bogrie Hill and the moors of Stroquhan and Craigenputtock, and six miles west of Dunscore, against a background of morasses and bleak hills, is the remote moorland farm of Craigenputtock.

To this two-storeyed, fir-shadowed farmhouse, "16 miles from a baker", Carlyle brought his wife soon after marriage. It was both impregnable shelter and impregnable fortress, sunk, quiet as a grave, in a curlew-haunted land.

So lonely was it that two previous tenants had gone mad. Another had taken to drink. Yet it had the kind of quiet that appealed to Carlyle, the quiet he needed for his work. Here he forged fiercely his first masterpiece, *Sartor Resartus*. Here, too, he wrote, appropriately, his essay on Burns. And here he and Jane Welsh Carlyle were

happy . . . as happy as ever they were. Emerson found them so
when he visited his friend . . .

> . . . among wild and desolate heathery hills and without a single
> companion in this region out of his own house. There he has his wife,
> a most accomplished and agreeable woman. . . . Truth and peace and
> faith dwell with them and beautify them.

And when sunlight falls across the study where *Don Quixote* was
once read by friendly lamplight we hear the laughter of Jane Welsh
Carlyle as she writes to her dear "Bess" in Edinburgh:

> My tea is done, and my coffee is done, and my sugar, white and
> brown: and without a fresh supply of these articles my Husband
> would soon be done also. . . .
> Craigenputtock is no such frightful place as the people call it.
> Till lately, indeed, our existence here has been made black with smoke:
> and confusion unspeakable was nearly turning our heads. But we
> are beginning to get a settlement at last, and see a distinct prospect of
> being more than tolerably comfortable . . . I read and work and talk
> with my Husband and never weary. . . .

Lag's Fearful Death

From memories so appealing and persons so rich and lovely it is
with reluctance that we turn to the third name in this contrasted trio.
Some two miles from Dunscore village is the massive ruin of the
Tower of Lag, home of Sir Robert Grierson of Lag, notorious for his
persecution of the Covenanters. His remains lie in the old churchyard not far from Ellisland. Tradition has it that a corbie perched on
his coffin all the way from Lag to the grave.

But one established circumstance—and a most macabre one—of
the burial of that grim personage is that Grierson had grown so
grossly fat at the end of his life that a breach had to be made in the
wall of the house before his corpse could be carried out. As for the
manner of his dying, well, that was as tortured as any death suffered
by his victims. During his last days men stood in a line from his
death-chamber to the Nith passing along buckets of water to douse
the hellish fires of his gouty limbs, and it is fearsomely recorded that
"the instant his feet touched the water it fizzed and boiled"!

Let us turn quickly from him to happier things, and welcome back
Robert Burns in convivial rantin', roarin' fashion.

South of the Tower of Lag, on the road from Dunscore to Ellisland, is the farm of Laggan. In the autumn of 1789 William Nicol—
one of the masters of the High School at Edinburgh and Burns'

companion in his tour of the Highlands—held a housewarming at Laggan. Burns came over from Ellisland and brought his friend, Allan Masterton, a writing-master in Edinburgh.

"We had such a joyous evening," says Burns, "that Masterton and I agreed, each in his own way, that we should celebrate the business."

Burns' way of celebrating made the housewarming immortal, for he wrote a song which Masterton set to music.

> *O Willie brew'd a peck o' maut,*
> *And Rob and Allan cam to pree;*
> *Three blyther hearts, that lee-lang night,*
> *Ye wad na found in Christendie.*

> Chorus: *We are na fou, we're nae that fou,*
> *But just a drappie in our e'e;*
> *The cock may craw, the day may daw,*
> *And ay we'll taste the barley bree.*

Friars Carse

We go further along that same road from Dunscore to the Nith to meet Burns again in convivial mood. At the end of the road, on the banks of the Nith, two miles from Auldgirth, is the house of Friars Carse, where Burns spent many an hour with "fine, fat fodgel" Francis Grose at the hospitable table of Captain Riddell, and on Friday night of 16th October, 1790, Burns acted as arbiter in a bacchanalian contest for *The Whistle*. In his own preface to the poem he wrote on that occasion Burns tells of the giant Danish gentleman who carried with him "a little ebony whistle which, at the commencement of the orgies, he laid on the table, and whoever was the last able to blow it was entitled to carry it off as a trophy of victory".

After three days and three nights of hard drinking Sir Robert Lawrie of Maxwelton won the whistle, leaving the Dane under the table, "and blew on the whistle his requiem shrill". On the night when Burns acted as judge there were three contestants: Sir Robert of Maxwelton, Robert Riddell of Glenriddel and Alexander Ferguson of Craigdarroch.

William Hunter of Cockrune, a servant at Friars Carse at the time, has left this account of the contest.

> Burns was present the whole evening. He was invited to attend the party to see that the gentlemen drank fair and to commemorate the

day by writing a song. I recollect well that when the dinner was over, Burns quitted the table and went to a table in the same room, and there he sat down for the night. I placed before him a bottle of rum and another of brandy, which he did not finish, but left a good deal of each when he rose from the table after the gentlemen had gone to bed. . . .

When the gentlemen were put to bed, Burns walked home without any assistance, not being the worse for drink. When Burns was sitting at the table, he had pen, ink and paper. He now and then wrote on the paper, and while the gentlemen were sober, he turned round often and chatted with them, but drank none of the claret which they were drinking. I heard him read aloud several parts of the poem, much to the amusement of the three gentlemen.

At Ellisland Burns' wife was waiting for him, and of that night she remembered that he "came home in his ordinary trim".

Notice, by the way, how the name of Lawrie of Maxwelton has crept into this story of Dunscore and notice also the name of Ferguson of Craigdarroch. He carried off the Whistle that night. His father had also won a Dumfriesshire prize—none other than the noted Bonnie Annie Laurie. But Annie's home, **Maxwelton,** lies just over the frontier of Dunscore parish. It would be too much, surely, for Dunscore to possess that as well!

Isle Tower

About a mile further down the right bank of the Nith from Ellisland, beyond the Laggan Burn, is little Isle Tower, a handsome survivor of ancient Scotland, and the house Burns lived in while Ellisland was being built. Isle Tower is one of the oldest inhabited buildings in Scotland and a memorial of the gratitude of Robert the Bruce.

When the Bruce was a fugitive in south-west Scotland, a Ferguson follower saved the future King of Scots from drowning near this spot in a flood of the River Nith. When King Robert came to the throne he granted the lands around the scene of the deed to the Fergusons, directed that the property should be known as the "Isle", and gave the family permission to bear the lion rampant on their arms.

The lion rampant and the initials of John Ferguson are seen in the carved panel over the gate at the entrance to the Castle. The date carved there, 1587, is apparently the date when Isle was completed, though the tower was originally built, it is believed, in 1414. It is a charming little tower, crow-stepped and turreted and beautifully preserved.

Each floor of the tower is a single apartment, and the floors are linked by a wheel stair—built with a right-hand twist so that defenders should have the advantage with their swords if any attacker forced an entrance.

Other interesting features of the little tower are a secret recess above one of the small square wall cupboards and the iron yett at the entrance with its bars interlaced in the unique Scots style.

DURISDEER   *The Queensberry Marbles*

Durisdeer is in Upper Nithsdale, six miles north of **Thornhill,** and the road up to it is an enchanting one. But the finest approach is from the north, between the wild bleak walls of the Dalveen Pass, that noble defile which leads down through the hills from Crawford's wind-flattened moors. The Dalveen competes with neighbouring Mennock Pass for the title of grandest pass of the Southern Highlands.

Tucked away in its little woodland niche at the foot of all this grandeur, Durisdeer hides in its church a treasure quite remarkable in so Scottish a scene. This is the sumptuous marble monument brought from Rome to grace the Douglas mausoleum in the north transept. The two sculptured figures represent James, second Duke of Queensberry, and his Duchess. On this monument the virtues of the Duchess, who died 2nd October, 1709, are extolled in language grand as marble itself.

> . . . who being sprung on the father's side from the very illustrious families of Burlington and Cumberland, on the mother's side from those of Somerset and Essex, tempered the splendour of her lineage by her winning disposition, heightened it by greatness of spirit, and rendered, by the seductive allurement of her wit and beauty, her sterner virtue pleasing and acceptable to her most loving husband, while he was engaged in the ever-changing affairs of state.

Included in those ever-changing affairs was, of course, the inveigling of Scotland into the Parliamentary embrace of England in the Union of 1707, and it would certainly need all the Duchess's seductive allurements of wit and beauty to take the Duke's mind off the macabre event of the day when the Union was signed, for on that day his heir, Lord Drumlanrig, murdered and roasted and began to eat a spit-boy in front of the kitchen fire at Queensberry House in Edinburgh.*

* See *Edinburgh and the Lothians* volume of *Queen's Scotland.*

DURISDEER

The epitaph for the Duchess concludes with the statement:

> James, Duke of Queensberry, has caused this monument to be erected with this hope and only solace, that under the same tomb where he has placed these beloved ashes, he will place his own.

That mournful hope was realised in less than two years: he died on 6th July, 1711. And on the panel behind the figures of Duke and Duchess four cherubs carry aloft a scroll recording the fulfilment of his wish.

On the breast of the Duke a scar marks where the Garter Star was plucked away by some sacrilegious thief, and a broken finger of the Duchess shows that she was also attacked and despoiled of her gold ring. She wears her coronet and an ermine-edged robe. The monument is flanked by two marble cherubs, weeping, tears welling on to their cheeks.

An iron trapdoor gives access to the burial vault containing the remains of 12 Douglas kinsmen of the Duke.

One of these is his son, Charles, third Duke, whose wife was that celebrated and eccentric beauty Catherine, patron of John Gay and friend of Congreve, Pope and Walpole. She gave great parties at her London home, but promptly at midnight turned out all those she did not want to stay for supper. Even those who stayed got no meat, for meat suppers were not her custom; they had to be content "with half an apple puff and a little wine and water". Even in her seventies she was exquisitely beautiful and insisted on dressing in the style in vogue when she was a young girl. She, too, is buried at Durisdeer. She died in London in 1777, "from eating too many cherries"!

A more sombre memorial at Durisdeer is that one recording the martyrdom of Daniel McMichael, a Covenanter shot dead by orders of Sir John Dalyell in 1685.

> On the 2nd Sabbath of October 1842 an appropriate and impressive sermon was preached by the Rev. Peter Carmichael, Penpont, . . . nigh to the spot of Daniel McMichael's martyrdom. By the proceeds of the collection made by a large and respectable congregation is this plain but respectable memorial erected . . .

> *As Daniel cast was in Lyons den*
> *For praying unto God and not to men*
> *So Lyons thus cruel devour me*
> *For bearing witness to truth's testimony*
> *I rest in peace*
> *Till Jesus rend the clouds*
> *And judge twixt me and those who shed my blood.*

The "factor's stone" in the churchyard—decorated with a retainer in livery—covers the remains of the children of William Lukup, Master of Works in 1685 at Drumlanrig, the Queensberry seat then being built by William, first Duke and father of the one so grandiloquently entombed at Durisdeer.

EARLSTON   *The Rhymer's Town*

Though seven centuries have come and gone since True Thomas lay on Huntlie Bank and saw "a ladye come riding down by the Eildon Tree", his memory is still green among the green haughs of Leader and in the little town of Earlston, his own Ercildoune.

Thomas is our first Scottish poet, but a misty, unresolved figure belonging to the day when fact and faerie were more closely interwoven than in our hard-headed times. His very name is in doubt. Was he really Sir Thomas Learmont of Ercildoune, or simply Thomas Rimour?

His tower, held together in an armour-plating of ivy, stands unassumingly in a potato-field, upon which a factory and a garage and a telephone-exchange turn their uninterested backs. The Edinburgh Borderers' Association bought it in 1895 and affixed a tablet to assure its immortality. Recently, however, the National Trust, after examination, stated—alas!—that it could not have existed in the Rhymer's 13th century. But the generations which hearkened and will hearken to Thomas the Rhymer's prophecies pay small heed to a prosy announcement from a National Trust. It is still and always will be "Rhymer's Tower".

Thomas lived there all his life—from, perhaps, 1219 to, probably, 1299—except for the seven years that he spent in Elfland with the Queen of Faerie. She it was who gave him the tongue that cannot lie —to foretell, for instance, the succession of Robert Bruce, the sudden death of Alexander III on the cliffs at Kinghorn, the union of the Scots and English crowns under one of Bruce's blood, and much else besides. Scores of wise and prophetic saws have since been attributed to Thomas, and—as we have seen at Bemersyde—he was proved right again as recently as 1919.

As we leave the Rhymer's Tower behind us and make for Earlston's main street, two things catch our eye. The first, a modern drinking-fountain set in the wall, is a practical memorial to John Young, Earlston's beloved physician and family doctor for fifty years, before ever the "National Health" set in. The second is the comely spacious Square, beautified since 1953 by a fair rose-garden, laid out on what was formerly a patch of worn grass as an apt and imaginative commemoration of Queen Elizabeth's crowning.

Built into the east wall of the Parish Church is an ancient small stone, with restored letters stating: AULD RYMR RACE LYEES IN THIS PLACE. It came from an older church, replaced by this present one, which was built in 1892 by that dominant disciplinarian, Dr William Mair, minister of Earlston for thirty-four years, moderator of the General Assembly in 1897, and writer of Mair's *Digest*, which is still the basic authority on Scots Church Law. In the tower is the old bell cast by Jan Burgerhuys, of Middelburg in 1609.

Among the quaint gravestones is one which simply says:

> *Time how short*
> *Eternity how long.*

As you descend the steep hill where a church has stood since the reign of the Sair Sanct, David I (1124–1153), you look over the town's roof-tops and the bijou gasworks to the Black Hill, famed for its views over Tweed and Leader's "troutful streams", and bearing on its ancient face the wrinkles of three concentric rings of ramparts built there in prehistoric times.

Modern Earlston is busy with saw-mills, tweed-mills, gingham-mills, quarrying, building, haulage. And its young men play, as they work, energetically. Rugby is strongly—one might say fiercely —supported; Carolside Cricket Club has a long history and lovely grounds; and True Thomas has bequeathed his name to the Rhymers Football Club.

But its chiefest charm lies now, as it did in the past, in the views and walks which Sir Walter knew and loved. The beechwoods stretching away to Birkinside. The road to **Mellerstain** ablaze with autumn. The confluence of the waters at Drygrange.

> "... *with the milk-white yowes*
> *Twixt Tweed and Leader standing*".

House of Cowdenknowes

And mansions where the names are as lovely as the places—Carol-side and Leadervale, Redpath Rig and Cowdenknowes. Many before Sir Walter came and saw and loved these gentle wooded haughs: King David in 1136, his son Prince Henry seven years later,

James IV, who "campit an nicht in Ersilton" on his way to Flodden, Prince Charles in 1745 on his southward march to Berwick.

Cowdenknowes—of the old ballad of the *Bonnie Broom o' the Cowdenknowes*—is a fine 16th-century building "where Homes had ance commanding". The initials of the Homes are on the lintel of the south-east doorway, along with the date 1574. True, Thomas left a curse upon Cowdenknowes:

Vengeance, vengeance! When and where?
Upon the house of Cowdenknowes, now and evermair.

But curses sit lightly on this lovely place, where Mary slept on her way from Edinburgh to Jedburgh and planted a chestnut tree. That tree is gone, and so is the Hanging Tree used—so we are told here— to hang Covenanters. Though in Lauderdale and the Merse the sentence on them was more often a fine than death. Indeed, this region must be the native heath of the Borderer who, when setting off to fight Bonaparte, refused to take any money with him. "They may kill me if they like, but they'll get nae siller aff me."

ECCLEFECHAN · *The Sage's Birthplace*

There is a picture of an aged woman. It is like scores of pictures of its period—a hundred-odd years ago—and the face bears the wrinkles and years that we have seen on the faces of thousands of old women. The dark hair, smoothed heavily down from a centre parting, is seen only at the temples, where two smooth triangles of it are left uncovered by the enveloping hood of white ruched torchon lace which ends under the chin with a bow meticulously and symmetrically tied. The hood outlines the face to an almost geometrical oval, and its whiteness throws into harsh contrast the weathered tints of the ageing skin. From this grotesquely wide white-lace frame the face stares out at us questioningly. It is a stare half of bewilderment and half of suspicious impatience. For behind the antiquely wrinkled forehead is surprise at being called upon to sit thus, clasping a book uncomfortably still, while a painter fellow scrawls and daubs on the square of canvas on an easel.

It is a formidable face with a big bold nose and a heavy chin; the whole visage possessing that masculine heaviness into which a lifetime of work and responsibility can cast a woman's face, and the skin is seamed with thought and worry.

It is the face of the woman who came to this village as Margaret Aitken, second wife of James Carlyle. It is the face of the woman who cleaned and cooked, washed and polished in the house where her picture now hangs on the wall. It is the face of a mother, a Scots mother, and it is like millions of others of her hard-working, dour generation. On a December afternoon in 1795 this mother gave birth to a boy, and thought the process no more remarkable than any other mother would think it. But the boy was Thomas Carlyle. The child born in this modest room became one of the great men of his day—became known as "The Sage of Chelsea", an odious soubriquet which ranks among other nauseating nicknames in the "Bard of Avon" class. Because of that this house has become a museum. And because of that the mother had to sit for her portrait and feel bewildered about it. That dour bewilderment is, we feel, shared by the village, a dour, plain place which is still bewildered at having so often to sit under the gaze of portrait painters and tourists. For it is just a typical workaday Lowland village.

The traveller hurrying along the road from Carlisle to **Lockerbie** sees the sign Ecclefechan and a straggle of houses along the side of the main road. But that is not the real Ecclefechan. The village lies off the road, a quiet street of cottages with a burn flowing before the doorsteps; the whole scene surely not much changed since the days when the Carlisle–Glasgow stage sounded its horn night and morning.

The house where Carlyle was born is known as the "Arched House". The burn that runs down the street and past its door is the *Kuhbach* (cow brook), still "gushing kindly by", as described in *Sartor Resartus*.

The room where Carlyle was born is the big room above the kitchen. For years it was said he was born in a little room across the landing. The reason for this mistake is at once amusing and understandable. A tenant of the house, embarrassed by the stream of visitors, used to show them that little room as the birthplace. It saved having to show them into the larger room where he and his family lived and tried to avoid being trooped over by tourists.

It is a modest museum for so majestic a great man. There are lots of interesting pictures and photographs, but the exhibits most appealing, and indeed most revealing and interesting, are the domestic objects of everyday use, the things which that mother as well as Thomas handled. A roasting jack, a horsehair sofa and an eight-day kitchen clock. Or the brass jelly-pan, the tea-caddy and the china soup ladle. Carlyle's walking-stick, felt hat, tobacco cutter and ingenious spring clothes-pin used as a paper clip. . . . How such things quicken the imagination and make us see not the towering genius of Thomas Carlyle, but the native of Ecclefechan.

A narrow street leads to the village churchyard where Carlyle was buried on a "cloudy, sleaty day" in February, 1881. It is fitting that the grave of this man who hated ostentation should be a simple granite slab, so unpretentious that it is difficult to find.

The churchyard also contains a headstone to Archibald Arnott, Napoleon's medical attendant at St Helena. A later Ecclefechan Dr Arnott left an odd 19th-century "memorial", an iron plaque affixed to a wall above the village burn, which reads: "1875. 209 feet of the burn below this spot was arched over by Dr Arnott at his own expense". He had, it seems, no regard for *Sartor Resartus*.

ECCLES *Tweedside Parish*

The parish of Eccles has the River Leet along part of its eastern boundary, and for its southern boundary nearly four miles of Tweed, quiet and deep-flowing between rich, level fields.

Confused ruins of the Cistercian convent at Eccles, founded in 1165 by Gospatrick, Earl of Dunbar, and burned down in 1545 by Hertford, are to be seen at the west side of the churchyard, and the east wall of Eccles House was probably part of the old Nunnery. The bell in Eccles Kirk bears the words *Feare God yee people of Eckles. 1659. I.R. J.R.*

Other ancient things in this parish include Leitholm Peel, a ruined Border tower just north-east of Stainrig House; a bastel house called Bite-About, on Printonan Hill; and a wheel-headed 15-foot-high stone cross by the roadside, a quarter of a mile south-west of Crosshall Farm.

The memory of a great judge and philosopher is kept alive at Kames, birthplace of Henry Home (1696–1782), who, when he was raised to the Bench in 1752, took the name of Lord Kames. His most notable works were *Elements of Criticism* and *Sketches of the History of Man*. The title of another, *Loose Hints on Education*, conjures up in the modern mind a series of Ronald Searle schoolgirls and schoolboys, but assuredly its contents were very much more solemn.

ECKFORD   *The "Bad Old Days"*

Two remnants of the "bad old days" are to be seen at Eckford Parish Church. Outside are the jougs in which offenders were placed, and among the gravestones in the churchyard is a watch-tower built in the days of the Resurrectionists.

In the parish, which includes Cessford, Kirkbank and Caverton, is Haughhead, which belonged in the days of Charles II to the zealous Covenanter, Habbie Hall. Here Richard Cameron received his licence to preach.

EDDLESTON   *The Man Who Did It*

Lead a Scot to the entrance of the mansion of Portmore in this north Peeblesshire town and tell him why the house became famous. Then watch the reaction. He might approve and nod his head; or disapprove, and even mutter an oath.

For Portmore was the birthplace of William Forbes MacKenzie, a man who has left on Scottish life a stamp that has endured now for more than a century. He it was who secured in 1852 the passing of that magnificent or infamous—have it how you will—Public House Act which closed public houses on Sundays in Scotland.

Another local mansion takes us further back in history. This is Black Barony, which was the former home of the Murrays and later Lords Elibank. The original Border Black Barony was built in 1412, but in the 17th century it was transformed into a massive château-like residence.

Further—much further—back in history we go when we walk into the hills encircling the village, for there abound traces of ancient habitations, including five prehistoric hill forts. The two best preserved are at Northshield Rings and Milkiston.

The Boy who Dreamed of Spires

Some two miles from Eddleston, on the road to **Peebles,** is the attractive roadside cottage which, at the beginning of the last century, was the workshop of Andrew Noble, joiner and wheelwright. To this cottage there came on 14th June, 1809, a young lad, son of a Pentlands shepherd, to begin his apprenticeship.

Here the story we have to tell of him is like a story from any book of fairy-tales. The lad became a millwright at Galashiels, and one day, when he was tramping along the road with his tools on his back on his way to that town, a coach overtook him near Elibank Tower and stopped. The gentleman in the coach leaned out and asked the lad if he would like a lift. The lad noticed that this traveller, a kindly, talkative gentleman, was lame, but not until he had been set down at Galashiels did he know his name: it was Walter Scott.

Sometime later, when the lad was sketching at Melrose, the poet came up and looked over his shoulder, but the young artist was too timid to speak. By that time the lad was embarked on that study of Gothic architecture which was to be his absorbing passion—a passion born, maybe, on the day when his father first took him to Rosslyn chapel and the whole wonder of it burst suddenly upon him. Pursuing his study, the boy tramped to London and went on to France, working as a millwright and spending his free hours staring at Gothic arches and spires, dreaming—as young people do ambitiously dream—of the day when he might design such things himself. But his dream was different from many such youthful dreams in that it came true. He did design a Gothic spire, one of the most famous in his native country, one known and recognised throughout the world. But he saw only the beginning of its building, for he was drowned in a tragic accident before the work was finished.

The boy was George Meikle Kemp, and his spire was the Scott Monument, the extravagant Gothic memorial which enshrines the statue and the memory of that same lame and kindly gentleman who once gave him a lift on the road to Galashiels.

At Redscaurhead a bronze tablet with a miniature of the Scott monument commemorates him: "George Meikle Kemp, Carpenter and Architect. Born 1795. Died 1844." And in the Scott Monument is a bust of him.

EDNAM   *Two Poets, Two Songs*

This pretty little village on Eden Water's banks was the birthplace of two poets, both of whom wrote songs that are known and sung by millions.

South of the village a 52-foot-high obelisk commemorates the birth at Ednam Manse on 11th September, 1700, of James Thomson, who, although he wrote *Rule, Britannia* and some ludicrous verse dramas, also wrote *The Seasons* and was a poet of note.

Also born at Ednam was Henry Francis Lyte, author of *Abide With Me*, that loveliest of hymns, and far more worthy of a monument than *Rule, Britannia*, though probably far less in need of one.

EDROM   *Ghosts and Corpses*

It is among the wide and level acres of Edrom parish that the waters of Whiteadder and Blackadder come at last together. At their joining stands the village of Allanton. Allanbank nearby, on the north bank of Blackadder, is still believed by the superstitious to be haunted by the ghost of pathetic "Pearlin Jean".

Allanbank was owned in the 17th century by a family of Stuarts, one of whom played the villain in the sad tale of Pearlin Jean. Sir Robert Stuart wooed and won the lovely Jeanne—a Flemish Jewess, some say, others a Parisienne, others an Italian.

In Paris one morning he harshly left her forever, striding out of the house and into his coach. Decked in the silks and the "pearlin" lace that was to give her her name, poor little Jeanne ran after her lover and tried to mount the carriage. The postillion was roughly ordered to drive on, the girl was thrown to the ground, and the wheel passed over her head.

When in due course the steely-hearted Stuart reached his home at Allanbank, there in the dusky autumnal evening, above the arched gateway that led to his estates, sat the dreadful figure of his murdered mistress gazing down with bloody head upon her slayer. From that day the sad ghost of Pearlin Jean, rustling in her silks and laces, walked the corridors of Allanbank. Seven ministers, all at one time, were not sufficient to exorcise her spirit. The villagers are proud of their sad, sweet ghost; and when the house was pulled down in the 19th century an old woman anxiously inquired: "Where will Pearlin Jean gang, noo that the hoose is dismolished?"

Furthest back in history Allanbank was a fortalice known as East Nisbet, where Ramsay of Dalhousie in 1355 defeated an English army, and later East Nisbet became the Castle of Blackadder.

The village of Edrom, in the north-west corner of the parish, retains one movingly beautiful relic of its 12th-century church—a gracious Norman arch, elaborately carved, standing a few yards west of the parish church, and forming the entrance to a much more modern burial vault. There are traces, too—diagonal buttresses and carved shields—of Robert Blackadder, Archbishop of Glasgow in 1499, whose family lived in these parts, and whose memory is kept green in Glasgow Cathedral.*

* See *Glasgow, Kyle and Galloway* volume of *Queen's Scotland*.

McGall was Buried Twice

Edrom churchyard was the scene of one of the most sensational cases in the history of corpse-snatching—that macabre exercise which was as prevalent in the early 19th century as smash-and-grab is in our day and age. A Duns publican and a Whitelaw farmer friend were driving back one night from Gifford Fair when they met on the road a gig going in the opposite direction. On the seat were three figures. Something about the posture of the centre figure— probably a certain devil-may-care indifference to what was taking place around him—roused the suspicions of the publican and his friend. They gave chase. Two of the men in the other vehicle sprang out and ran into the night. The centre figure remained where he was, and the publican and farmer found their suspicions confirmed; it was the corpse of a man by the name of McGall, buried shortly before at Edrom. A culvert a mile from Edrom where his coffin was found is known to this day as McGall's Brig. An Allanton woman, Mary Manuel, who had dressed McGall for his first burial, had to dress him again for his second.

The incident led to a riot in Duns when the gig had been claimed by the owner and was to be handed back to him. The blacksmith smashed open the door of the coach-house and an indignant crowd dragged it to the market place. Although the Riot Act was being read to them, the citizens of Duns paid no heed; instead they smashed up the vehicle and made a bonfire of it.

Further up the Whiteadder is the modern mansion of Broom-house, which incorporates the walls of an old peel tower. Here, at Bawtie's Grave, lies the body of a handsome Frenchman, Sieur d'Arcies de la Bastie or de la Beaute, a knight appointed by the Duke of Albany as Warden of the East and Middle Marches of the Merse and Teviotdale in place of Alexander Lord Home, executed in Edinburgh, in 1516. The Homes were revenged a year later, meeting de la Bastie near Fogo and pursuing and slaying him, sticking his head on the mercat cross at Duns.

Two miles south of Duns, but still in Edrom parish, stands hand-some Nisbet House with its two circular towers, built during the reign of Charles I by Sir Alexander Nisbet on the site of an old moated castle. The arms of the Kers, and their motto FORWARD, appear above the original old doorway.

Until a century ago there was a mineral spring of proved medicinal

Duns   **Square and Town House**

Duns Castle   **Gateway**

Duns   **Parish Church**   **Dumfries:Burns Memorial**

Ecclefechan   **Carlyle's Birthplace**

Ecclefechan   **Margaret Carlyle's Parlour**

Eildon Hills   **From Bemersyde**

Ecclefechan   **The School**

Galashiels   The Border Reiver

virtue, known as Duns Spa, about a mile from Duns, on the Edrom side of the Langton burn. But a 19th-century drainage scheme caused it totally to disappear, as happened also with St Mary's Well at Whitekirk in East Lothian.

THE EILDON HILLS   *The Mystic Peaks*

Bold on the landscape of Tweeddale rise the triple peaks of these noble hills. As we follow the winding roads around **Melrose** we see them again and again, looking, because of their strange isolation, far higher than a modest 1,300 feet. They catch the eye and capture the imagination, as they have done through the centuries, summoning into the mind strange legends and mystic thoughts.

There was, we are told, only one big hill here until the familiar demon of the wizard Michael Scott cleft them into three.

The Romans knew them well, and on the north-eastern hill built a great camp, and many Roman relics found here are to be seen in the National Museum of Antiquities in Edinburgh. Before the Romans, it is believed, the priests of Baal sacrificed here to the sun-god, and on these slopes Thomas the Rhymer "conceived and delivered to superstitious ears the fortune he darkly foresaw in store for his native country".

To Walter Scott the hills served as a kind of grandstand to romance: from here he could look over the territory he loved and wrote about. "I can", he said, "stand on the Eildon Hills and point out 43 places famous in war and verse."

On the middle hill is now an indicator guiding the eye over the magnificent panorama, from the Cheviot in the south to the Lammer-moors in the north. Here we can gaze out to the heights of Liddes-dale, Eskdale, Ettrick, Yarrow and the Gala uplands, and below us are the lands of the four Border abbeys—**Dryburgh, Melrose, Kelso,** and **Jedburgh.**

ENTERKINFOOT   *The Rescue at Keltie's Linn*

Near the village of Enterkinfoot—on the main **Thornhill–Sanquhar** road—is the ruined church of Kirkbride, of which Robert Reid wrote his Covenanting poem.

> *Bury me in Kirkbride,*
> *Where the Lord's redeemed anes lie!*
> *The auld kirkyaird on the grey hillside*
> *Under the open sky;*

Under the open sky,
On the breist o' the brae sae steep,
And side by side wi' the banes that lie
Streikt there in their hinmaist sleep.

Enterkin Pass, cut into the breast of the Lowther Hills, between the heights of Thirstane and Stey Gail, was described by Dr John Brown as more impressive, with "its sudden and immense depths", than Glencoe or Glen Nevis. The pass is famous in Covenanting history for the daring rescue of a minister and five Covenanters at Keltie's Linn. Twelve intrepid rescuers, led by James and Thomas Harkness of Closeburn, attacked a company of dragoon, frightening them to submission by shooting down their commander, Captain Kelty.

Higher up the glen is Katie's Pool, scene of another of Reid's verses:

Wow! but the braes are dour to speel,
And, what wi' loupin' hags and burns,
It's richt weel-pleased I am to kneel
Beside thee till my breath returns.

ESKDALEMUIR *The Fair of Trial Marriages*

The village of Eskdalemuir stands 600 feet above sea level in the exposed valley of the White Esk. The whole of this wild countryside is dotted with the traces of ancient camps, the most striking of which is Castle O'er, or Castle Overbie, about a mile up the valley from Eskdalemuir Church. This was a Roman station, linked with the camps of Middlesbie and Netherbie by a causeway.

The Black Esk, rising on the hill known as Jock's Shoulder, joins the White Esk some five miles below the village, at the King's Pool; so called because a Pictish king was drowned in it when attempting to cross the ice on it. Nearby, at Yetbyre Farm, is another camp, an oval Saxon one.

Eskdale was the scene of the annual Hand-Fasting Fair, at which unmarried lads and lassies paired of for a year's "trial marriage" until the next Fair, when, if all had gone sweetly, they wed. But if the year's trial had been unsuccessful, then the parties went their way and tried again, any children of the Hand-Fast going with the unsatisfied party. Robert II is said to have engaged in such a Hand-Fast with Elizabeth More before he married the Earl of Ross's daughter, and Robert III is claimed to be a Hand-Fast child.

ETTRICK *The Shepherd's Resting Place*

Near the banks of Ettrick Water, and wrapped thickly around with birch and fir, are the church and manse of Ettrick. Beyond are the hills of Ettrick parish: "all one mighty sheepwalk", says the Ordnance Gazetteer of Scotland, "wave upon wave of long, green, rounded hills, whose rich grass feeds enormous flocks of Cheviots." Here in this churchyard, appropriately in the midst of such country, lies the genial Border poet, James Hogg, the Ettrick Shepherd.

Beside his grave how very many good stories we could tell. And out of each one of them would bustle the happy personality of a man who was surely excellent and lovable company. Walter Scott found him so. Exasperating he was sometimes, good-naturedly opinionated, wrongheaded, almost irresponsible, but ever a man after Scott's heart—a good man, a generous man, and one who loved his fellows, his landscape and his legends.

Hogg is another of Scotland's poets sprung from the soil. Self-taught, adventurous in his craft as he was in life, Hogg sings with sincerity and unsophisticated artistry songs of natural beauty. Psychology and all its kindred sciences have failed to find the key to this mystery of the born poet. Hogg cannot be explained by schooling or hereditary. He had but a year at school. At the age of seven he was herding ewes on the hills of Ettrick, and in his teens he was a full-time shepherd. Indeed, practically the only thing that was ever taught to him was herding sheep. And that teaching did him little good, for as a sheep-farmer he was a notorious failure, again and again losing money in the job, and once bankrupting himself at it. Yet in the thing he taught himself, in the craft of writing, he rose triumphant. Many of his songs are as well known and flow as easily from the lips of Scots as those of Burns. Many, like those of Burns, are recastings of earlier songs, but many are the inspired outpourings of his own poet's heart and ear. His prose did not enjoy during his life the acclaim it deserved, but the recent successful revival of his *Confessions of a Justified Sinner*—a study in suggestive terror—indicates that perhaps he was ahead of his time.

Although Lockhart could never quite forgive Hogg for trespassing into *The Domestic Manners and Private Life of Sir Walter Scott*, he could not entirely resist the warm friendliness of the man. Who could? We owe to Lockhart this picture of Hogg's beginnings as a poet.

Hogg, coming into Edinburgh with a flock of sheep, was seized with a sudden ambition to see himself in type, and he wrote out that same night *Willie and Katie*, and a few obscure booksellers gratified him by printing accordingly.

And Lockhart's story of Hogg's first visit to Castle Street is too delightful to miss.

> When Hogg entered the drawing-room Mrs Scott, being at the time in a delicate state of health, was reclining on a sofa. The Shepherd, after being presented and making his best bow, forthwith took possession of another sofa placed opposite to hers, and stretched himself thereupon at all his length; for as he said afterwards, "I thought I could never do wrong to copy the lady of the house."

This friendly, neighbourly man has good company here in Ettrick churchyard. Here are Tibbie Shiel and Will o' Phaup, and also the Rev. Thomas Boston, minister of Ettrick from 1707, and author of *The Fourfold State*. He has left us this sketch of his last communion service:

> There were very nearly 800 communicants, great numbers of them from a considerable distance. The hospitality of the farmers and all those who had it in their power to accommodate and support them during the preaching days, was beyond all praise. At one farmplace they accommodated nine score; at another they had half a boll of meal baken, besides a quantity of loaf bread; they killed 3 lambs and made up thirty beds.

Those beds, it would seem, must have been crowded!

Hunting Ground for Kings

The name Ettrick Forest is the popular and historic name for most of Selkirkshire. Once it was a forest, wooded thick with oak, and a favourite hunting ground for Scottish kings. Pitscottie tells us how James V, commanding his lords and barons and freeholders to gather in Edinburgh, "with a month's victuals" on an expedition against thieves on the Borders, "also warned all gentlemen that had good dogs to bring them, that he might hunt in the said country". Argyll, Huntly and Athole and other Highland noblemen accepted this invitation.

> The second day of June the King past out of Edinburgh to the hunting, with many of the nobles and gentlemen of Scotland with him, to the number of twelve thousand men; and then past to Meggitland,

and hounded and hawked all the country and bounds; that is to say, Pappert-law, St Mary-laws, Carlavirick, Chapel, Ewindoores, and Longhope. I heard say, he slew, in these bounds, eighteen score of harts.

Also on this expedition apparently he slew a pack of freebooters, including Johnnie Armstrong. But after this jaunt James turned 10,000 sheep into the forest to graze there, and now no trace of the "forest" remains.

Execution at Tushielaw

Four miles down Ettrick Water from Ettrick village, beside the road to Selkirk is a farm, a hotel and a burn, all bearing the sturdy Border name of Tushielaw. Standing forlornly beside the road is the medieval stronghold of Adam Scott, whose head James V put on a spike in Edinburgh after his hunting "purge" of the Borders when he also dispatched Piers Cockburn at St Mary's Loch and Johnnie Armstrong at Teviothead. Scott was known in his day as "King of the Border", and to others as "King of Thieves", and tradition has it that he was hanged on his own gallows tree—an ancient ash conveniently spreading its branches near the tower.

The moorland road from Tushielaw to Hawick passes the farm of Buccleuch where Walter Scott and James Hogg met.

EWES   *The Bell in the Tree*

At Kirkton in Ewes, three miles north of Langholm on the way to Hawick, a church bell hangs in the fork of a tree by the roadside. The bell was hung in this convenient spot when the old church was demolished. Apparently it looked so attractive there when the new church was built in 1867 that it was never moved.

Well into the 18th century Ewesdale was impassable for vehicles and the Lords of Justiciary had to ride on horseback from Jedburgh to Dumfries. One of them was Lord Kames. "What lang black dour-looking chiel is yon?" Armstrong of Sorbie asked. "That," replied Lord Minto, "is a man come to hang a' the Armstrongs."

On Sorbie bridge a tablet commemorates the birth at Sorbie, half-a-mile from Ewes Church, of the poet, the Rev. Henry Scott Riddell, author of *Scotland Yet*, who was incumbent at Caerlanrig, Teviothead, and is buried there.

EYEMOUTH   *The Smugglers' Town*

Fish-guts and stinkin' herrin'
Are bread and milk for an Eyemouth bairn.

So, most impolitely, sang the bairns in the neighbouring villages. The slandered bairns of Eyemouth no doubt had a suitably impolite reply to hurl at their neighbours, as they played on the doorsteps in the narrow, twisted wynds of their native town.

The higgledy-piggledy architecture of those closely-packed houses is thought to be quite deliberate, designed by men and for men bent on jouking the excisemen. It has been said that there was as much of Eyemouth underground as there was above. Double walls and cellars, steps that lifted bodily out of the staircase, even the stool on which the young wife sat to nurse her baby—all these might be cunning hiding-places for contraband.

The only exciseman ever welcomed in the "free-trading" town of Eyemouth was one Robert Burns, when he came in 1787 to be made a Royal Arch mason!

The Water of Eye, which we have seen dancing in its sparkling country freshness from Grantshouse to Ayton, flows at Eyemouth into a picturesque harbour, busy with boat-building, the gutting and packing of fish, and all the other activities of a cheerful East Coast fishing-port. Green mounds rise on each side of this harbour, making a fine frame for the sandy beach and the high pier, the smoking lums of houses close-packed round their livelihood, the rows of bright boats in the river.

The westernmost of these bold promontories, lying like a huge animal, snout on paws, is called The Fort, having had elaborate defence-works twice built upon it, and twice destroyed, during the 16th century.

On the remains of one of the earthworks, called the King's Mount, the coastguard's watch-house stands today. The eastern, known as Gunsgreen, carries the golf-course on its shoulder, as well as a solid Georgian mansion which is now a boarding-house, but was obviously planned for more adventurous living, being fitted with many ingenious contrivances for the storing of smuggled goods. Cromwell visited Eyemouth in 1650, and the nearby tower now used as Eyemouth Golf Clubhouse is associated with his name.

The little town, so full of character, has not succeeded in escaping the infectious rash of modern uglinesses; but the steep, modern, jerry-built streets are redeemed by the perfect cameo of sky and sea that lies at the bottom of each one. Prefabs perched above the unattractive rail-terminus and the disused factory in the ravine where runs the Water of Eye have still the bright boats to look on, and those unalterable acres of blue, blue sea.

Still spoken of with the hushed voice of personal sorrow is the Eyemouth Disaster of Friday, 14th October, 1881. That Black Friday dawned calm and bright, though some of the older fishermen noticed with foreboding that the glass had never stood so low. By eight o'clock the fishing-fleet had sailed from the harbour, Harmony and Press Home, Fiery Cross and Janet, Six Brothers, Industry, Lass o' Gowrie, Myrtle and Forget-Me-Not, close on 30 boats from Eyemouth alone. About midday there came a horrible sort of stillness. The sky was darkened, and with an appalling suddenness a kind of hurricane descended, tore the boats' masts from their sockets, ripped their sails away like wastepaper, and lifted whole boats clean out of the water. Some overturned and disappeared. Others struggled back, only to be thrown on the rocks outside the harbour and their crews drowned within sight of their waiting women.

Some half-dozen boats in all got safely home. Burnmouth and Coldingham and Cove, as well as Newhaven and Fisherrow, lost ships and men, too, on that dreadful day. But 129 fishermen of Eyemouth lost their lives—almost half of the whole adult male population of the town—and for days and weeks folk would go out along the coast east and west, searching and waiting for the bodies of their missing men to be tossed back to them by the indifferent sea. No wonder the grandchildren of those fisher-folk still lower their voices when they speak of Disaster Day.

The Murder at Linthill

A short distance inland, on the east bank of the Eye Water, stands wooded Netherbyres, once the home of Sir Samuel Brown (1776–1852) of the Royal Navy, the suspension-bridge expert, responsible for the old Brighton chain-pier, and for the Union Bridge which crossed the Tweed near Paxton. And on the west bank, a little further inland, overlooking the confluence of Ale and Eye, is the mansion-house of Linthill, which was the scene in 1751 of the notorious murder by her butler, Norman Ross, of the wealthy widow Mrs Patrick Home, the Lady Billie, who lies buried in the old church of Bunkle.

The dastardly butler hid himself in her room, and when he thought she was asleep crept out to rifle the iron-bound box in which were stored her valuables. She awakened, and instantly grappled with the robber. He cut her throat, and, leaving her for dead, proceeded with his rifling. The old lady, dying but indomitable, groped her bloody way along the wall to the bell-rope and summoned the other servants. Norman Ross leapt from the window, broke his leg, was taken, tried and hanged. As for Lady Billie . . . at her funeral the cortege and the mourners had gone some distance towards Bunkle before it was discovered that the coffin had been left behind. As though the poor murdered corpse had not received indignity and notoriety enough.

FAST CASTLE *The Bones of a Plot*

The bones of a man, dug from his grave, were brought into court for judgment. He had been dead nine years, this John Logan of Restalrig, before they discovered that he had been implicated in the Gowrie plot to kidnap King James VI, and now the only way they could punish the rascal was to condemn his bones for high treason.

Fast Castle, perched on a ledge on the precipices of Berwickshire's coast, are the bones of the castle where the plot was hatched. To this place, had the plot succeeded, the kidnapped King would have been brought.

John Logan of Restalrig's bones surely looked no more sinister a bundle in the dock than do these fragments of Fast Castle. You first see the ruins when you reach the brow of the steep grass slopes three miles north-west of St Abb's Head. Far below your toes, on the rock precipices above the waves, is Fast Castle—a few jagged stumps, old witch's teeth sticking out with a grin from thin sea-licked jaws. In certain lights it is difficult at a distance to distinguish the scraps of man-built wall from its surrounding rocks, which, channelled by waves and eroded by time, copy the Castle's demolition with gigantic gestures of immemorial decay.

You step and slide down the steep grass slope, and find when you get to the level of the Castle that you can reach it only over a chasm which separates its rocky perch from the mainland. You step warily across the narrow bridge of packed rocks which has taken the place of the drawbridge that once was slung across the gap. At last you are in the precincts of the Castle, poised dizzily between sea and sky, waves thundering 70 feet below you and gulls wheeling above you.

It was never a big fortress. On top of that sliver of rock there was never room to spread. But it was a mighty important fortress, of big nuisance value to whoever held it, English or Scots, and could be used by either of them as a kind of corsair lair from which, secure against all attack from the land, they could sally out across the waves. At sea-level below the keep is a cavern which a boat could use as its harbour, and its crew climb rocky steps to the fortress above. Fast Castle was important enough, for instance, for the Marshal of Berwick to be sent, in 1510, with no fewer than 2,000 men to wrest it from the 10 Scots then inhabiting it.

It is doubtful who built it, though James VI, looking at the venomous tuft of building clutched on so niggardly a spot, said whoever it was "must have been a knave at heart".

In the 16th century it belonged to the Homes, and then passed by marriage into the hands of Logan of Restalrig. Logan was a wonderful fellow. Apart from cooking up a plot against his sovereign as he sat on this grim little perch he also sold to the great Napier of Merchiston—who, as creator of logarithms, ought to have known better—the idea that there was a vast undiscovered treasure lying concealed under Fast Castle. Cunning Logan drew up a contract under which, it seems, Napier, in return for the expense of finding the treasure, would be given one-third of it: such a contract as might be drawn up by anyone selling the Brooklyn Bridge. But it cost the genius Napier quite a tidy sum before he saw through Logan.

Fast Castle is usually described as the Wolf's Crag of Scott's *Bride of Lammermoor*, although the writer himself never strongly supported that deduction. However, it is grim and romantic enough to serve as such, and although so little of it remains, it is undoubtedly one of the most exciting ruins to be found on the coast of Scotland.

FERNIEHURST   *Where War is Forgotten*

The English are back at Ferniehurst, ancient stronghold of the Kers which the Earl of Sussex demolished nearly 400 years ago. But nowadays they come unarmed and with rucksacks on their backs instead of armour, for this Border Castle on the banks of Jed Water near **Jedburgh** is now a youth hostel, open to all, Scots or English or any other kind who is weary of foot and light of purse.

These wanderers enjoy the shelter of one of the Border's loveliest castles. Ancient muskets in the guest hall remind the visitors of battles of the past, but in the vast banqueting hall with its two fireplaces and stone walls those whose forbears fought hotly and bloodily for possession of it meet as comrades.

Enchanting is the tower doorway, with the corbelled base of a characteristic Ferniehurst turret beside it and the carved armorial plaques above it. Within the Castle, perhaps more exciting as a showplace than are the grand embrasured rooms, is the old kitchen with its barrel-vaulted roof, cobbled floor and remains of the original fireplace.

Further up the river hummocks in the grass outline the site of the chapel founded 1,000 years ago by Ecgred, Bishop of Lindisfarne.

FLOORS CASTLE — *Mansion of the Golden Gates*

A mile from the centre of Kelso is Floors Castle. In all Scotland the seeker of domestic grandeur will find nothing grander than Floors, and certainly few things grander in all Europe.

On one day of the week visitors are allowed to penetrate into the park—enclosed by one of those fabulous unending ribbons of high wall such as ducal owners can lavishly wind around their princely parkland. But the house is so immense, so spread, so much an army of turrets and cupolas that it is best seen from a distance. The finest view of it is from the road to Melrose. There we can gaze at Floors across the Tweed, which noble river flows—almost, it seems, slinks like a peasant—just below the bland and insolent gaze of the terrace-enthroned and aristocratic Floors.

You spend, if you are curious about such things, a half-hour trying to count the graceful ogee-capped turrets which sprout so luxuriantly all over the roofs of the main building and the flanking pavilions. Then you give up. It is easier to do it by multiplication. . . . At each corner of the main building one tower, on each tower four turrets . . . and so on.

The great residence—often described as now the largest inhabited mansion in Britain—is a blue-blooded sight indeed. It has not the architectural refinement of comparable Drumlanrig, but if by virtue of nothing more than that tremendous array, that veritable forest of turrets, it is perhaps more exciting. It was built in 1718 by that versatile playwright-architect Vanbrugh. The work of this creator of Blenheim, the very breather of sumptuosity, should surely have been big enough and grand enough for any duke. But the wealthy Roxburghes wanted even more, and in the 19th century Playfair was commissioned to embellish and extend it. He it was who made it into a beautifully extravagant Tudor palace.

Its magnificence is inspiriting. It makes us quite joyful to think that it still lives and is still lived in. It is the home of the ninth Duke, wealthy sportsman with 60,500 rich Border acres lying around his walls, and even in this dun-coloured age, when great wealth is worn more like disgrace than ermine, Floors has put on mighty shows.

When the present Duke came of age the whole place was floodlit. Forty Mayfair chefs were brought to cook the banquet. When he married, 1,000 guests knelt on cushions of cloth-of-gold. Four hundred wedding presents included jewels, ermine, crystal and £30,000-worth of gems from the Duke's mother. The Duke gave his bride a diamond tiara.

At the end of Roxburgh Street, one of the narrowest of Kelso's thoroughfares, are the "golden gates" to Floors, gates built as recently as 1929 but already legendary and emphasising the magnificence proper to the ducal seat. They are flanked by handsome lodges and are crowned with wrought-iron flourishes of acorns, thistles and lilies laid thick with gleaming gold-leaf. They work by remote control, so that when the gatekeeper hears the hooting of the ducal horn the gates do a kind of "Open Sesame" act and the ducal equipage sweeps on unhindered up the half-mile of tree-lined drive to the wondrous palace.

It is all so right, so appropriate, so much in keeping with the lavish turret-tipped array of the princely home beside the Tweed.

FOGO   *Hogs and Trotters*

Some six miles from Duns, and set amid lush woodland, is the hamlet of Fogo. From the quiet road a lych-gate leads to the tiny country church with its softening ivy-draperies.

At the west end of the church is an outside stair leading to the Laird's loft, the gallery reserved for the exclusive worship of the Trotters of Charterhall, whose privileges seem to have included the not unenviable one of being able to slip quietly away down their private stairway when the sermon showed signs of going on beyond the customary sixty minutes. The Hogs of Harcarse had a gallery at the east end, facing the Trotters, but without their major privilege of an escape route. Hogs and Trotters have left their painted heraldic panels in their lofts, the former dated 1677, the latter, 1671.

Outside on the south wall of the church is another panel, undated and unnamed, depicting three figures in Queen Anne costume, two men and a woman, linked together in companionable cheerfulness, which is somewhat belied by the scroll across their breast, VIVE MEMOR LETHI, "Live ever mindful of Lethe", or "In the midst of life we are in death". Over all are the words

> *We three served God, lived in His fear,*
> *And loved Him Who bought us dear.*

The 17th-century lairds of Charterhall would be startled to see their lands now, for during the war an aerodrome levelled great stretches of it; and it was while piloting an aeroplane from here that Richard Hillary, the brilliant young author of *The Last Enemy*, crashed into a hillside and died. When we visited Fogo the redbrick R.A.F. quarters were standing roofless and empty, and the runways were being used, deafeningly in this quiet country, for motor-racing and motor-cycle-racing.

FOULDEN   *Why Queen Mary Died*

It was to the church at Fugeldene—"valley of the birds"—that Commissioners from Elizabeth of England came in 1587 to meet the Scots, to explain to them why the Queen had executed Mary and to vindicate that deed. Near the ivy-clad church stands a Tithebarn, which the minister used for storing the grain given to him as stipend. Such structures are less common in Scotland than in England, though there is a fine example at Whitekirk.*

One of the best-preserved antique gravestones in Scotland lies in the graveyard here, commemorating the Hon. George Ramsay of Dalhousie, who was born in Fife and died at Foulden Bastel in 1592.

> *And now I have more quyet rest*
> *Than in my native soyl.*

GALASHIELS   *The Braw Lad's Town*

In the sheltered valley of the Gala—which carves its chattering way between busy mills—is this little industrial Border town, which can give us, all at one glance, a picture of smoky industry and green

* (*Queen's Scotland, Edinburgh and the Lothians*, p. 261.)

countryside, a montage of jostling slatey roofs with reeking lums and rolling hills and a river sweeping through them.

Though of ancient foundation—a settlement of "shiels" beside the Gala—where Melrose pilgrims enjoyed hospitality, the town offers none of the dramatically obvious tourist attractions. No castle here nor abbey. But from its market place we catch seductive glimpses of the meadows and woods curving off in attractive sweeps towards **Abbotsford, Melrose** and **Selkirk.**

On the north-west façade of the municipal buildings is the town's crest, expressing the brusque humour of the "braw braw lads o' Gala water". It depicts a fox trying to reach plums hanging from a tree, and the inscription below declares tersely: "Soure Plums".

This recalls an incident in 1337, when, at a spot known as the "Englishman's Syke ", Galashiels folk discovered a party of English soldiers searching for wild plums in the woods. The "Syke ran red for three days and nights". Thereafter the villagers have always jokingly referred to "The soure plums o' Galashiels".

The Braw Lad and his entourage still receive sprigs from the sour-plum trees when they ride out to Englishman's Syke on the occasion of the "Braw Lad's Gathering".

The day of pageantry opens with the sounding of the chimes from the Memorial Tower, and thousands gather to watch and cheer the triumphal fordings of the Tweed and the ceremonial annual visit to Abbotsford. Leading the entourage are the Braw Lad and his Lass, and at the Ceremony of Sasine at the old Town Cross the Braw Lass mixes the red and white roses of the houses of York and Lancaster, thus recalling the marriage of James IV and Margaret Tudor. The Cross, in Scott Crescent, bears the inscription:

> Near the site of this Ancient Cross, Margaret Tudor of England was given sasine of her Dowry of Ettrick Forest on her marriage in 1503 to James IV of Scotland which led to the Historic Union of the Crowns in 1603.

The past is poignantly linked with the present at the end of the Gathering when the Braw Lad dips his standard in homage at the War Memorial.

This war memorial, in Corn Mill Square, perpetuates the bold history of Galashiels with a striking statue of a mounted Border Reiver by T. J. Clapperton below a clock-tower designed by Sir Robert Lorimer.

Of Galashiels' past the most noteworthy survival is the beautiful 15th-century mansion, Old Gala House. It was the home for four centuries of the Lairds of Gala, and is now the headquarters of the Galashiels Arts Club.

The growth of modern Galashiels dates from 1790, when Scotland's first carding machine was built locally. After that things changed quickly. The old thatched cottages disappeared, and in their place went up those homes which Dorothy Wordsworth described as "ugly stone houses".

On a June morning nearly a century and a half ago Robert Southey received an Edinburgh-franked letter from a Scottish friend.

> You are quite right in apprehending a Jacquerie; the country is mined below our feet. Last week, learning that a meeting was to be held among the weavers of the large manufacturing village of Galashiels, for the purpose of cutting a man's web from his loom, I apprehended the ring-leaders and disconcerted the whole project; but in the course of my enquiries, imagine my surprise at discovering a bundle of letters and printed manifestoes, from which it appeared that the Manchester Weavers' Committee corresponds with every manufacturing town in the South and West of Scotland, and levies a subsidy of 2s. 6d. per man—(an immense sum)—for the ostensible purpose of petitioning Parliament for redress of grievances, but doubtless to sustain them in their revolutionary movements. . . .

The correspondent who gives us this vivid glimpse of turbulent life in the "village" of Galashiels was Walter Scott—"Shirra" of Selkirk.

Scott's worst fears were not realised. The revolution never came, and six years later Scott received on an October morning an invitation in verse inviting him to be an honoured guest at the annual procession and festivities of the Galashiels weavers. Penned by the popular "Galashiels poet", a weaver named Thomson, Scott was promised:

> *Your favourite dish is not forgot*
> *Imprimis, for your bill of fare,*
> *We'll put a sheep's head i' the pot—*
> *Ye'se get the cantle for your share:*
> *And we've the best o' Mountain dew*
> *Was gathered whare ye mauna list,*
> *In spite o' a' the gauger crew,*
> *By Scotland's "children o' the mist".*

GATELAWBRIDGE

Near Langlee, on the Galashiels–Melrose road is a tablet with the inscription:

> At this spot on his pathetic journey from Italy home to Abbotsford and his beloved Borderland Sir Walter Scott gazing on this scene for the last time "Sprang up with a cry of Delight." July 11th, 1832.

Galashiels today has expanded from a village to a thriving town over two miles in length, chief centre of Scotland's tweed manufacture and home of the Scottish Woollen Technical College with its own mill where the students put theory into practice and learn the art of manufacturing the tweeds for which the Border towns are famed.

This is an appropriate moment to remind English visitors that the word "tweed" has nothing at all to do with the Tweed, but comes from a clerical error—by an English clerk—who thus wrote the Scots word "tweels", meaning woollen fabrics, in that way.

GATELAWBRIDGE   *A Famous Leap*

Robert Paterson—the Old Mortality who carved so many Covenanters' gravestones—was tenant at Gatelawbridge Quarries, and near the village of Gatelawbridge, north-east of **Thornhill,** is a glen much frequented by the men he honoured with his epitaphs.

This is the wild gorge of Crichope Linn. In this romantic dell is the spot where a Covenanter leaped to safety from his pursuers across the 90-foot chasm, and also a recess among the rocks known as Souter's Seat, where a cobbler sat and repaired the boots of his Covenanter comrades.

GLENCAPLE   *Burns' Indiscretion*

In **Caerlaverock** parish, six miles down the left bank of the Nith estuary from **Dumfries,** is the seaside village and one-time port of Dumfries, marked on maps as Glencaple, but locally known as The Auld Quay. No longer do schooners from over the seas tie up here, but shrimpers and a huddle of rowing-boats still take advantage of its shelter.

Burns must have taken many a walk down the river bank to The Auld Quay. Once, below the village, a smugglers' boat ran aground, and Burns, wearing a sword in his official capacity as an exciseman, led a party across the sands to capture it. While they all waited for the arrival of a superior officer, Burns sat down with pencil and paper.

> *The Deil cam fiddlin' thro' the town,*
> *And danc'd awa' wi' th' exciseman;*
> *And ilka wife cries "Auld Mahoun,*
> *I wish you luck o' the prize, man."*

And so on, into one of his rollicking songs.

GOLDIELANDS   *Castle with a View*

Among other things, Goldielands tower is famed for possession of one of the finest views in the Border. This ancient peel stands on its own green ridge of ground above the Teviot two miles south-west of **Hawick.**

It is square and massive, and, as is usual with Border peels, there is about as much masonry within the walls as there is open space inside them. Originally there were two towers, but sometime after 1789 one of them was demolished.

The lairds of Goldielands were a branch of the Scott family— descendants of Walter Scott (1532–96), who was the natural son of the famous Sir Walter of Buccleuch. The first owner of Goldielands was probably the celebrated "Laird's Wat" of the Raid of Redeswire.

Local legend has it that the last laird of Goldielands was hanged over his own gateway for reiving, but historians discount that.

"Gaudilands" gets a mention in the Border ballad of *Jamie Telfer o' the Fair Dodhead.*

GORDON   *The Tinklers' Village*

Outstanding in the main street of the fresh little village of West Gordon is a round clock-tower above an iron-barred gateway. Half-a-mile away is the 16th-century L-shaped tower Greenknowe— beautifully set on its green knoll and making its name self-explanatory. The carved lintel over the entrance doorway bears the date 1581, and the tower was once occupied by Walter Pringle, noted covenanter and author.

A Border version of the by-word "Six of one and half-a-dozen of the other" goes: "The horners o' Hume are as good as the tinklers o' Gordon": horners and tinklers being the travelling packmen (also called muggers and besom-makers) who dealt in horn spoons or cuttys, earthenware, brooms and the like. And from this village the Gordon tribe—Jean Gordon was the original "Meg Merrilies"—took their name. (See Yetholm chapter.)

GRANTSHOUSE   *The Highlander's Inn*

Grantshouse is but a century old, having grown from a huddle of workmen's huts at the summit (370 feet above sea-level) of the projected Edinburgh-to-Newcastle railway as surveyed by Mr George Stephenson.

A kindly Highlander, by name Tommy Grant, is supposed to have made and mended boots for the railway workers, and later to have opened an inn for them, always referred to as Grant's House.

GREENLAW   *"Hell's Hole" in Church*

This little town sunning itself on the banks of the Blackadder was from 1696 until 1853 the county town, with all that that meant of county buildings, sheriff court, trials and executions, pomps and circumstances. From that date, **Duns** and Greenlaw divided the honours between them until 1903, when Duns ran away with the prize.

The former County building stands in the centre of the village green, on the spot once adorned by the mercat cross. In 1829 this Cross of hexagonal shaft with lion rampant was pulled down and thrown aside as worthless. But in 1881 the shaft, with its capital but no lion, was discovered in the basement of the old church, and re-erected against the west wall of the church tower, where it now stands.

This church tower is unique, having been built to look like a church tower but to serve as a jail. At the foot of it there is a sinister great gridiron of a gate. Similar gratings cover the four narrow windows, set one above the other on the south wall. On the east side of this grim old relic stands the church, which in 1712 was lengthened to join the jail. To its west side adhered the courthouse, since removed.

The prison was called Hell's Hole, and a bitter rhyme referred to this three-in-one all-purposes structure in these terms:

> *Here stands the gospel and the law,*
> *With Hell's Hole atween the twa.*

The last public execution in the county took place here on 2nd April, 1834, when an Irishman, Mannes Swinney, was hanged for robbery and assault, and his body buried within the precincts of the jail.

Under the Greenlaw heading it might be of interest to quote an ancient rhyme, still current in Lauderdale, if only to suggest that even in those unsophisticated days gentlemen seem to have preferred blondes:

> *The lasses o' Lauder are mim and meek,*
> *The lasses o' the Fanns smell o' peat reek,*
> *The lasses o' Gordon canna sew a steek,*
> *But weel can they sup their crowdie!*
> *The lasses o' Earlston are bonnie and braw,*
> *The lasses o' Greenlaw are black as a craw,*
> *But the lasses o' Polwart are the best o' them a'.*

GRETNA GREEN   *The Notorious Marriage Racket*

Gretna Green is just the kind of place the "tripper"—intent on a lark and a laugh—likes to come across on a day's jaunt. As he crosses the Border on his road he is diverted by oddities. Along the route are roadside legends . . . "last public house in England" . . . "first in Scotland" . . . or such like. All the messy and ridiculous trivia of tourism shrilly and untidily call his attention to the fact that he is leaving one land and entering another.

By the time he reaches Scotland's first village, Gretna Green, the tourist nudging has risen to a vulgar shout. Painted signs, as bold as though they announced Bearded Ladies or Monstrous Dwarfs, shout violent contradiction at each other; one declaring that this way lies one thing, and the other directing the sightseer elsewhere. The place lacks only pin-tables and hurdy-gurdies to make it one whole fairground. There is, it appears, intense and placarded rivalry about just where the eloping couples were spliced.

Amid such barking the traveller enters Scotland! The crossing of the Border could have been signalised with so much dignity and beauty. Strange that no one ever thought of making it so and that it has been left instead to the fun-fair mentality to make it a kind of seaside-postcard joke.

The traveller who comes north in search of the real beauty of Scotland—the Scotland of memorable history and unspeakably lovely landscape—would do best to avoid this Gretna Green route and, if he comes from Carlisle, keep to the right, following the Edinburgh fingerpost for Longtown and Langholm instead of the

Glasgow fingerpost for Gretna and Lockerbie. Better still, let him enter Scotland by the route further to the east by Carter Bar and Jedburgh.

This is not to scoff at Gretna Green's history of runaway marriages. That history is, indeed, a fascinating story—altogether too interesting to have deserved vaudeville buffoonery.

Gretna Green became famous for runaway marriages because of the tremendous difference between the marriage laws of England and Scotland. It was the first place reached by young lovers when they fled from England to Scotland. At home in England their parents had legal power to stamp on and strangle young love, but Scotland's laws took no notice of outraged Montagues or Capulets.

Parental consent for the marriage of minors has never been asked for in Scotland. In quite recent years this essential difference in the marriage laws has leaped into public prominence again; particularly so in 1953, when wealthy 18-year-old Isabel Patino eloped to Scotland with 20-year-old James Goldsmith. This runaway marriage had all the trimmings of romantic elopement—the most exciting of these trimmings being the pursuing father of the bride.

It was a kind of obstacle race for the runaways. If only they could keep out of papa's reach for 25 days and stay for that length of time in Scotland no power of parents or law could prevent their marriage. For in Scotland the only question asked of those who would marry is "Are you over 16?" and if they are, the only condition is that they have been resident in the country a certain number of days. Then, even if the boy and girl are still at school, they are considered old enough to choose their life partner.

Brides Aged 12!

In fact, as late as 1923 a girl of 12 and a boy of 14 could be married in Scotland with no question of whether parents were agreeable to the precocious union or not. So it is that Scotland—dour moral Presbyterian Scotland, the country where it is hard to get a drink on a Sunday—is still the one country in Europe which smiles on young love, still the country of runaway marriages, still the land of Gretna Green.

It was not until 1940 that the "anvil marriage" became invalid, but even today it is easier to be married in Scotland than anywhere else. Paris enjoys the reputation of being the honeymoon capital, but compared with Scotland it is a poor place for romance. Any couple wedding in France must live in the country for a year before they can marry there: in Scotland 25 days' residence and 7s. 6d. is enough.

After only 15 clear days in the country any couple over 16 years old can pay a fee of 1s. and enter their notice of marriage, and buy a 1s. 6d. certificate of marriage. Seven clear days later they can present themselves to any Registrar. In the presence of the Registrar and of two witnesses not under 16 years old they accept each other as man and wife. They pay the Registrar 5s. If they wish, they can, for an extra 2s. 6d., have a copy of the precious marriage lines. That is all.

England tightened up its marriage laws as long ago as 1754, but the law was not extended to Scotland, so young lovers did the natural thing and ran away over the Border to marry at the first place they came to—which was usually Gretna Green and sometimes Coldstream. By 1771 Gretna Green was being described by Pennant as "the resort of all amorous couples whose union the prudence of parents or guardians prohibits".

Scottish law at that time demanded no more than a declaration of marriage by the contracting parties, and the "priest" for such ceremony could be anyone—ferryman, tollkeeper or landlord. The fees of these self-appointed priests varied from 2½d. to £100. The popular legend is that at Gretna Green the "priest" was the village blacksmith. There is not the slightest proof that this was ever so. That this popular tale is a lie seems in accord with the general gimcrack showmanship that has grown up around the place.

Until 1826 the marriages customarily took place in the toll-house or the King's Head Inn, and later at Gretna Hall, where the old marriage register can be seen. There are 1,134 entries from 1825 to 1855. Among them are some famous names. Lord Archibald Drumlanrig, heir of the Marquis of Queensberry. Robert Brinsley Sheridan, grandson of the dramatist. John Peel, the celebrated huntsman. And an ostler at a tavern in Spilsby, Lincolnshire, who walked the whole 240 miles with his bride.

The country around Gretna Green is delightful undulating farmland; the road westward to Dumfries is enchanting; but the screaming signposting of Gretna Green does the territory a disservice.

HASSENDEAN   *The Lost Church*

Across the Teviot from **Denholm** is Hassendean, the place of the lost church. Until 1690 Hassendean had its own ancient church, a

Norman building much loved by the people of the valley. But the parish was annexed to the neighbouring parishes of Minto, Wilton and Roberton, and the powers that were declared that the old church must be closed. The folk of Hassendean fought hard and long against this brutal order, but at last, in 1690, the revered building was torn down, despite the riotous opposition of the men and women.

Today not even the ground on which it stood remains! A century later, in 1796, the site of the church and graveyard were swept away by the fierce flooding of the Teviot.

The mansion-house of Hassendean perpetuates the name of an ancient barony belonging for many generations to a branch of the Scott family. Its peel tower, near the mouth of the Hassendean burn, has vanished, except for a fragment which survives in the gable of a cottage. Its one-time owner, Sir Alexander Scott, fell at Flodden.

Once, too, there was at Hassendean a monastic cell, called Monk's Tower, on a tract of land still referred to as Monk's Croft.

Hassendean, under variations of Halstanedean and Hazeldean, figures in several of the Border ballads—most attractively, perhaps, in *Jock of Hazeldean*.

HAWICK   *A Border Capital*

Sunk in the valley of the Teviot, with rolling green patchily wooded hills all around it, is this grey stony town. Above its roofs spring tall purposeful-looking chimneys which sometimes conspire to spread a mantle of hazy smoke across the roof-tops. In the streets we hear the rattle and clank of industry.

This is the Hawick of today. A working town. A prosperous town. Yet also a holiday town, for it is every summer the headquarters for Border explorers. But, more than anything else, it is the town of the callants, with a spirited statue in the main street to remind us of the valour of the lads of Hawick at **Hornshole** in 1514.

We come down to it from the higher reaches of the Teviot—a glimpse of pantiles or a roundel or a gable awakening us to the knowledge that we are entering an inevitably historic Border Burgh—and we come to a halt on the kerb-edge of the High Street. It is a busy street, not handsome and not old, but broad and straight, and the buildings show traits of squat practicability inherited from earlier Scots domestic architecture. No. 51 is Hawick's surviving example of a fortified house. Halfway along is the over-adorned tower of the Town House, built in a kind of workaday baronial and completed in 1887 in pompous replacement of the building which was there until 1884—a pleasant little building with an outside stair, a graceful clock-tower and arched pends at ground level.

On the staircase of the present House, and in the Council Chambers, hang valuable pictures—among them water-colours by the late Tom Scott, R.S.A. Appropriately enough, one bears the bold title "1514" and shows the return of the Hawick callants from Hornshole with the flag captured from the English marauders.

Turn off High Street, and we are immediately engulfed in history. There is, for instance, the Round Close—a huddle of hoary old houses that seem to be continually whispering to each other memories of their 17th-century heyday. A tablet on a wall of the Tower Inn states that here Wordsworth and his sister Dorothy stayed in 1803, and they were eventually joined by Sir Walter Scott.

The Black Tower

In Towerdykeside there is a door-knocker which still knocks as loudly and truly as in the year of its origin—1677. That door itself is set in an eight-foot-thick wall built of what are now the oldest stones in the Burgh.

This was once the Black Tower of Hawick, stoutest and most valiant fortress in all the Borders, standing guard over the land for 300 years. Other towers were blasted apart and burned. But not the Black Tower. In the very middle of the path invariably followed by the ruthless harriers from over the Border it stood, a dour oblong citadel of unyielding defiance.

When Earl Douglas fell at Otterburn and his natural son, Sir William, became the founder of the family of Douglas of Drumlanrig, the tower became known as Drumlanrig Tower.

In 1675 the Tower passed with the Barony of Hawick to the Duke of Monmouth and his wife Anna, Duchess of Monmouth and Buccleuch. In part of the building today there is still a room called "The Duchess' Room", once favoured by her. Often the Duchess came to stay here with her family, always attended by all the pomp and circumstance of a Royal visit—as befitted one who liked to style herself as "ane michtie Princess".

In 1679—by then not so accustomed to defending itself—the

Tower was laid low by Covenanters before the battle of Bothwell Brig. They looted the store of militia arms.

In 1773 the venerable stronghold's distinguished career came to an end. In the process of converting it into an inn, much of the original masonry was unfortunately destroyed, but the very old eight-foot-thick wall giving on to Towerdykeside is certainly a relic from the Tower's more glorious days.

St Mary's Church, not far from the Tower, was the scene of the capture of Sir Alexander Ramsay in 1342 by Sir William Douglas. Sir Alexander, the brave warrior who had captured Roxburgh Castle from the English, was carried off to **Hermitage** and there starved to death.

The Hawick Cornet

But of all monuments of Hawick's past that gallant equestrian statue in the High Street is the one which most stirs Hawick's heart, for this commemorates the victory of a band of youths of Hawick over English soldiers at Hornshole in 1514.

When the alarm came to the town that the English were at Hornshole there were no men to go out to battle. All of them had fallen at Flodden the year before. So the callants—the youths of Hawick—sallied out, routed the English at Hornshole and came back with a banner wrested from the enemy. Scotland's heart was still bleeding over the tragic defeat at Flodden, so the little victory at Hornshole seemed a bright blaze in the dark skies of mourning Scotland.

And the statue stands as a year-long reminder of Hawick's great annual festival of Common Riding. It's the week when Hawick goes gay. The busy town relaxes; shops and factories close for two days during the week of celebration. The Riding possibly has pagan origins, for the war song which reverberates through Hawick's streets during the festival week is *Ter-ibus ye Tyr ye Odin*, the ancient invocation "*May Thor and Odin have us in his Keeping*".

It is, of course, certain that the festival is linked with that custom of examining the marches in the days when Hawick bailies, armed with pistols and supported by a large contingent of townsfolk carrying clubs, staves, spears and scythes to aid them in any argument that might arise with proprietors, rode out to make sure that there had been no encroachment on common land by neighbouring land-owners.

Then in 1514 came the unforgettable exploits of the callants, and, in commemoration of this deed, the standard-bearer and flag were introduced into the Common Riding ceremony.

The custom of electing a Cornet—a young, unmarried Hawick townsman—to carry the flag, may have started even before a record of the names was kept. The existing roll is headed by James Scott who carried the colour in 1703. Since then, every single year has had its Cornet, except the war years.

The Cornet is elected by the Town Council at its monthly meeting in May; the Burgh Officer, accompanied by Drum and Fife Band, marches to the Cornet's home to inform him of the appointment, and the Cornet rewards him with a gratuity of a shilling. Then the Cornet and his right- and left-hand men—the Cornets of the two preceding years—"walk the bounds", visiting various streets and buildings with historic associations. At certain times during the next few weeks the Cornet and his supporters also visit Bonchester, Lilliesleaf, Mosspaul, Denholm and other villages.

The date of the Riding is determined by reference to the pre-1752 calendar. From that is reckoned the Friday and Saturday of June which are not sooner than the 5th and 6th, and not later than the 11th and 12th.

On the Thursday of the week before, as the clock of St Mary's Church strikes six in the evening, the Drum-and-Fife Band escorted by Town Officers carrying their halberds, march through the streets playing the age-old "Teribus", and the Cornet and his party try out their horses in a preliminary "chase" from Haggishaw to Nipknowes.

On the Thursday of Common Riding Week the colour is bussed with ribbons by the Cornet's Lass, carried into the Town Hall, and presented to the Provost. The Lass invests the Cornet with his sash of office over his traditional green coat, and the Provost places the precious flag in his care, charging him to return it unsullied at the end of the ceremonies. The roar of the stirring "Teribus" fills the building, and from the balcony of the municipal buildings the Burgh Officer reads the ancient proclamation of the March Riding: "warning all the said Burgesses to attend the Provost, Bailies and Council that day in the best apparel to the end aforesaid".

Led by the bands, the Cornet and his lads march round the Town. On the way a ladder is placed against the statue of the original Hawick Callant, and the bronze flag clutched in that outflung bronze arm is bussed with ribbons.

On the following morning the band rouses the town at six o'clock. There is the rollicking breakfast given by the Cornet for his friends and supporters in the Tower Hotel, and another by the Provost in the Council Chambers. At both gatherings, oak leaves are distributed after the meal.

An old version of the Common Riding Song is sung on the steps of the Tower Hotel, and then Cornet, supporters, Provost, Magistrates, Town Council and other officials ride in procession round the town, and on to the Moor, where the whole cavalcade of riders gallops madly in "The Cornet's Chase", a stirring re-enactment of the capture of the Hornshole trophy.

The next ceremony is that of the taking of curds and cream at St Leonards by the Cornet and his men. At the furthest extremity of the Common the Cornet cuts a sod. At the race-course he plants the flag in the paddock, and receives the customary riding crop from the Provost. The Cornet dips the flag three times at the Coble Pool in deference to an ancient boundary of Burgh property. Arriving at Millpath, the proclamation is read to the effect that the Marches have been ridden.

> For as much as the Provost, Bailies, and Council of the Burgh of Hawick, with the burgesses of the said Burgh, have this day ridden the meiths and marches of the Commonty of Hawick, as has been in use yearly since time immemorial, without interruption or molestation of any sort. Therefore, if any nobleman, gentleman or others, having lands lying contiguous or adjacent to the said Commonty, shall find themselves leized or prejudiced in any sort by the marching, they are hereby required to state their objections thereto to the Provost, Bailies and Council of the said Burgh within forty days from this date otherwise they shall be held to have acquiesced in the said marching.

The stirring words of "Teribus", sung with great fervour from hundreds of throats, boom across the green hills of Teviotdale.

At the Cornet's Ball the highlight is the Cornet's Reel, danced exclusively by the Cornet and ex-Cornets usually immediately after midnight. When the week's Festival comes to a close, the crowd roars "Teribus" more lustily than ever. The Marches have again been ridden as in centuries past, the "emblem grand" has been "safe oot" to the extremity of the "Commonty" and is now "safe in" with its honour unsullied and unstained.

Every year exiled "Teries" find their way home from all parts of the globe. The civic reception given these sons of Hawick on the

Wednesday of Common Riding Week has become, in recent years, one of the highlights of the Festival.

> *It's no in steeds, it's no in speeds,*
> *It's something in the heart abiding;*
> *The kindly customs, words and deeds,*
> *It's these that make the Common-Riding.*

Vertish Hill is part of the town's Common, and nearby is Burnflat, birthplace of Robert Paterson, Old Mortality. Harden House, a few miles west of Hawick, was the home of "Auld Wat" of Harden who married Mary Scott, the "Flower of Yarrow" and whose son married "Muckle Mou'd Meg".

Hawick is now a Border capital of the woollen industry with two dozen famous hosiery and knitwear factories. The introduction into Hawick of four hand-knitting machines by Bailie John Hardie set the town off on its road to industrial prosperity. That was in 1771, when the native Cheviot sheep provided wool for knitting the coarse stockings worn with knee-breeches. But today the rarest yarns in the world—lamb's-wool from Australia and cashmere from Tibet among them—come to Hawick's ultra-modern factories to be knitted into lovely garments, styled by leading couturiers for sale throughout the world.

HERMITAGE *Castle Dolorous*

A man boiled in lead. Another nibbling crazily the corn which trickles meagrely into the dungeon where he will die. Another—this one a dark mysterious nobleman who has captured the heart, or perhaps no more than the body, of a Queen—lying wounded and dreaming up a dolorous future.

Those are the kind of men who have played their part in the 700 years of Hermitage's history. And how well such actors suit their stage, this Hermitage, this bitter and powerful lump of frowning castle which lodges—like a stone in the gall—in a rift in the hills near the cold northern end of Liddesdale.

Turn from the main **Langholm–Hawick** road and climb up to Hermitage. Stand in its shadow. Shiver in its malevolence. It is a pilgrimage that you ought to make if you would feel to the uttermost the rough hard blow of Scotland's past. For here is all that is dour in Scotland's history. All that is grim and bloody and cruel and savage is brutally housed in this glowering stack.

Legend has laid upon it such a weight of horror, such a bat's breath of dire prophecy slavers through it, that local people have all their lives expected it to fulfil the curse supposedly destined for it and see it sink shamefully into the ground. Yet, defying this super-stition, Hermitage's two towers stand stoutly, and one glance at them is enough to convince us that mortal life is all too short for us ever to witness Hermitage's massive disappearance to the underworld. And although such a withdrawal would without doubt relieve the landscape of a terrifying monument, it would at the same time most undeniably take from it a certain savage nobility.

It is a castle of two giant towers, two mighty brown ferocious twins, whose walls are slitted with narrow windows and ominous loopholes. The principal feature of the Castle—the one which we shall on first acquaintance remark upon and which we shall always recall when we remember the place—is the high and powerful arch which links these two great towers. It is a very frown of an arch, a heavy browed thing knitting the whole façade into one intolerable threatening glare.

The whole of it stares upon a burn which, trickling down a little glen, might in happier surroundings have prattled prettily but here, even on the brightest day, drools a lament. On the banks of this water are the remains of a chapel built as a hermit cell. The coming of this recluse changed the name of the stream from its original Merchin Burn to its present Hermitage Water. His coming also gave the 13th-century Lord of Liddesdale a name for his new fortress.

This lord, one Nicholas de Soulis, was given sole right to build a stronghold on these lands, and it is believed that he did so some time about 1244. A cruel wicked man he was, according to legend, engaging in all manner of hideousness and black arts in his castle. So cruel and so detested was he that one day his neighbours and vassals rebelled and carted him off to Nine Stane Rigg, the stone circle a mile away, behind the present school and farmhouse of Hermitage. There, in a big copper pot, they boiled him in lead.

> *They rolled him up in a sheet of lead*
> *A sheet of lead for a funeral pall.*
> *They plunged him in the cauldron red,*
> *And melted him, lead and bones and all.*

Thus John Leyden on this local legend. Although official history records that the Lord of Liddesdale died in jail at Dumbarton Castle, the boiling-in-lead seems more in tune with harsh Hermitage.

In the next century Sir William Douglas, fair "Knight of Liddes-dale" and styled "Flower of Chivalry", seized in the church of St Mary at Hawick the gallant Scottish patriot, brave Sir Alexander Ramsay of Dalhousie, and dropped him into the Hermitage dungeon and left him there to starve to death. Above the dungeon was the granary, and through some cracks in the wall grains of corn trickled down. Enough grains came down to protract Sir Alexander's agony and keep him alive for 17 days.

Two hundred years later James Hepburn, fourth Earl of Bothwell, was there, lying sick with the grievous wounds inflicted by the famous Border freebooter, "little Jock Elliot". Only 30 years old is this James Hepburn, but already a strange uneasy power in the land, and such a one that when news of his death reaches London the Spanish Ambassador de Silva writes: "The Queen has lost a man whom she could trust, and of such she has but few."

But not yet has Queen Mary lost her Bothwell. News of his illness reaches her at Jedburgh and she gallops out to wild Hermitage to sit for two hours beside the sick-bed, comforting her husband's murderer ". . . to his great pleasure and content".

That day's riding cost her dear. It gave her such a fever that she lay ten days dangerously ill at Jedburgh. But if her visit plucked up the heart of the sick Earl and helped his recovery, then that, and not her ten-day fever, was the fiercer price she paid for the journey.

Twenty-one years later—in 1587—Mary's son, James VI, granted Bothwell's nephew, Francis Stuart, last Earl of Bothwell, the Castle and lands of Hermitage. Through him it passed to the Buccleuch family, who have now given it over, together with the adjoining ruin of St Mary's Chapel, to the Ministry of Works.

HORNSHOLE   *The Hawick Callants*

Hornshole—the place remembered so gloriously in **Hawick** history—lies two miles east of the burgh, on the bank of the Teviot, where an old stone bridge crosses the river.

On a patch of grass where the roads divide stands a simple monu-ment—a stone pillar, surmounted by a circle, upon which is carved a saltire, and the date 1514. On the pedestal the date is repeated above the words "Lest we forget".

To this spot in 1514 came one of the bands of English troops who roamed through the Borderland, looting and pillaging at will, con-fident in the knowledge that the death-roll of Flodden had reduced the garrisons of all the neighbouring Border Burghs to mere handfuls of old men and boys.

This party, led by the notorious Abbot of Hexham, decided to camp at Hornshole for the night. News of this travelled swiftly, and the alarm bells were rung in Hawick two miles away. The town had no soldiers to send. But its "callants"—teen-age youths with no experience of serious warfare—rode to Hornshole, charged into the enemy, killed some, pursued the others across country and captured their ponies.

They captured also the English flag and with it rode in triumph back to Hawick. The golden saltire on an azure field has been Hawick's banner ever since.

HOUNAM   *Where Border Heather Grows*

Tradition has it that heather will not grow on the Borders and that attempts to nurture it have always failed because of some deficiency in the soil. But there is at least one Border spot where it does well, and that is around the shores of Heatherhope Loch near Hounam, south-east of **Morebattle.**

The view of this fine loch often surprises visitors with its Highland aspect—not only because of the heather around its banks but the wild sloping hills surrounding it. Its waters slake the thirst of **Kelso** folk 11 miles away.

HOUNDWOOD   *Queen Mary's Wedding Ring*

Two miles down the main Berwick road from Houndwood Church lovely old Houndwood House stands among her trees, gazing over fields that slope gently to the Water of Eye. Parts of the ground floor date from the 12th century, and the vaulted cellars contain the bones of long-dead monks. Some of those bones protrude from the white-washed walls, for all the world as though one were intended to hang one's cowl on them.

Houndwood's façade, regular and austere with the mathematical beauty of a Bach fugue, hides all sorts of eerie, age-old things, still in the 20th century being just discovered. Man-sized niches under the floor. A "priest's hole" in the wall. Windows blocked up for centuries. Even a wailing child-ghost, known to some as "Chappie", because she knocks and knocks on door and window, and never ceases to weep.

Mary Queen of Scots paused here once upon a time, and every

night along the vaulted stone passages the hooves of her ghostly horse can be heard to clatter by. The housemaids now who shiver and bury their heads in the blankets are the great-great-grand-daughters of the housemaids of long ago who used to shiver and hide and hear those same hooves: and they know it is so.

In 1868, when a tree was blown down in the garden, there was found at its roots a wedding-ring of Queen Mary's, initialled and dated, and unmistakably a wedding-ring. Did she, perhaps, wear her wedding-rings rather loosely? That one is to be seen in the National Museum of Antiquities in Edinburgh.

Across the road from Houndwood House stands Howburn Farm, blinking in the sun beside the single-arch bridge that takes the road across the Water of Eye and south to Chirnside. Young bullocks splash contentedly in the shallow water.

There is no memory now of the day—no one knows just when, probably in the 14th century—when the Plague struck Howburn. Except in this grim old rhyme:

> *Howburn stands its lee lane,*
> *Howburn folk are a' gane.*
> *The Pest has come by the water down*
> *And hasnae left a soul i' the town.*
> *The nettles grow on the hearth-stane,*
> *And lang they'll grow, ere there again*
> *A house will be seen at Howburn stead;*
> *For a' the folk o' Howburn's dead.*

HUME   *Sentinel of the Merse*

The rocky height above the pretty village of Hume has held a castle for centuries. But not the castle we see here today. That one is a kind of dummy fortress, erected in 1794 by the last Earl of Marchmont.

Its ancient predecessor was demolished in 1650 by Cromwell's orders. Through 400 years it had been the Sentinel of the Merse. Standing so high, it could catch the first glimpse of a danger-signal from the fords across the Tweed and send its beacon-blazing warning not only to all the Border country, but to Edinburgh, Haddington, Dunbar; even to the shores of Fife.

And even this present fortress kept its eyes peeled for danger. On the 31st January, 1804, a watcher at Hume Castle saw a flare, as he thought, from Berwick. This, then, was Napoleon Bonaparte's invasion of the island! It was in reality Northumberland charcoal-burners. But the excited watchman lost not a moment in setting light to his beacon, and sending the summons to arms through all the Border country.

Although the alarm was false, Borderers are still proud of the way their forbears leapt to answer it. Yeomanry and volunteers rode 40 and 50 miles and more to reach their posts. Sir Walter Scott himself was in Cumberland on that night, but within 24 hours he and his horse had reached Dalkeith, 100 miles from his starting-point.

Home Guard readers of these words will recall the summer night in 1940, when just such a false alarm was sent out through the Borders, though then church bells were used instead of beacons to warn us of Hitler's paratroops descending from the skies. The response—of course—was the same. And once again the alarm proved to be a false one.

In these peaceful times Hume Castle makes a peerless viewpoint, greatly enhanced by the Berwickshire Naturalists' Club's gift, in 1931, of an excellent indicator.

The Border version of the boys' game, *I'm the King o' the Castle*, is supposed to refer to Governor Cockburn's arrogant reply to Colonel Fenwick in 1650, when called to surrender Hume Castle:

> *I Willie Wastle*
> *Stand firm in my castle,*
> *And a' the dougs in your town*
> *Canna ding Willie Wastle down.*

The three churches of Stichill, Hume and Nenthorn are now united under one minister.

HUTTON   *Auld Wives and Swine*

This parish rejoices in another of the scurrilous rhymes which Mr Henderson (1800 64) made it his delight to collect:

> *Hutton for auld wives,*
> *Broadmeadows for swine,*
> *Paxton for drucken wives*
> *And salmon sae fine.*
> *Crossrig for lint and woo'*
> *Spittal for kale,*
> *Sunwick for cakes and cheese*
> *And lasses for sale.*

All the places thus immortalised are in Hutton parish.

The mansion-house, Hutton Castle, stands on the south bank of the Whiteadder about a mile from Hutton village. The oldest part is a small square peel tower of remote antiquity, to which a variety of more modern architecture has been attached. It is now the residence of Sir William Burrell, the shipowner whose long life of stalking down and capturing masterpieces in Europe and Asia resulted in that astounding mass of beauty known as the Burrell Collection, gifted by its owner in 1944 to the City of Glasgow.*

The elegant suspension bridge spanning the Tweed near Tweed-hill House was the first of its kind in Britain. It was built in 1820 to the design of Samuel Brown (1776–1852), a naval officer living at Netherbyres, near Eyemouth. Not far from Tweedhill House is Paxton House, massive, heavy, superb, designed by the Adams, and standing in fine grounds which run right to Tweed's edge.

The little village of Paxton, whose church is now united with Hutton and Fishwick under one minister, is said to be the birthplace of the tune of *Robin Adair*, sung to the words:

> *Paxton's a fine snug place, Robin Adair,*
> *It's a wondrous couthie place, Robin Adair;*
> *Let Whiteadder rin a spate,*
> *Or the wind blow at ony rate,*
> *Yet I'll meet thee on the gait, Robin Adair.*

Paxton House with its wealth of delicate plasterwork, including some luxurious overmantels, is one of the great Border homes built in the late 18th-century classical style. Among its possessions is exquisite Regency furniture fashioned for it by John Trotter of Edinburgh.

In 1655–56 Hutton Church underwent considerable repairs, and we find an entry in the Session records: *Feb. 3, 1656. Given out of the boxe to Mrs. Dune in Barwick 8s. 9d. for timber to the kirk.* That kirk was rebuilt in 1765, and replaced in 1835 by the present-day one. The bell in Hutton Church bears the following inscription:

SOLI . DEO . GLORIA . IOHANNES .
BURGERHUYS . ME . FECIT . 1661 .

When the false warning of Napoleon's invasion in 1804 was sent out from Hume, the Volunteers in this district made Hutton their rallying-point, and spent a night under arms in the old church.

* An account of this fabulous collection can be found in *Queen's Scotland, Glasgow, Kyle and Galloway*, pp. 19–21.

The Tweed   **Yair Bridge**

Hawick   **The Cornet**

Galashiels   **War Memorial**

Gretna Green   **The Blacksmith's Shop**

Gretna Hall   **Marriage "Church"**

Hermitage   **Bothwell's Castle**

Hume   **The Dummy Castle**

Jedburgh   **The Abbey**

The Town Clock

Queen Mary's House

INNERLEITHEN *The Blacksmith's Town*

Alexander Brodie was a blacksmith of Traquair who went to London to make his fortune and then came back to his native hills and here at the junction of Leithen Water and Tweed built Innerleithen's first woollen mill.

Today it is a thriving little industrial conglomeration, a squarish town, all straight built with a workaday Main Street. But it doesn't, as has so unjustly been said of it, sprawl. It is indeed deliberately compact, a model in that respect to many a town that has straggled away up any likely valley and smudged the whole landscape around. Around Innerleithen the grand sweeping Tweed countryside is almost untouched.

Above the town is the famed St Ronan's Well, which was bringing invalids to the place about the time when Alexander Brodie opened his mill, and then became known throughout the world by Walter Scott's novel. That was in 1824. Five years later Hogg instituted the Border Games, which are still held annually.

In the 12th century a bastard son of Malcolm IV was drowned in a pool in Leithen Water, and his body lay for a night in the church at Innerleithen, for which service the King granted it privilege of sanctuary.

Cardrona Keep

Two miles up the Tweed from Innerleithen, on the other bank, can be seen the old Keep of Cardrona, one of the long line of towers whose beacons warned of English invasion or other dangers. It was one of the laws of the marches that "he who did not join the array of the country upon the signal of the beacon lights, or who left it during the continuance of the English invasion without lawful excuse, should suffer forfeiture of his goods and have his person placed at the warden's will".

The "Stannin' Stane" in the field near Cardrona railway station might mark the grave of some Scot who fell in battle at this spot.

JEDBURGH *Welcome to Scotland*

Jedburgh is the loveliest town in the Borders. That is our own choice, though we risk trouble from all its Border neighbours for stating the choice so boldly. It is a gentle informal sandy-visaged town, its streets and closes grouped with a great deal more natural grace and, it seems, altogether more casually than is customary in Scottish towns. It is just the right size too; small enough to be given a nodding good-morning on a breakfast-time stroll; and big enough to be lively and throng and well-furnished with shops.

We smiled when we read one of the briefest descriptions of Jedburgh. A learned Scot, casting around for some phrase to sum up the place, described it as "the nearest Scottish town to Newcastle"! A back-handed compliment, if ever there was one. Though, of course, not inaccurate. Jedburgh has certainly meant no more than that to generations of English invaders—not only those English who came with sword and fire centuries ago, but also those English who come nowadays with business to do at Jedburgh mills or with money to spend on Border holidays.

To all the countless travellers who come northward over the Border by way of Carter Bar, Jedburgh is the first Scottish town on which they set their eyes. This Carter Bar route is undoubtedly the grandest and most exhilarating way of entering Scotland, but even if it were not, the road would still be worth taking for nothing more than the visit to Jedburgh.

The descent from Carter Bar is one of the most memorable journeys you can make in Britain. The road sweeps downward with an almost Alpine verve, over the shoulders of the hills; and all the time the contours of Teviotdale unfold before you, rolling countryside draped with a mantle of glistening bracken, the folds shadowed with thick woodland. It is a sight you will never forget—this first sight of Scotland—and you share it with centuries of travellers who have come down the Cheviot road before you.

You share it with some marauding 16th-century Englishman. Surely impatience quickened his blood when he glimpsed below him his destined victim, the town of Jedburgh, then spurred his horse downhill on his way to "this nearest Scottish town to Newcastle". Perhaps before dawn his head was being kicked over the bloodied turf in footba' celebration of another Jeddart victory.

After the swift descent of the moorland hills the last few miles to Jedburgh are gentler. The road is bordered with fat hedgerows and stalwart trees. The greenest of pastures spread around us and the happiest of burns clatter down to join the Jed. The road twists about the hem of steep woodland, crosses a bridge, climbs a hill . . . and suddenly we are in Jedburgh.

The town's centre is an open space about the mercat cross; a *place* not dourly square but as irregular in shape as an oak-leaf curled lop-sided by frosts; and the whole weathered sandstone face of the town bears perpetual autumn tints. From the mercat cross a street climbs uphill to the Castle. Other streets ramble off downhill to the river-bank. All around are peaked roofs and crow-stepped gables framing little vignettes of the steep pastures and wooded hills beyond the town. In the midst of it all is the Abbey.

Of the four Border Abbeys Jedburgh is the most intact and the most powerfully impressive, standing admirably on a natural terrace above the town's centre, its 86-foot-high tower dominating the whole scene. Like its sister abbeys—Melrose, Dryburgh and Kelso—it was founded in that great period of building in the 12th century. Like them it was stripped of its valuables and set ablaze by English invaders. The ruins comprise the Abbey Church, dedicated in 1147 to the Virgin by David I, and a part of the sub-vaults of the Refectory.

The most precious remains are the great West doorway and the rose window, St Catherine's Wheel, in the gable. This West doorway and the Abbey's 14th-century cloister doorway were described by Sir George Gilbert Scott as "two of the most exquisite gems of architectural art in this island".

On each side of the nave are three tiers of arches. The basement storey consists of clustered pillars which support deeply-moulded pointed arches. In the triforium are semi-circular arches subdivided by pointed ones. The clerestory is a detached arcade of 36 arches, also pointed; the wall behind every alternate two is pierced for windows.

The nave is 129 feet long, and the west end was roofed in at triforium level and used as Jedburgh's parish church until as late as 1875. Then the Marquis of Lothian provided the town with a kirk and, beginning a restoration of the Abbey, had the false roof taken away. Later clearing away of modern accretions has restored the nave to its original austere and beautiful proportions. Now it represents the maturity of Early English architecture in Scotland. The factory and the black steel chimney at the east end represent Border money-grubbing of the 20th century.

The north piers of the tower, Early Norman, are the oldest part of the building, and in the Abbey's museum are sculptured stones which show us how profusely the early building was decorated, among them carved bosses and corbels and a floriated cross, and one slab exuberantly carved with a pattern of foliage where birds and beasts and winged dragons are seen eating fruit amid the branches.

During this century, under the devoted and inspired direction of Sir Rowand Anderson and Mr J. Wilson Paterson, difficult and at times dangerous restoration work has been done at Jedburgh. When the crust of modern encasing walls and buttresses was stripped away every old stone was replaced in its original position. Previous to this the Marquis of Lothian had done much work. When the cloister doorway showed signs of serious decay he had a facsimile of it carefully executed and built on the site of the West Processional doorway in the same wall.

The result is an abbey as intact as ever we can hope to find in Scotland, unless by some miracle of spiritual regeneration we experience again that sublime fury of building which 800 years ago raised four great religious houses in these valleys in 40 years.

In the North transept, above the great window, is a stone bearing the arms and initials of Blacader, that 15th-century Archbishop of Glasgow who built the lovely Blacader aisle at Glasgow Cathedral. This North transept has been walled in: it is the burial-ground of the Kers of Ferniehurst and their descendants, the Lothian family.

Also buried in the Abbey is the historian Dr Thomas Somerville, uncle and father-in-law of Mary Somerville. Mary, known as the Rose of Jedwood, born in the manse of Jedburgh in 1780, was a formidable blue-stocking. Her famous scientific works include *The Connection of the Physical Sciences* and *Microscopic and Molecular Science*. A Chantrey bust of her was placed in the great hall of the Royal Society and her name was commemorated in the foundation of Somerville College and in the Mary Somerville scholarship for women in mathematics at Oxford.

Jedburgh's War Memorial, built at the southern end of the Abbey, incorporates a handsome stairway leading to the Abbey ramparts.

Queen Mary's House

Next in importance to the Abbey as a place of high and romantic antiquity is the tall house in Queen Street known as Queen Mary's House. Here—in what was styled at the time the Lord Compositor's House—Mary Queen of Scots lodged for a month when she visited the town in 1566 to preside over a justice court and grant the Town

Charter. During that visit news came to her that James Earl of Bothwell had been wounded in a fight with the Liddesdale free-booter Jock Elliot. James was, they told her, dangerously ill, and in a frenzy Queen Mary rode to his bedside at Hermitage Castle 20 miles away.

The story has it that she did the whole ride, there and back, in a day and then went to bed stricken with a fever. She was, undeniably, near to death, for her ladies opened the windows of the house so that her soul might fly free. But she recovered, and years later, at the nadir of her ill-fated fortunes, she was heard to sigh, "Would God I had died in Jedburgh". There were many who shared that mournful wish with her. One of the relics preserved at Queen Mary's House is the facsimile of Queen Mary's death-warrant signed by Queen Elizabeth.

This pretty house is now a museum—one of the most pleasant in all Scotland; a three-storey honey-coloured house with high crow-stepped gables and a turret stair. It was bought for the town in 1928 for £750. The steep roof, once thatched, is now covered with red tiles, but otherwise the house is every bit as Queen Mary must have seen it. Indeed, it has a markedly authentic air. Solid and sound though it is, it looks outspokenly just as a 16th-century Scottish mansion must have looked, and was lived in right up to 1928.

When modern plaster and partitions were removed it was dis-covered that the first floor comprised one Great Hall and a with-drawing room to the south. The fireplace has been restored. The room where Queen Mary lay ill is in the staircase turret, and on the walls is a piece of tapestry depicting the meeting of Jacob and Esau, which is reputed to have been there when the Queen was there.

Other interesting relics include Queen Mary's watch and thimble-case; a letter of hers to the Laird of Cessford dated 25th September, 1566; and a bronze cannon presented by her to Sir Thomas Ker of Ferniehurst. Also there are stocks, halberds, pennons, a drawing of the flag captured by the Weavers of Jedburgh at Bannockburn, and the "hangman's ladle"—an iron scoop which the town hangman was allowed to dip into every sack of meal or corn that came to market.

The house is surrounded by a lovely garden in which grows a pear-tree known as "Our Queen Mary Tree". It was sent by Queen Mary, consort of King George V, from Sandringham and planted on 29th November, 1934—the wedding day of her son, the Duke of

Kent—on the site of an earlier pear-tree, "Queen Mary's Tree", blown down in a winter gale.

Another house associated with the royal Stuarts is the one in Blackhills Close in Castlegate. Here Prince Charles Edward stayed for a night in November, 1745, and in 1935 the Jethart Callants Club affixed a tablet here to commemorate the Prince's stay.

In Abbey Close is recorded another Jedburgh visit—this by William Wordsworth and the indefatigable Dorothy. They were called upon at this house by an advocate well known in Jedburgh legal circles. This man of law had pretensions, too, to be a poet, and asked William and sister Dorothy if they would bear with him while he read to them part of a yet unpublished work which he was thinking of calling *The Lay of the Last Minstrel*. Walter Scott was a frequent attender at the Circuit Courts in Jedburgh and made his first appearance as an advocate in a criminal trial there in 1793. A bronze tablet on the County Buildings records Jedburgh's proud association with Scott.

Jedburgh is prodigal with such engraved records. In Canongate—where Border lairds once had their town houses—is a tablet on a house adjoining Dean's Close which tells us that Burns lodged there in 1787 when he came to receive the freedom of Jedburgh. Jedburgh was the first town to give him such public honour. His diary suggests a pleasant visit: "Walked out with some ladies to be shown Lovers Lane."

Near the foot of Canongate, on the north side, is yet another tablet, marking the house where was born Sir David Brewster, inventor of the kaleidoscope and lenticular hereoscope and founder of the British Association.

The bridge from the Canongate to Richmond Row is officially recognised as a "monument of national importance". Believed to be as old as the Abbey, and indeed to have provided passage for the stones used in the building of the Abbey, it is one of the few three-ribbed bridges still in existence in Scotland.

Castle was a Jail

At the top of Castlegate is Jedburgh Castle, built in 1823 as the County Jail. It occupies the site of the ancient Castle of Jedburgh destroyed in 1409 by order of the Scottish Parliament so that the English, who had just been driven out of it after holding it for 63 years, could never again make such use of it.

In medieval times the Castle was a favourite home of Scottish kings. It was the scene of the wedding feast of Alexander III, who married his second wife, Jolande, daughter of the Count of Dreux, at Jedburgh Abbey in 1285. This was six months before his death on the coast of Fife, and legend has it that at the height of the wedding festivities the spectre of Death stalked through the banqueting hall.

Jeddart or Jethart

It is claimed that there are as many as 84 different spellings of Jedburgh. The popular local ones, Jeddart and Jethart, are in fact nearer the old form, Geddewrd, than the official Jedburgh.

In the old fighting days the battle-cry "Jethart's Here" heralded an onslaught by the men of Jedburgh, and many a time the cry rallied the Scottish forces. The story is supported by a letter the Earl of Surrey sent to Henry VIII. Reporting on the storming of Jedburgh, the Earl comments feelingly that he "found the Scottes at this time the boldest men and the hottest that ever I saw in any nation".

The Jedburgh men were feared for the ferocious weapon they carried: the Jeddart staff was an eight-foot pole surmounted with an axe or a vicious hook.

In the last Border battle—the Raid of Redeswire—the Jedburgh men, led by the Provost, "the Bauld Rutherfurd", arrived on the scene at the crucial moment and routed the English 10 miles south of the town.

A memory of those bloody days is said to be preserved in the riotous game of Handba' with which the men of Jedburgh celebrate the coming of Candlemas. It is a glorious rough-and-tumble. The "Doonies" come from down-town—below the mercat cross—to challenge the "Uppies". Shop windows are barricaded. Play surges through the streets and often spills over into the Jed, where Uppies and Doonies deliriously duck each other. The object is to put the ball "out of play". This is done by cutting the ball. The Doonies have the right to cut the ball in the Goose Pool at the Townfoot Brig—the same pool where Jedburgh witches were once ducked—and the Uppies in the water above the Abbey Cauld.

One grim legend is that this game is a relic of the time when the men of Jedburgh came home from their battles and celebrated victory by playing footba' with severed English heads.

Certainly the annual game began as football, but in the 18th century the Town Council forbade this playing of football within the streets because *"sometimes both old and young near lost their lives thereby"*. Some time later handball was substituted. In 1849 the Council tried to stop this as well and the magistrates fined a number of prominent citizens for defying the prohibition. This was too much for Jeddart Callants. They took the matter to the High Court in Edinburgh. There they won their appeal. The right to play Candlemas Handba' on Jeddart streets was held to be sanctioned "by immemorial usage".

Jeddart Callants have their annual festival each July. They rally at the Rampart and go in cavalcade to the old castle of Ferniehurst and on to Lintalee, where the English invaders were routed by the Borderers.

Among the many beauty spots around the town is the Sunnybrae Scaurs, praised by John Ruskin in his *Modern Painters*, and at Prior's Haugh, a meadow beside the river at Hundalee Mill, is the revered Capon Tree. This wide-spreading oak is honoured as the sole survivor of the ancient Forest of Jed, and is reputed to be around 1,000 years old.

KELSO   *Scotland's Lost Capital*

"The most beautiful village in Scotland!" In the days when he said this of Kelso, Scott—so romantically and so generously wrong on many occasions—was probably right. The things that prevent us saying that of Kelso today are things which happened after Scott's day—two fiercely ugly churches, a congregation of post-war houses and the loss of the piazza in the square.

Even with such handicaps Kelso can still make a good case for a beauty prize. Much, of course, it owes to its exquisite setting. It is lapped in one of the most luxurious curves of the Tweed. Its immediate surroundings seem to be all rich feudal parkland and dreamlike woodland. Beyond are hills of pasture-land, shimmering fold on fold of it piling up to distant clean moorland heights, and on the horizon are the outspokenly handsome Eildon Hills.

The Tweed itself pays lavish homage to the town. Newly enriched and enchantingly tinctured by the amber waters of the moorland Teviot, it spreads wide and sumptuous as it approaches Kelso, and thus insists that the bridge by which we enter the town should be long and low and graceful. Tweed and Teviot meet under the very walls of the town, near enough for many cottage windows to enjoy perpetually this loving union of the two famous Border rivers. This view impressed Burns enough to make him pull off his bonnet and stand in silent prayer.

In actual building Kelso is among the very best that Scotland can show in the way of towns. Do not, however, expect to find anything declamatorily Scottish. Kelso is not decked out with exaggerated native eccentricities. It has not that almost morbid Scottishness such as we see, for instance, in a town like Culross. No. In Kelso the gaunt crow-stepped lum-hatted Scot beloved by the romantics— and by Edinburgh—has relented, his grim-visaged austerity quite caressed away by the seducing contours of the Border landscape. Here he is soft and gentle. Here, untroubled by Presbyterian conscience, he has agreed to live graciously—even fatly—in sleek abbey lands.

To do so he laid out airy streets of well-built houses with walls of pale clean stone and roofs of ink-blue slate. He designed, too, that great joy of Kelso, its admirable and ample market square—on one side a comfortable wide-paunched coaching inn, and on the other a town hall with piazza and cupola.

This square must once have been the loveliest small town square in Britain. It is still one of the most handsome, despite what was done to it in later years. The town hall's piazza was filled in with windows to provide room for offices at ground level. And at the corner of the little lane leading to the Abbey a bank was built—a building of that clean spare modern bricky handsomeness which would be so suitable for a Welwyn Garden City.

These are the only notable changes in the square. They are, admittedly, only tiny details in so expansive a scene—like two pimples on a lovely visage, not more noticeable nor, sadly, any less.

It is strange how blind we were in the 19th century. Or careless. And strange, too, how even today, with evidence of 19th-century stupidities on every hand, we still think we can get away with it, still think that messing about with a little corner here or a little corner there will do no harm to the entire picture.

We feel more offended about such things in Kelso than we would elsewhere. Kelso is so very nearly unspoiled that spoliation shrieks more loudly here. Thus we look uneasily at what so prettily remains and hope that in future ages neither wealthy banks nor blear-eyed town councils will have the power to tamper.

First the parkland and the wide Tweed. Then the big square and broad inn. . . . These are the features which give Kelso a particularly well-fed urbane air. It is this air which strangers from other lands—particularly the English foreigners who have newly crossed the nearby frontier—find unexpected. The writer himself confesses that when he came for the first time into Kelso's market square—it was on a winter afternoon, when the yellow sun, flooding low, touched with gilt the curved crowns of the cobbles so that they looked like an orderly scattering of buttercup petals, and every street corner was dramatised with triangles of purple shadow—he also found this vision of a Scottish town unexpected.

And when on the following morning, looking down from a window, he saw the square all silent and motionless—except for the postman plodding a dark-blue whistling diagonal across the cobbles—he thought the whole scene, because of its leisure and its regular square pattern of cupola and roof, very French. Later in the day the impression was intensified. This was when he was walking through the parkland of the princely Floors Castle—the true name, of course, is *Fleurs*—and saw the town lying obediently outside the "golden gates" of this ducal chateau. "How very French!" he thought. And wrote it, too. Only later did he discover that others had said and written just that. Others, too, had said "How Flemish!" and had traced that resemblance to the Flemish influences of weaving days.

So much for first impressions. Later acquaintance shows such impressions as superficial. Basically Kelso is as Scottish as . . . oatmeal. All its graceful amplitude and all its fat tranquillity demonstrate just what the Scot can do in matters domestic when his landscape is charitable enough to allow it. If all his land were like this lush Borderland, then all his homes might be like Kelso.

One might dream on this and speculate that had the capital of the nation grown here instead of in a place bitten by east winds and shrouded with haar, then Calvin and John Knox might never have won a hearing and to this day there would have been fat monks angling in the Tweed and the ample inns would not on the seventh day become suspected haunts made sordid with the humiliating ritual of book-signing.

But we must be careful. We must not let the charming tranquillity of the scene—that sleepy quilt of cobbles and the glimpse of an abbey tower dozing in a honey-coloured haze at the end of one narrow street —trick us into seeing Kelso as some Rip Van Winkle backwater beyond the current of Scottish life. It is not that, and never was.

Indeed, Kelso's story is so richly studded with all the things which make up history books—the comings and goings of kings, the mustering and marchings of armies, the growlings and roarings of politics—that a diary of the things that have happened here would serve as an outline, a kind of chronological index, of the history of all Scotland through all the ages of English raids and Stuart kings from the day when David I founded the Abbey to the time of the two Rebellions.

For three centuries the town was the target of the English, the necessary first prize in any invasion, the essential key to open the highway into the heart of Scotland. That scrap of ruin beyond the square—the remnant of the despoiled Abbey—is lasting evidence of the vicious severity of England's last assault.

In Kelso one king was killed and another was crowned. To Kelso came Queen Mary herself, and that at a most historic period in her career, for her visit was during her desperate liaison with Bothwell. At Kelso, too, at the ancient cross of Roxburgh, the Old Pretender was proclaimed King James VIII, and at Kelso, 30 years later, Prince Charles Edward, poised for his invasion of England, stayed for two days, and the spot where his horse cast a shoe is fancifully marked in the street.

Since then Kelso has relinquished warlike ways. In the last two centuries she comes into the pages of history in civilian and quieter habit. But those entrances, though less clamorous, are no less important. Her ways have become the ways of commerce and invention, ways as important and significant in modern times as kings and armies were in ancient days.

We discover, for instance, that in the last century the first building to be illuminated with gas in Scotland was a fishmonger's shop in Kelso. That in this century Kelso had Scotland's first public dispensary, founded in the 18th century and now the Kelso Dispensary and Cottage Hospital at Maxwellheugh. That Kelso's *Chronicle* was only second in the powerful line of Scotland's provincial newspapers—a fact that might to many seem even more important than the crowning of the third James.

Rennie's Great Bridge

And that fine five-arch bridge by which we have entered the town across the Tweed made architectural history when Rennie built it 150 years ago. It was the first bridge designed with an elliptic arch.

It served Rennie as his prototype for the Waterloo Bridge which he built across the Thames and which served London until the reign of Herbert Morrison. The relationship of the two bridges was recently commemorated in a happily imaginative way: two lamp-posts from Rennie's Waterloo Bridge have been planted on Rennie's Kelso bridge.

One of Rennie's three-shilling a week labourers at Kelso was a ploughman's son who became Sir William Fairbairn, part designer of that ingenious ugly tubular bridge across the Menai Straits. Fairbairn was a native of Kelso, as also was another eminent engineer—Sir James Brunlees, who laid the first railway across the Alps.

Until 1955 the carriage-way of the bridge conformed to the pattern of Kelso: it was laid with cobbles, like Kelso's square, but the County Council over-ruled the town and insisted on macadam.

Kelso is famous, too, in the hymn-books. Mary Lundie Duncan, born in Kelso manse, wrote many hymns, including the lovely *Jesus, tender Shepherd, hear me*. And Horatius Bonar, minister of the North Parish Church before the Disruption, wrote, among others, *I heard the voice of Jesus say*, and *A few more years shall roll*. St John's-Edenside Church was built for him, but he had gone to Edinburgh before it was finished.

Walter Scott's Home

Kelso town and its surroundings awakened in the young Walter Scott his "love of natural scenery, more especially when combined with ancient ruins or remains of our fathers' piety or splendour". To the farm at Sandyknowe, near **Smailholm,** six miles from Kelso, he was sent as a baby, and when, as a schoolboy, he was given a rest from Edinburgh High School, he came to stay for six months in Kelso with his "kind and affectionate aunt", Miss Janet Scott "in a small house, situated very pleasantly in a large garden . . . which extended down to the Tweed". The cottage, Garden Cottage in the Knowes, has been completely rebuilt since his day, and is now known as Waverley Lodge, but it bears on an outside wall a bust of Scott, and above one of the doorways a carving of Maida.

During his stay at Kelso young Walter attended the Grammar School—its site is now occupied by the Abbey Row School. There he was under the tutelage of Mr Lancelot Whale, who, not unnaturally, had a "supreme antipathy to puns. The least allusion to

Jonah, or the terming him an odd fish, or any similar quibble, was sure to put him beside himself."

Near the school are the graves of Scott's Aunt Janet, his great-grandfather "Beardie" and his uncle, Captain Robert Scott.

The six months Walter Scott spent at this country grammar school can now be recognised as one of those "accidents" of early life which, apparently without significance, in later years resurrect themselves, assert their influence and determine inexorably the future. For it was in the classroom at Kelso that there was born the partnership—that great, rewarding, productive and yet disastrous partnership—of Walter Scott and the brothers Ballantyne. At the grammar school he met, as fellow students, James and John Ballantyne, later to be respectively the printer and the publisher of nearly all his works.

So all that immense flood, that rich outpouring of romance, can be thought to have begun in the days when Walter Scott whispered in the classroom to James Ballantyne, "Come, slink over beside me, Jamie, and I'll tell you a story".

And two decades later the first two volumes of *Border Minstrelsy* came off the press of the *Border Mail* in Kelso's Bridge Street—so beautifully printed that bibliophiles in Edinburgh handled them in wonder and then asked "But where is Kelso?"

The Abbey

If in Kelso we have sought the paths of the young Scott—his aunt's house, the garden where he lay beneath a plane-tree rapt through the summer hours in the magic of the *Reliques*, the site of the school he went to—then also we have followed, affectionately, the halting footsteps of the lad below the shadow of Scotland's loveliest ancient monument—the Abbey of Kelso, one of those "ancient ruins of our fathers' piety".

Be sure of this, wherever else we go in Scotland, whatever grandeur of scenery or romance of history would take us by other routes, we must, if we have hearts and eyes at all, make our way to Kelso's Abbey.

Little remains of the once great Abbey founded by David I more than 800 years ago. Little but enough. Enough to light the dullest eye and quicken the slowest heart. The grandeur of even the little piece bequeathed to us rebukes those who were impertinent enough to think little of it, and prick up their mediocre spires in its shadow.

Kelso Abbey was through 200 years one of the supreme ecclesi-astical powers in the land. Its Abbot took precedence over all others in Scotland. The Abbey was immensely rich: it gathered in the revenues of 37 parishes, all the forfeitures within the town and county of Berwick, several manors and vast numbers of granges, mills, fishings and other Lowland properties.

It grew in power and magnificence. Then, in the 16th century, it fell. On 20th June, 1523, the invading English demolished the vaults and the chapel of St Mary. They tore off all the roofs and set fire to the monastic buildings. This destruction they continued in 1542 and 1545.

The last raid is famous in history, for it is marked by the heroic defence of the Abbey by the burgesses and monks. Only 100 strong, they held out against Henry VIII's force of mercenaries—a kind of United Nations army of "liberators" in which every country was represented except Russia and Turkey. Driven into the tower itself, the little garrison held out till nightfall. During the night some escaped; in the morning the invaders forced an entry and butchered those who remained.

From 1649 the transept, roughly ceilinged and with a thatched prison above it, served as Kelso's parish church until, on a Sunday in 1771, part of the roof fell in during a service. The worshippers, running out, remembered a prophecy ascribed to Thomas the Rhymer that the kirk would fall when it was at its fullest. So they did not go back. Later, as we have seen, they built churches of their own.

In the Vatican library is the manuscript of a traveller who de-scribed the Abbey as he saw it in 1517. Research that has been made on the basis of this clue has established that what we see at Kelso is only the extreme west end of the greatest of the Border abbeys.

It is believed that the church of St Mary, up to 300 feet long, consisted of a long nave with seven or eight bays. There were transepts at each end and a tower at each crossing. The square Galilee porch and ante-church at the west end was balanced by a projecting presbytery from the choir at the east end.

Of this great church remains some of the ravaged façade of the west end, the transepts, the battered tower, two bays of the nave. The face of the north transept is as it has been for 800 years. Par-ticularly notable is the triple-tiered arched Galilee porch, the two remaining tower arches—beautiful Early Pointed—and the lavishly ornamented intersecting arcades of the side walls.

Do not fail to notice the rich and characteristic Norman decoration—particularly the network pattern on the pediment above the arch and the carving on the remaining half of the western archway.

But all these are the details beloved by scholar and architect, and, richly as they do reward us for examination, it is the general effect of the ruin—the whole solemnly beautiful congregating of tower and arch and window of mellow softened stone—which composes the great joy of Kelso.

Roxburghe Cloisters

In 1919 the Abbey was presented to the nation by the eighth Duke of Roxburghe, with the family retaining burial rights in the cloisters. South of the church an ancient Gothic arch is now the entrance to cloisters built as a memorial to the ninth Duke and his Duchess, and nearby is Kelso's war memorial.

We must, of course, find some happiness in the thought that we have reached the time of life when such relics as Kelso's Abbey are protected and preserved. But that does not restrain us from deploring the bitter encirclement of railings—ornamental and adequately designed though it is—which is clasping tightly around the base of the building and spikily intrudes into every vision we have of the ruin, so that we must always see its venerable frame enchained —handcuffed, as it were like a saint still held captive by heretics. Surely now that the English can be trusted not to make more forays across the Border and now that the anger of the Reformers has centuries ago evaporated there is no need for such protection.

"Ugliest Parish Church"

Near the Abbey is the parish church, built in 1773 and much altered in 1823 and 1833, described as an "octagonal structure, and has the peculiarity of being without exception the ugliest of all the parish churches in Scotland but an excellent model for a circus".

We have devoted a separate chapter to the princely house of **Floors,** whose parkland sweeps up to the streets of Kelso, but the title of its owners, the Dukes of Roxburghe, reminds us that Roxburgh is actually the original name for this territory.

Roxburgh Castle

The old town of Roxburgh grew up nearby that royal castle of Roxburgh where Alexander II was married and Alexander III was born. Some few roots of the Castle can still be seen on the peninsula between Teviot and Tweed. In the reign of David I, Roxburgh was one of Scotland's four royal burghs: the others were Edinburgh, Stirling and Berwick. Which reminds us of our dream, earlier expressed, of what might have been the ways of Scotland had this corner of the land and not Edinburgh become the site of the nation's capital. But Roxburgh lay too near the frontier of enemy England and suffered in the sacrificial policy of the Scots, who, for reasons of strategy, laid low all that could be used by the English.

James II it was who employed this "scorched-earth" policy against the foe. The town and Castle had been held by the English for 100 years when the 29-year-old King attacked it in 1460. He was killed on 3rd August that year when he was watching the discharge of his greatest cannon, The Lion. The cannon burst and he was fatally wounded. In the park of Floors Castle a holly tree is pointed out as marking the spot where James II was killed.

His eight-year-old son was carried by the nobles to the Abbey and there crowned King James III of Scotland. The widowed Queen fought on and encouraged the troops. The English capitulated, and then, to make sure that "the place which the English had held for more than 100 years might thenceforth cease to be a centre of rapine and violence, or a cause of future strife between the nations, the victors reduced it to a heap of ruins".

Wealthy Beggar Gemmels

The nearby village of Roxburgh, on the left bank of the Teviot, stands on the site of the "New Roxburgh" built as an "overflow" town from David I's "Old Roxburgh". In the churchyard is the tomb of Andrew Gemmels showing the noted Border character who, wearing his beggar's blue gown, caught the eye and fired the imagination of the young Walter Scott.

Gemmels, who was immortalised by Scott as "Edie Ochiltree", was one of the most popular gaberlunzies of his day. And one of the wealthiest. He had, indeed, a vested interest in begging. In his latest years he was heard to lament—as many a super-tax payer today laments—about the harder times he had lived to see. Why, he declared, begging brought him in £40 a year less than it had done in earlier years! But he could ride his rounds on a good blood-mare and sit down to a game of brag with the Laird of Gala—the laird sitting, of course, indoors, and the beggar sitting on a stool in the yard—for a fat stake of silver.

Before he died, in a bed made up for him on a cart in the barn at the farm of Newtown, Andrew was asked what money he had on him. "Bow, wow, wow, woman!" he retorted. "Womenfolk are aye fashing theirsels aboot what they hae nae business wi'."

He carried with him two combs for his beautiful silver locks, and had a set of teeth, very white, which he got in his 101st year. He died on 31st March, 1793, aged 106. Old Jamie Jack of Roxburgh dug his grave and was paid for with the shoes Andrew had bought in Selkirk on his last begging round.

One feature immediately noticeable in Kelso is its rich collection of occupational names on the corners of its streets—Horsemarket, Coalmarket, Woodmarket, Oven Wynd and Distillery Lane.

The coal, wood and horse markets have gone, but the September ram sales still attract breeders from many parts of the world, and even Kelso's capacious square cannot hold the crowd when visitors pack the town each July for the annual Agricultural and Industrial Show of the Border Union Agricultural Society.

On the score of names, surely Kelso would take any prize there might be for a display of the most unusual family names on the signboards of its shops. We hope the tradesmen concerned will not take offence if we, in passing, mention three which caught our eye as we made a farewell stroll around that big market square—J. S. Bookless, A. Titilah and Jas. Cowe Burgon.

At Berrymoss, about a mile from Kelso, is the race course, opened in 1822.

East of Kelso is the frontier parish of Sprouston, where, at Hadden Rigg, the Scots, in 1549, routed a brave English force of 3,000 horsemen.

KIRKMAHOE   *First Steamer Trip*

Four miles north of Dumfries, on the quiet road running near the east bank of the Nith, is the village of Kirkton in Kirkmahoe parish. Further north is Dalswinton, on the site of the fortress of the Comyns and home of Patrick Miller, who in 1788 let the farmland of Ellisland, across the Nith, to Robert Burns.

That same year, on 14th October, Mr Miller—enthusiastic believer in the future of steam power for navigation—launched on the loch in his parkland a boat fitted with a steam engine and demonstrated the practicability of steam navigation for the first time. Burns is reputed to have been a passenger on that occasion. The engine used is now in South Kensington Museum.

Writing of Miller, Carlyle said: "He spent his life and his estate in that adventure, and is not now to be heard of in these parts, having had to sell Dalswinton and die quasi-bankrupt, and, I should think, broken-hearted." Carlyle must have been repeating careless local gossip, for Patrick Miller's late career hardly bears out that gloomy story. It hardly seems likely that a "quasi-bankrupt" should be deputy-governor of the Bank of Scotland, which Miller later was. When almost 80 he was still an enthusiast for progress, introducing florin grass into Scotland, and, again refuting Carlyle's story, he died at Dalswinton in December, 1815.

KIRKPATRICK   *The Bruce Country*

North of the main road from **Gretna Green** to **Ecclefechan** lie the hills of Eskdale, but they are too far away to give any grandeur to the immediate scene. South of the road gentle Kirtle Water ambles pleasantly along through wooded banks towards the sandy Solway, but out of sight. The road itself, with its unceasing stream of Glasgow–England traffic, can be wearisome and dull, and the village of Kirkpatrick—whose full title is Kirkpatrick-Fleming—seems little more than a crossroads conglomeration of cottages. But beyond the road, on both sides of the hedgerows, is a tract of Scotland seldom explored by visitors, yet stuffed with interesting memorials of the past.

This muted countryside is territory closely associated with early Scottish history; with Bruce and, long before him, the Romans. Across its low hills and shallow valleys English and Scots marched and countermarched at the dawn of Scotland's fight for her independence.

You will indeed be shown here—if you can believe in such things —the very cave where Bruce hid from the English. You might even be lucky enough to see a spider.

On the bank of Kirtle Water, about midway between Gretna Green and Kirkpatrick, at Redhall Castle, seat of the Flemings, 30 Scots held out for three days against the English, and when the attackers set the place on fire they chose to perish in the flames rather than surrender.

Further down the Kirtle Water stood Stonehouse Tower, another ancient Border fortalice that has disappeared from the scene.

Along the road to Ecclefechan, near to Kirtlebridge but still in the parish of Kirkpatrick-Fleming, is the old Merkland Cross, supposed to mark the spot where in 1484 a Master of Maxwell, Warden of the Marches, was assassinated after a successful skirmish with the Duke of Albany and the Earl of Douglas.

KIRTLEBRIDGE   *A Lovers' Grave*

Kirtlebridge clusters beside the main road midway between **Kirkpatrick** and **Ecclefechan**. Some two miles north-east, enfolded by a loop of Kirtle Water, is the burial-ground of Kirkconnell. Here are the graves of "Fair Helen of Kirkconnell Lee" and Adam Fleming, two 16th-century lovers whose tragic death forms the subject of one of Scotland's saddest ballads.

Helen had the misfortune to be courted by two ardent suitors, Adam Fleming of Kirkpatrick and Bell of Blackethouse, one of that famous landowning family known as "the Bells of Middlebie". She favoured Adam, but Bell of Blacket warned her that if he ever saw her with Fleming he would slay him. One day Bell surprised the lovers as they walked beside Kirtle banks, and the faithful Helen flung herself in front of Adam to save him from the assassin's shot. She fell dead and Adam Fleming drew his sword and hacked the murderous Bell to pieces. Adam Fleming is said to have gone abroad and fought in Spain before he came to lie beside Helen in the tree-shadowed burial-place.

> *I wish my grave were growin' green,*
> *A winding-sheet drawn owre my een,*
> *And I in Helen's arms lying*
> *On fair Kirkconnell Lee.*

Across Kirtle Water from Kirtlebridge is sturdy Bonshaw Tower, seat of the Irving family. The last of the line, Sir Robert Irving of Bonshaw, died in 1954. He was the noted captain of the *Queen Mary* who was in command when the liner regained the Atlantic Blue Riband, and one of his great feats was to dock his mighty craft without the aid of tugs in New York during a dockers' strike.

A near neighbour of Bonshaw is the old baronial pile of Robgill Tower.

LADYKIRK
Gratitude to God

The charming Tweedside village of Ladykirk is graced by one of the last churches to be built in Scotland before the Reformation, a lovely building which is a King's thankoffering to God for salvation from death.

In 1499, crossing the river here at the head of his army, James IV was overtaken and almost overwhelmed by one of the sudden spates of the Tweed. He narrowly escaped drowning, and thereupon vowed to build a shrine and dedicate it to "Our Lady" in gratitude to God for his deliverance.

There it stands as he built it, a joy to behold and noteworthy indeed in a countryside where almost everything of ecclesiastical beauty has been replaced by the 19th-century's idea of the elegant, the commodious, the comfortable.

It has a stone-slabbed roof in the fashion of medieval Scottish building—like the roofs of Seton, Corstorphine and Borthwick—and the short crocketed pinnacles of the massive buttresses stand bravely up around the overlapping stone flags of the roof. The square three-storeyed tower at the west end seems to have been constructed—like many church towers in the north of England—with a view to defence. The base-course and moulded string-course round the walls and buttresses of the church are continued round the base of the tower, which is apparently coeval with it, except for the four-sided dome with its funny little belfry above. This dates from 1743, and may have been the work of the elder Adam.

On the inside of the western gable, a marble records a 1743 restoration. How the heart sinks at the thought of an 1861 "Restoration", but this time it seems to have confined itself to cleaning, heating and re-seating.

Under the marble plaque is a brass one, on which Marianne Sarah Robertson, Baroness Marjoribanks of Ladykirk, expresses her thankfulness to the merciful Providence that protected this parish and its inhabitants on the 14th day of October, 1881, when a windstorm of unusual severity proved so disastrous in its effects to persons and property both on sea and on land—in other words, on the day of the Eyemouth Disaster in 1881. Thus the centuries are linked, as this pious Victorian lady follows the example of her long-dead Stuart

Sovereign, in making a tangible thankoffering to God for deliverance from sudden storm.

In the bed of the river just opposite Norham Castle there was found a stone cannon-ball, 57 inches in circumference. This, we can reasonably assume, was emitted by Mons Meg when she was here in 1497, for we know that the "great iron murderer called Muckle Meg" could fire a granite ball "the weight of a Carsphairn cow".

LANGHOLM   *Eskdale's Muckle Town*

So many bridges, so many waterways! Why, at first glance this Muckle Town of the Langholm seems like a little Venice. A very grey Venice, of course, very muted and dour, but nevertheless excitingly cut up with rivers, so that any Langholm housewife must cross at least a couple of bridges on her shopping rounds. And every good church-going burgess must cross a bridge at least once a week, for even the church has its own bridge.

Langholm prides itself on being Scotland's "most Border" town, for it stands on the very threshold of Scotland. It is only eight miles from England, and many of these foreigners who live on the other side of the Border are within daily sight of Langholm's prominent landmark, the noted Monument.

The Monument is a 100-foot-high obelisk of white sandstone on the top of Whita Hill. It commemorates one of the "Four Knights of Eskdale". These were four brothers of the Malcolm family of Burnfoot. All four were knighted for service to their country. The one of the Monument was a General: Sir John Malcolm, Governor of Bombay and author of a history of Persia. Another brother was an Admiral: Sir Pultney Malcolm, who served under Nelson. His Monument is beside the Town Hall in Langholm Market Place.

But what is a mere family of knights to Langholm? This little town is quite disproportionately rich in famous sons. William Julius Meikle, author of *There's Nae Luck Aboot the Hoose*, was born in Langholm in 1734, and another poet—a far greater one—Hugh MacDiarmid was born in Langholm. One of the peculiarly Scottish subjects that has moved this distinguished modern poet to verse is Langholm's Common Riding.

> *Drums in the Walligate, pipes in the air,*
> *Come and hear the cryin' o' the Fair.*

A' as it used to be, when I was a loon
On Common-ridin' Day in the Muckle Toon.

The bearer twirls the Bannock-and-Saut Herrin',
The Croon o' Roses through the lift is farin',

The aught-fit thistle wallops on his thigh;
In heather besoms a' the hills gang by.

And so on, capturing—not only by his words but also in delirious infectious rhythm—the high spirits and gaiety of Langholm's festival every last Friday in July. The ceremony stems from 1759, when Bauldy Beattie the Town Drummer was employed to repair the boundary marks. For more than half a century Bauldy walked the Marches and proclaimed the Langholm Fair at the Cross. In 1816 the Riding on horseback was instituted and also the horse races. The following year the ceremony was graced with its first Cornet.

The day opens with a Hound Trail, after which comes the Presentation of the Town Standard, the Dressing of the giant thistle and the Crown and the crying of the Langholm Fair by the Town Crier standing on the back of a horse. The main event of the day is the Cornet's Chase, and it is a stirring sight to see some 200 horsemen galloping up the steep Kirk Wynd.

Horse races, athletics, wrestling and an evening of dancing on the Castleholm complete Langholm Riding's joyous round of activities. The Crying of the Fair is done in good traditional style, and here is an extract from the Second Crying which serves to show the spirit of the whole:

> THIS IS TO GIVE NOTICE that there is a muckle Fair to be hadden in the muckle Toun o' the Langholm, on the 15th day of July, auld style, upon his Grace the Duke of Buccleuch's Merk Land, for the space of eight days and upwards; and a' land-loupers, and dub-scoupers, and gae-by-the-gate swingers, that come here to breed hurdums or durdums, huliments or bruliments, hagglements or bragglements, or to molest this public Fair, they shall be ta'en by order of the Bailie and Toun Council, and their lugs be nailed to the Tron wi' a twalpenny nail; and they shall sit doun on their bare knees and pray seven times for the King and thrice for the Muckle Laird o' Ralton, and pay a groat to me, Jamie Ferguson, Bailie o' the aforesaid Manor.

Ruined Langholm Castle was the home of the Armstrongs, kinsmen of the famous freebooter, Johnnie Armstrong of Gilnockie, some four miles away down Eskdale near Canonbie.

The market-place at Langholm is in the old part of the town, and here it is that Langholm's sound building in white freestone from Whita Hill is most apparent. The overall appearance is modest, almost drab, though most of the houses are soundly built. The new part of the town, Meikleholm, was founded in 1778 as Langholm laid plans to flourish into an industrial town. In 1788 a cotton factory was founded here and did much trade with Glasgow and Carlisle, but Langholm's real importance as a cloth-making town was established when it began making plaids and check trouserings for shepherds in 1832. Not long after that it became a noted centre for tweed.

Prospering, it built in 1846 its big Gothic church. The town certainly needed a new place of worship. The old church—the "kirk up the wynd"—was extremely primitive. For the most part the feet of the worshippers rested on the bare soil. People with means had boards laid down, whilst others provided themselves with plaited straw. Weeds of various kinds grew inside the kirk.

The present church, on the Eldingholm where Wauchope joins the Esk, adds to the number of Langholm's bridges its own bridge over the Wauchope.

By the way, when one of Langholm's bridges was being built a lad called Thomas Telford worked on it as an apprentice. Well, a lad who was to become one of Britain's most famous bridge-builders could start life in no better place then Langholm.

LANGTON   *The Curse of the Cornysyke*

If ye pass owre the Cornysyke
The corbies will get your banes to pyke.

The burn of the Cornysyke flows through the parish of Langton, and the French knight Sieur de la Bastie had been warned to cross it at his peril. But he did when, pursued by the Homes of Wedderburn, he galloped from Langton Tower, making north-east for Dunbar. He got through the town of Duns, but his horse stumbled and his pursuers caught up with him. His subsequent fate we have told in our Edrom chapter.

In the disused burial-ground are traces of the 12th-century church of Langton, abandoned when a modern church was built in 1798 at Gavinton. That in its turn was replaced in 1872 by the present one.

A pleasant little piece of antique competitive advertising has come down to us in connection with the farm of Choicelee, on the Langton Burn.

> There's as good cheese in Choicelee
> As ever were chow'd wi' chafts:
> And the cheese o' Cheshire
> Is nae mair like the cheese o' Choicelee
> Than chalk's like cheese.

LAUDER *The "Long-haired Boys" Were Hanged*

Slap in the middle of the unspeakably wide yet most times almost empty High Street of Lauder is the Town Hall. As you come into this town—high up in breezy wide-horizoned Lauderdale, the only royal burgh in Berwickshire—this town hall is the first thing that catches your eye.

It is a stern little building, terribly bald, almost ugly in its utter lack of decoration. Yet it is strangely lovable, a real "character", a veritable odd old man of the Borders. Stare at it along the broad street and you will see that you could never call its front a façade. No, it is a real honest-to-goodness *face*. Look at it. There are two eyes; two square windows scowling, or squinting, under the forehead of its peaked roof. Just below these windows, of just the right proportion and accurately placed in the very position of a nose, is the door. From the bottom of this dour straight nose the outside stair droops down in the very pattern of moustache and whiskers. And, to complete this Lauder visage, is a narrow lum hat on which a clock serves as cockade. This, you will be thinking, is a whimsical and fanciful description of a severe stony civic building. But you'll see it for yourself. And you, too, will be struck by how right this description is when you see how this Lauder Town Hall does gloot and glour down the High Street.

The upper storey was used as the Town Hall. In the tower is the bell used for summoning meetings of the Town Council. Below is the vaulted windowless jail which was used up to 1840 for the dark confining of criminal and civil offenders.

In front of the Town Hall is the site where Lauder Cross once stood. The Cross has gone, and so have the Kirk of Lauder and the sinister bridge which both figured in a wholesale hanging nearly 500 years ago. There's a deed that gives Lauder a most notorious position in Scotland's bloodier history.

The dread story begins 60 yards from the west front of Lauder's great Thirlestane Castle. There a sycamore tree marks the site of the pre-Reformation kirk where in 1482 the Scots nobles came to a deadly decision—to murder those favourites of their sovereign, King James III, who formed his Council.

Among those marked for death were Cochran, Torphichen, Rogers, Ramsay and the rest. They were the intelligentsia of their day, the long-haired boys. Why, these men talked to their king about such things as music and painting and books, and at the time the rude sword-wielding barons felt the same about such things as Lord Beaverbrook feels about the British Council today. The barons despised highbrows; the brains of these barons were much nearer to the saddle than to the head. They were proud, too, of their ancient lineage, and fiercely offended that the King had gathered around him men of lowly birth, "mushroomes sprung upe out of the dregs of the commons".

Archibald Douglas, Earl of Angus—who would surely have beaten Goering in any grab for the gun at the mention of the word "culture" —volunteered to take the lead in wiping out the intelligentsia, and by doing so he earned his immortal title of "Bell-the-Cat".

The story of this Lauder purge has probably never been more succinctly told than by Robert L. Mackie, in his delightful *A Short History of Scotland*. He tells how the angry barons pursued King James as he marched south with his army in the new war against England. Mackie goes on:

> At Lauder they overtook him: then a sudden timidity seized them. They all wanted the King to surrender his power to them, but not one of them dared to face the angry monarch. Lord Gray, seeing them hesitate, told them the story of the cat and mice. Still they hesitated, then the young Earl of Angus calmly remarked "I will bell the cat", and set off for the royal tent to demand the surrender of the detested councillors. He came back a few minutes later to their meeting place in Lauder Kirk with the news that the King had flatly refused.
>
> While they debated what their next step should be, a knock was heard, and the door opened to reveal a gorgeous figure—Cochran, the most hated of all the King's low-born friends. The sight of the favourite, all gorgeous in black velvet and gold, with a chain of gold about his neck, and a horn tipped with gold at his side, was too much for the nobles. "A rope will suit you better," cried Angus, as he snatched the chain from his neck.
>
> "My lords, is this jest or earnest?" exclaimed Cochran.
>
> "It is good earnest," was the ominous reply. The nobles rushed

from the church to the royal quarters, seized every one who they thought looked like a member of the Council, and hanged six of their captives, including the gorgeous Cochran, over the bridge at Lauder. Cochran died as he had lived, protesting that he should have been hanged in a silken cord, and not in "ane tow of hemp, like ane thief".

The actual position of the bridge has never been established, but in 1827, when drains were being dug in the castle grounds, a stone vault was discovered containing a number of skeletons.

Seven years later, on Monday, 4th January, 1489, the next James rode to Lauder to the hawking. *"Laddis ran with the king at the halking, and the childer chasit dukis in the dubbis and set them up to the halkis"*—a happier scene this than the one seven years before . . . except perhaps for the ducks in the dubs.

The present church of Lauder is almost as bald a building as the Town Hall and has likewise been decried as unlovely. But, again, its stark simplicity has something almost endearing. It was built in 1763 in the rare form of a Greek Cross (of four equal arms). It possesses two silver Communion Cups given in 1677 by the notorious second Duchess of Lauderdale, by whom the Duke was "a little wife-ridden", and there is a six-bushel-sized bell given by Treasurer Maitland in 1681.

In the graveyard is a very small stone bearing a proud glimpse of wide horizons: *George Renwick's Burying place who hath been in Europ Asia Africa.*

From a 19th-century Gazetteer we quote also, without comment:

> On the south-west and the north-east sides of the main street are two thoroughfares, almost altogether unedificed, and bearing the absurd names of the Upper and Under Backsides.

Thirlestane Castle

Screening these two thoroughfares is the park wall of Thirlestane Castle, seat of the Maitlands, the Earls of Lauderdale. Until the 16th century the Castle was known as Lauder Fort, and it was the famous John, Duke of Lauderdale, who "wonderfully adorned it with Avenues, Pavilions, Outer Courts and Stately Entries with large Parks and Planting". And John also it was who added to the Castle —to quote our old friend Bailie Nicol Jarvie—the whigmaleeries and curliwurlies and open-steek hems.

It seems probable that the Duke employed as his master-mason

Robert Mylne, principal master-mason to Charles II—whose work at Edinburgh's Heriot's Hospital we have admired—and, as his architect, Sir William Bruce, famous as the designer of Holyrood-house and Kinross House.

Today, Thirlestane Castle is indeed an impressive sight. Ten circular towers, ogee roofs and pointed turrets, a great central stair-case, leading up to the wide first-floor terrace, ponderously balus-traded and flanked by two pavilions.

The reason for those six semi-circular towers projecting at irregular intervals along the side walls seems to have been the dubious one of providing direct access from the ground, by way of the wheel-stair contained in each, to bedrooms on the upper floors.

The old dungeons, with some instruments of torture, are still preserved. The interior of the Castle is ornamented in a style of richness and grandeur probably unequalled in Scotland, and among the treasures are notably one by Sir Peter Lely. Janssen's fine portrait of the Duke of Lauderdale with the second Duke of Hamilton hangs in the National Portrait Gallery in Edinburgh.

He was a strange person, this John, Duke of Lauderdale; a paradox of a man; profligate and voluptuary Covenanter; scholar; professedly a godly man, but a false coiner and extortionate; "the evil genius of Presbyterianism".

"You're like a Lauderdale bawbee, as bad as bad can be," was the local by-word. And the local landowners had cause to know John's methods. Home of Bassendean! Pringle of Greenknowe! Swinton of that ilk! All of them had estates and money forfeited by the Duke on trumped-up charges of one kind and another; though we shall see in the Westruther chapter how he relented towards one at least of his tenants, the winsome Midside Maggie of Tollis-hill.

On the Greyfriars Monument in Edinburgh, the first and last of the Martyrs named are James Guthrie and James Renwick. Guthrie, minister of Lauder from 1642 to 1649, was an upright, fearless, difficult man. He was executed on 1st June, 1661, and his head exposed for 27 years on the Nether Bow of Edinburgh. The last Covenanting Martyr, James Renwick, in 1686 addressed the last conventicle held in Berwickshire, in the Greencleuch, near Broad-shawrig. There the young Renwick lectured, prayed and preached from before mid-day till the setting of the sun, wearing the short sword which he never laid aside. Two years later, he was executed,

THE BORDER COUNTIES

aged only 26—the last of the company who "glorified God in the Grassmarket".

One of Lauder's most recent acquisitions is the gold chain of office for the Provost. The chain, designed and made by the Edinburgh artist, Miss Elizabeth H. Kirkwood, has a pendant of gold displaying in enamel the arms of the burgh—the figure of the Virgin with the Holy Child in her arms. The pendant is bordered with golden ears of corn, symbolising agricultural Lauderdale. The double chain is fashioned with diamond-shaped links, showing alternately the thistle of Scotland and the fleur-de-lis of the Virgin. The chain was provided by subscription when the Council issued a public appeal. They issued this appeal because they had possessed for some time Provost's robes of office purchased from a bequest. But the robes could not be worn because there was no chain to go with them. When this was made public Lauder folk and friends of Lauder from as far afield as Germany sent the cash to buy the chain.

LEGERWOOD   *A Treasure Preserved*

Legerwood sits in the hills of Lauderdale, four miles away from **Lauder**—as the crow flies. But the crow's way is not the way you can go. You must go down Lauderdale some four miles on the road south to **Earlston** and then turn up the side road east into the hills.

There you will find a lovely thing—Legerwood Church, with its noble chancel and its exquisite Norman arch existing sublimely; appealing beauty that has weathered 800 years of Scotland's story.

Too few such relics of ancient glory remain in Scotland for us to hurry away from even the simplest of them. Two forces destroyed the bulk of them. The Reformers, in high and righteous anger, swept some away. But not so many as they have been accused of. More destructive to Scotland's ancient churches was the apathy of generations of Scots who allowed these treasures to crumble or be despoiled; or to fall into ruin; or—perhaps even worse—to be "improved" by gross insensitive hands.

But a miracle preserved the Norman remains at Legerwood. The miracle happened in this way. To make for their own use a private burial-ground quite cut off from the rest of the church, some early Kers of Morriston blocked up the chancel arch. Hidden thus it stood, protected from the fury of despoilers and the bite of neglect until the year 1898. Then, during the ministry of the Rev. William

144

Rankin, the removal of the masonry and plaster revealed the lovely arch, one of the finest pieces of Norman work in the district. The arch has three semi-circular orders. The central and west consist of a wide hollow and a half round with a fillet between; the east order is of the plain square-edged type. On caps and abaci is a geometrical sunk-star ornamentation, and the enriched abaci, continued along the east wall of the nave, terminate at the interior angles.

Now the light of day pours in upon these lovely lines through the three long-hidden windows, north, south and east, round-arched and nine inches in width. There is a rediscovered round window, too, high in the east gable, its glass now depicting our Lord as the Light of the World.

The restoration of the chancel was the gift of W. van Vleck Lidgerwood, British Chargé d'Affaires at the Court of Brazil, and head of an Airdrie Iron Works.

Story of Brave Grizell

Against the east wall of the chancel stands the 17th-century monument to the memory of John Ker of Moristoun and his Lady, the Grizell Cochrane who, when scarcely out of her teens, saved the life of her father, Sir John Cochrane of Ochiltree. During the political troubles of 1685 Sir John was sentenced to death, but twice this intrepid daughter held up at pistol's point—on the lonely moors outside Berwick—the mounted messenger who bore the warrant of execution.

When, for the third time, the King was asked to sign the warrant, he relented and signed a pardon instead. The family of Sir John—clinging around him and shedding tears of joy—were wondering who their mysterious deliverer might be, when a stranger was shown in, clad in coarse cloak, coarser jerkin and concealing beaver. Without a word the stranger handed over the two death-warrants, now so mercifully out-of-date.

"By what name," eagerly inquired Sir John, "shall I thank my deliverer?"

The stranger burst into tears and, raising the beaver, revealed raven tresses tumbling about the sweet pale girlish face. It was Grizell. Remembering that other Grizell who saved her father Sir Patrick Hume at Polwarth, one cannot but feel that fathers in these parts were extraordinarily fortunate in the daughters they bred.

Perched upon high ground about a mile north-east of Legerwood church is Corsbie Tower, a tall tattered fragment of the Castle where was born Marion Cranstoun, mother of William Maitland of Lethington. A second ruined tower, Whitslaid, is found on a strong natural site, Leader's rushing waters guarding it on the west, and a deep ravine on the north.

An old and constant tradition, traceable to persons old enough to have talked with contemporaries of the event, affirms that Prince Charles Edward Stewart spent the night of 4th November, 1745, in a tent pitched under a plane-tree on Legerwood Farm. It seems quite certain that he passed through Channelkirk, Lauder and Legerwood, but spent the nights of 4th and 5th November at Kelso. The tradition, however, persists.

LILLIESLEAF   *Home of the Riddells*

The secluded village of Lilliesleaf beside the Ale Water is one of the prettiest and quietest retreats in the Borders. Many years ago it was famous as a haunt for artists, but the picturesque thatched roofs that attracted them have gone.

There was a church here in the 12th century, but no authentic vestige of it remains except the font which is now housed in the 18th-century church and used for 20th-century "incomers". The church was extensively altered in 1883, and again in 1910 when it was beautified by the addition of a Romanesque apse. It shelters a 12th-century stone coffin of infant size and a disused bell of 1745.

For seven centuries the place was dominated by the Riddells of Riddell, but since the fall of their dynasty in a spectacular bankruptcy in 1819 the estate is greatly diminished. Their mansion was destroyed by fire in 1943.

Two stone coffins were discovered at Riddell a century ago. One contained an earthen pot filled with ashes and bearing legibly the date A.D. 727. The other contained the bones of a man of enormous size.

LINTON   *Dragon Becomes Two Bears*

So much for legends! Above the main doorway of Linton's lovely Norman church is a carved tympanum. This stone panel, believed to be the only one of its kind in Scotland, is a memorial to Sir John Somerville who was knighted by William the Lion nearly 800 years ago and is believed to have been given his grant of lands in the parish of Linton because he slew wild beasts which were terrorising the local inhabitants.

Linton folk have all said for centuries that this beast was a dragon and that Sir John defeated it by revolutionary means. His "secret weapon" was a long stake mounted on wheels. Its warhead was red-hot peat which went down the dragon's throat. Despite the dragon's own flaming breath, this flaming peat ended its carccr.

In those days a dragon was called a "worm", and its Linton lair had been known for time immemorial as Wormington.

If anyone doubted the story he would be taken to the church and shown the Somerville carved panel, and the lively but muddled outlines of decayed carving would be pointed out to him. "Can't you see it now? There is the dragon writhing in its death agonies!"

Alas for legend! At the beginning of 1954, when an appeal was launched to provide funds for the restoration of the panel and other stonework of the ancient church, experts examined the stone and were able to reconstruct the scene. The dragon, they discovered, was no dragon at all: it was two bears!

But the appeal for funds was successful, and the Ministry of Works undertook the task of putting the stonework of lovely Linton Church into repair. The church, standing on its own small round hill just a mile from Morebattle, is a gently beautiful survivor in a territory where so much else has perished. This little pocket of Scotland, almost encircled by the frontier of England, lay in the very path of invasion. Up at Frogden Farm, north of the church, is a spot called the "Tryst", one-time gathering place of the moss troopers.

Nothing remains of the great fortalice of the Somervilles, Linton Tower, which once stood beside the parish church. It was utterly demolished by Henry VIII's soldiery.

LOCHMABEN   *Castle of the Bruce*

Here is one of the great " shrines" of Scotland's history. The Castle of Lochmaben was the ancestral home of the Lords of Annandale, ancestors of the royal Bruces, and King Robert himself spent much of his childhood in this corner of Dumfriesshire.

It has been deduced that the name Lochmaben means "many lochs", for this royal burgh was at one time surrounded by lochs. There are still seven in the neighbourhood. Three—Mill, Kirk and

Castle Lochs—are world famous as the only Scottish waters where the delicate vendace can be found.

On a heart-shaped peninsula in Castle Loch are the remains of Lochmaben Castle, once the biggest and strongest and most cunningly engineered fortress in the Borders. In the days of its prime it must have held a reputation for strength such as the Maginot Line or Hitler's Atlantic Wall once held in ours. It covered no less than 16 acres with its devilishly ingenious maze of ramparts and moats and drawbridges.

Its designers made every advantageous use of its position amid so much water. Arranged in layers of defence were four moats, each of which could be flooded in turn at the will of the defenders until, when the last moat was filled, the Castle became a well-nigh impregnable island fortress.

Some indication of the Castle's enormous size can be gathered from the knowledge that after it was abandoned it provided generations of Annandale folk with a rich quarry of ready-cut stone. From the Castle's bones they fed their building for more than 200 years. Thus, bit by bit, the great Castle of Lochmaben was gnawed away, until—in the colourful words of Francis Groome—"barbarian rapacity" so destroyed it that only "the heart and packing of some of the walls" was left, "huddled together and nodding to their fall". But at last it has been saved. Now officially protected as an ancient monument the remnants are being rescued from final disappearance by the Ministry of Works.

The Castle is believed to have been built late in the 13th century, and probably some of the stone for it was carted from Castle Hill, on the other side of the loch, where there are traces of a presumably earlier fortress. Tradition claims—without any documentary proof—that that early Castle was the birthplace of the Robert Bruce who became eighth Lord Annandale, Earl of Carrick, and later King Robert of the Scots. Certainly Robert spent much of his early life at the then new Castle of Lochmaben, and it was at Lochmaben, on the western approaches to the Castle, that in 1304 he intercepted and beheaded the messenger who, Bruce claimed, was carrying to King Edward of England the message from the Red Comyn plotting Bruce's death.

This encounter was the spark that set ablaze the Scottish War of Independence. For it led to Bruce's bloody duel with the Comyn at the Church of the Greyfriars in Dumfries, and that deed led in

Jedburgh Abbey   **West Door**

Kelso   **Bridge over the Tweed**

Memorial Cloisters   **The Abbey**

Drumlanrig   **"Castle For a Night"**

Kelso   **Floors Castle**

Kirk Yetholm   **Gipsy Village**

St Mary's Loch   **Head of Yarrow**

turn to Bruce at last coming out into the open against his liege lord King Edward of England and allowing himself to be crowned King of the Scots at Scone.

Seated on the Throne of Scotland, King Robert raised Lochmaben to the dignity of Royal Burgh. His charter was burned in a Border raid in the 15th century. Robert gave Lochmaben Castle to his faithful Randolph, Earl of Moray, hero of the capture of Edinburgh Castle from the English, and granted lands and privileges to the "King's kindly tenants", the inhabitants of the neighbouring "Four Towns", places now known as Heck, Greenhill, Hightae and Small-holm.

In 1409 the Castle came into possession of the Douglases, but when that family was overthrown it was raised to the dignity of a royal garrison, belonging personally to the King or to his sons and managed by a Royal governor. Governorship of Lochmaben was a nice job. It carried the then fat salary of £300 Scots a year, fishing rights on all the nine lochs, and every year the fattest cow in the parish, 39 meadow geese and "Fasten's e'en" hens. This went on until as late as 1730, when the inhabitants of Annandale rebelled against the Marquis of Annandale's exactions, went to law and wrested from the Court of Session a decree putting an end to the Lochmaben toll.

James IV liked the place and spent four years repairing it and building a large hall within it. Queen Mary visited it with her new husband, Lord Darnley.

LOCKERBIE   *Scene of the "Lamb Fair"*

Lockerbie is prominent in the farmer's calendar as the scene of the great August Lamb Sale. This famous Scottish "tryst" dates from the 17th century when the English dealers began coming north to buy stock from the Dumfries cattle and sheep farmers. On the hill beyond the town—known as Lamb Hill—there were often as many as 70,000 lambs gathered for sale, and around their lamb market the folk of Annandale crowded the booths and sideshows.

The folk of Lockerbie bought Lamb Hill for the town with the surplus of money raised to build their £10,000 red-stone baronial town hall.

Lockerbie suffers the discomforts but also the rewards of sitting on the main route from Glasgow to England. At peak seasons of the year 1,000 vehicles an hour pass along its main street. But tourist traffic and its eminence as a market town have made it so prosperous that it was listed recently as the eighth richest town in Scotland.

Its oldest relic—in fact, one could call it Lockerbie's "birthplace" —is the Old Tower, a tiny fortalice hiding behind the present-day police station, and which once did serve as the Town Jail. The Old Tower originally stood in a morass, guarded by natural moats of lochans, and under its protection grew the village, which eventually became Lockerbie. The Tower is built of whinstone with brown stone facings, topped with the later addition of crow-stepped gables. It was rescued recently from complete ruin by the public spirit of two Lockerbie tradesmen, joiner and slater, who gave their working time free for the job of putting a roof on the Old Tower.

In December 1593 the Johnstones of Lockerbie Tower formed a contingent in the last of the Border feuds at Dryfe Sands, two miles away, when, under the command of Johnstone of Lockwood, they defeated the Maxwells. The Lockerbie fighters' custom of slashing enemies across their faces to mark them for life added to the vocabulary of Scotland's history the ominous and famous phrase "a Lockerbie Lick". The Dryfe, which brings down the sand to form the level stretch of Dryfe Sands, is a little river notorious for disastrous inundations. It tore down the ancient church of Dryfesdale on Kirkhill and then ruined its sucessor.

To the Dryfe a Dryfesdale man owes the honour of having buried a wife and married a wife in one day. It happened in this manner. The man was a widower who, after mourning his departed wife for a decent spell, hastened to Dryfesdale Church with his second bride. As he crossed the bridge at the head of the bridal party he saw that the Dryfe was up to its tricks again, gnawing away yet another corner of the graveyard, Then he saw a coffin floating along on the torrent. He recognised it as the one in which he had interred his wife. He rescued the coffin. His bride and the guests assisted him to restore it to the graveyard, and then the party resumed the wedding procession.

Some five miles north of Lockerbie, west of the Glasgow road and beside a loop of the Annan, is Jardine Hall, seat of the Jardine family. On the opposite bank of the river is Spedlins Tower, the former Jardine home, once haunted by the angry ghost of a man who died because of the first baronet Jardine's bad memory. This baronet

rode off one day and did not remember, until he reached Edinburgh
and found the key in his pocket, that he had locked a miller—named
Porteous—in the Jardine dungeon. He sent the key back post-haste,
but the unfortunate man had died of starvation.

Time has embroidered to this horrible enough story the legend that
the dying miller had gnawed his own hands and feet in the last
throes of starvation, and that his spirit haunted the tower until it
was laid in the dungeon by means of a black-letter Bible.

LONGFORMACUS   *Capital of the Lammermoors*

Longformacus, a steep little hamlet clustered around with many
trees and a great variety of bridges, enjoys the title of Capital of the
Lammermoors, emphasising the blessed lack of centres of population
of any kind for miles and miles around.

Behind the little 1890's church—with its St Clair of Roslin coat
of arms, its ancient cross-carved stone in the vestibule and its fragment of a barbarous old joug—stands the huge Longformacus
House, a Georgian dwelling-house with symmetrical rows of
windows.

Westwards from there along a lovely leafy road we found workmen busy among great pipes and bridgework for the reservoir being
constructed on the Rawburn lands (or Rathburne, if you prefer it,
but still pronounced Rawburn).

Here the roads begin to peter out, and at last quite disappear
among an infinitude of *knowes* and *laws* and *shiels* and *cairns* and
rigs and *burns* and *cleughs*. One of the highest points in the whole
Lammermoor range is Meikle-Says-Law or Cesslaw, in the north-
west corner of the parish. Just short of that, on Byrecleugh Ridge,
about 4½ miles west of Longformacus village, near the Dye Water,
is a very extensive and very remarkable cairn called variously Mutiny
Stones, Mittenfull o' Stones, Meeting Stones.

One tradition says the stones mark the burial of a Pictish king.
Another, that they were collected by an army to perpetuate a famous
victory. A third, most dramatic of all, tells how the Devil, being
employed to build a cauld on the Tweed near Kelso, crossed and
recrossed the Lammermuirs, flying high above them, to fetch the
necessary stones from the sea-coast at Dunbar. These stones he
stowed about his person, for convenient cartage. One night of
exceptional darkness he made an error in altitude, and grazed one
hand on a whinstone hillside; and it was the mitten on this hand that

burst above Byrecleugh. Down fell the "mittenfull of stones", and the noise was heard two miles away at Blythe Edge.

Another tradition maintains that an ox-hide is buried here, packed with gold and precious stones, and there it will lie until someone has determination and courage and greed enough to search until he finds it. In the year 1866 Lady John Scott of Spottiswoode and Lord Rosehill dug right across the cairn near the centre. But the treasure was evidently not for them. So it must still be there, waiting for us, or for you, or for someone else, under the devil's mittenful of stones.

One thing seems certain—and this is not fancy, but fact—the Mutiny Stones are the only thing in Berwickshire which can be assigned with definiteness to the Stone Age, and they form the only example of this type of cairn occurring in south-east Scotland.

The two parishes of Longformacus and Ellem were united in 1712, and the ruins of the ancient church of Ellem (which was dedicated in 1243) can be seen on a slope above the north bank of the Whiteadder, close to the tiny hamlet of Ellemford.

MANOR *The "Black Dwarf's" Home*

At Manor, some four miles from Peebles, is one of the strangest cottages in all Scotland, and one of the most famous. It was the home of David Ritchie, the misshapen, pitiful dwarf who, even in his lifetime and long before Walter Scott immortalised him as "The Black Dwarf", had become a legendary figure in the Borders.

In his youth the little man had tried to earn his living in Edinburgh as a brush-maker, but the stares and jeers of the townsfolk drove him back to the quiet of Peeblesshire and the seclusion of the Manor valley. On ground belonging to the farm of Woodhouse he built himself a cottage—the one in which Scott visited him in the summer of 1797—but in 1802, the laird, Sir James Nasmyth of Posso, charitably built him a new cottage of stone and lime with a thatched roof. This is the one we now see, though its roof has been slated and a later building has been tacked on to the end.

The dwarf's original doorway—only three feet ten inches high—is preserved. The normal-sized door and window beside it were made when his sister came to live with him.

Scott was 26 when he walked over from Hallyards, the home of his friends the Fergusons, a mile away, to see "Bowed Davie o' the Wuddus". It was a quite unnerving experience. When Scott and

Ferguson were inside the cottage the dwarf double-locked the door, made a signal to his big back cat to leap on to a shelf, and sat staring at the two visitors, his tremendously ugly face curled into a grin.

The visit made a vivid and lasting impression on Scott. Nineteen years passed before *The Black Dwarf* was published, yet the description of David Ritchie was scrupulously accurate, and probably no other character in all Scott's work bears so close a resemblance to its original.

Nature had indeed played a gruesome prank with poor David. His body was broad and of almost normal size. His arms were as powerful and sturdy as those of a giant. His head was heavy and fashioned into malignant ugliness. But his legs were sadly twisted stumps, and his total height was only three feet six inches. Mungo Park, at that time a doctor in Peebles, describes his legs as being like corkscrews. "The principal turn they took was from the knees outward, so that he rested on his inner ankles and the lower part of his tibias."

Davie was immensely strong. Scott describes him so in his novel, but there are other stories telling of such amazing feats as butting over in a minute with his head and shoulders a tree which two men had been trying to fell for two days.

Yet, he seems to have been a gentle man, avoiding visitors but cheerfully kind to children and devotedly so to animals. Perhaps most affecting of all is the account of how, when he issued from his tiny habitation, his two she-goats would come and lick his hands. "You at least," he would say to them, "see no difference in form."

He was an inspired gardener. His lovely planting made his garden one of the wonders of the valley. He was also, it appears, a great reader. He loved Allan Ramsay's pastoral poems; he detested Burns. He could quote Milton and Shakespeare, and wished, he said, that there should be upon his tombstone the words:

> *Good friend! for Jesus' sake forbear*
> *To dig the dust enclosed here;*
> *Blest be the man that spares these stones,*
> *And curst be he that moves my bones.*

But in 1821, ten years after his burial, that wish prayer was disregarded by curious doctors. The bones were resurrected and carted off to Glasgow, and it is possible that below the stone erected over his grave in Manor churchyard the only relic of "Bowed Davie" now remaining is his skull.

In the garden of Hallyards is a lively stone effigy of Davie, clutching the staff by which he helped himself along the roads of Peeblesshire.

MAXWELTON HOUSE *Annie Laurie's Home*

"But for bonnie Annie Laurie I'd lay me doon and dee!"

He didn't, of course. Those who can profess such ardent and despairing passion rarely live up to it. In 1706 young William Douglas of Fingland forgot the snowy brow and swanlike neck and married Miss Elizabeth Clark of Glenboig in Galloway.

Nor was Annie—for whom the young Jacobite Lieutenant had written his lovely song—broken-hearted. Four years later, when she was 28, she wed 24-year-old Alexander Ferguson, that laird of Craigdarroch whose son won the Whistle in the drinking bout at Friars Carse in the parish of Dunscore. Indeed, William's love seems to have lain but lightly in Annie's memory. When her cousin, years later, mentioned that she had seen William Douglas at an Edinburgh ball, Mrs Ferguson's mild reply was, "I trust he has forsaken his treasonable opinions and is content." Jane Austen could have written it no better!

Annie Laurie's birthplace, the beautifully proportioned white-walled mansion of Maxwelton, set amid lovely lawns and shrubberies and lilies-of-the-valley, can be seen as we journey through the valley of Cairn Water to the village of Moniaive. A striking portrait of her is preserved at Maxwelton. But the neighbouring portrait of a handsome curly-haired youth is not that of her boyish lover: it is her future husband.

She became Mrs Ferguson, mother of four children, and a voluminous letter-writer. She outlived her husband by fourteen years, dying at the age of 81 in May, 1764.

In 1835 William Douglas's song was revised and set to music by Lady Jane Scott. The first verse is believed to be essentially as Douglas wrote it, but Lady Jane rewrote the second verse and added a third. The melody is that composed by her for the old ballad *Kempye Kaye*.

MELLERSTAIN *An Adam Masterpiece*

Some seven miles north of Kelso, just west of the road to Lauder, is the magnificent castellated mansion of Mellerstain, seat of the

Earl of Haddington. It was begun by William Adam and gloriously completed and adorned by his son, Robert.

The library of Mellerstain is one of Adam's masterpieces. By its use of coloured plasterwork it reminds one of his library at Kenwood, and Sacheverell Sitwell described the design of its plaster ceiling as "fine drawn as a spider's web on a frosty morning". In the centre is a medallion painted by Zucchi.

Above the book-shelves is a classic frieze, the panels of which are interposed with niches holding marble portrait busts by Roubilliac.

As at Kenwood Adam innovated here by introducing colour into his decoration. The walls and ceilings are pale green; the grounds of the panels pink; and the background of the friezes is pewter grey.

In the original dining-room, now used as a music-room, is a beautiful fireplace with the carved figures of War and Peace on its pillars. Above is Aikman's portrait of Sir Patrick Hume. Sir Patrick's daughter was Grizell, the heroine who saved his life by carrying food to him when he hid from Charles II's troops in the vaults of Polwarth Church.

Carrying messages between her father and the imprisoned Robert Baillie, who was later hanged in Edinburgh, she met Baillie's son, George. They fell in love and married. After exile in Holland they returned to Scotland, and in 1725 George Baillie began the building of Mellerstain. Portraits of Grizell's daughters, Grizell and Rachel, by Maria Verelst are in the dining-room.

The walls of the drawing-room are covered with their original green damask; the hangings are of brocaded Genoese velvet. A fascinating collection of period dresses, books and silverware is displayed in the Great Gallery up the main staircase.

The Italianate gardens are one of the glories of Mellerstain. Their terraces, stepping down to lovely formal lawns, lead the eye to magnificent vistas of the surrounding countryside.

MELROSE   *Medieval Picture Book*

Here is a monk telling his beads. Here is a musician angel with smiling eyes and curling hair. High up in the angle of two buttresses are a mason, fat-bellied and pop-eyed, with his chisel and mall, and a cook with his ladle. There is a pig playing the bagpipes, and again and again we can detect, amid the profuse adornment of plants and flowers, the comic curl of good Scots kale.

Such carvings are the joys we find when we examine the beautiful ruins of the Cistercian Abbey of St Mary at Melrose. All too little of the rich gaiety of medieval builders has survived in Scotland, but here in Melrose there is wealth indeed.

To the world outside, Melrose is perhaps the most famous of all Scottish abbeys. It owes much of that fame, undoubtedly, to the romantic gloss put upon it by Walter Scott. Few of us as school-children did not have put before us the verses from *The Lay of the Last Minstrel* which begin with the near doggerel couplet:

> *If thou wouldst view fair Melrose aright,*
> *Go visit it by the pale moonlight.*

We have grown older. We have learned that there is no Santa Claus and we have learned that it is most unlikely that Sir Walter ever saw Melrose by moonlight at all. Old John Bower, custodian of the Abbey in Scott's day, maintained that he never let Scott have the key for any night visit. To this Scott himself is reputed to have retorted:

> *Then go and muse with deepest awe*
> *On what the writer never saw.*
> *Who would not wander neath the moon*
> *To see what he could see at noon?*

Yet it became the custom for Scott's worshippers to make a moon-light pilgrimage to the ruin. If clouds obscured the rays, then old John Bower was ready with his tallow candle. This, he said, was really better than the moon. "It does na licht up a' the Abbey at aince, to be sure, but then you can shift it aboot, and show the auld ruin bit by bit, whiles the moon only shines on one side."

That maybe is a good way to see Melrose, to examine it bit by bit, for the Abbey is notable for the grace and delicacy of its stone carving. The most strikingly beautiful survivals are most certainly the two magnificent windows for which Melrose is famous; the great East Window and the window of the north transept. The East Window, whose "slender shafts of shapely stone" are described in the *Lay of the Last Minstrel*, forms almost the whole of the wall, and is surmounted by a shallow gable wondrously decorated. The centre carving of the gable is a group representing the Coronation of the Virgin.

The window of the north transept is an exquisite one. Its five slender lights are surmounted by delicate tracery flowing upwards to the famous "Crown of Thorns".

The remains of Melrose Abbey comprise the east part of the nave, the transepts, the chancel and choir and two piers of the central tower. The eight side chapels of the south aisle remain as burial-places of Border families, including the Scotts, lairds of Gala, and the Pringles of Galashiels, Woodhouse and Whytebank.

The remains of the tiled floor of the chapter house are one of the two known examples of tiled floor left in Scotland; the other was recently found at Glenluce in Galloway. Beneath the floor is buried a human heart enclosed in a lead cone-shaped container. It was always said that the heart of Robert Bruce, when it was brought back from Spain, was buried before the High Altar at Melrose, but it might well have been buried in the chapter house. Here also—near the entrance—was buried the second Abbot, St Waltheof. His shrine became a place of pilgrimage. In 1169, ten years after the Abbot's death, his body was uncovered and found still uncorrupted. It was still so in 1206 when surreptitiously viewed by a mason at work in a neighbouring tomb. An ancient house beyond Cloister Road has been fitted up as a museum of Abbey relics and there we can see three fragments of St Waltheof's shrine, still bearing traces of gilding with pure gold.

In the chancel are the tombs of Sir William Douglas, the Knight of Liddesdale; James, second Earl of Douglas, the victor of Otterburn; Alexander II; and, it is believed, Michael Scott the Wizard. Joanna, Queen of Alexander II, who died in 1238, was buried at the door leading from the north transept to the sacristy.

The story of the growth and destruction of Melrose follows the traditional Border pattern. The Abbey was founded in the reign of David I in 1136, superseding the ancient Celtic chapel of St Cuthbert founded down the Tweed at Old Melrose about 635. In 1322 Edward II pillaged and destroyed it and murdered many of the monks. King Robert the Bruce began its restoration, but in 1385 King Richard II set fire to it. The church was rebuilt, but in 1545 the English came again and destroyed it and pillaged the tombs.

By 1558 the monks were complaining that people in the neighbourhood were stealing the stone and lead. In 1573 Sir Walter Scott of Branxholm was accused of wholesale despoliation, having carried off stone, timber, lead and glass. Though he claimed he did so only to protect the materials from the English!

In 1618 part of the nave was roofed in to serve as a parish church. John Knox, a great-grandnephew of the Reformer, was minister. The stone images of the saints which stood in the niches miraculously survived the fury of the Reformation and were not thrown down and destroyed until 1649.

In the graveyard are the graves of Tom Purdie, Scott's forester, and Peter Matheson, his coachman. Also buried here is Sir David Brewster, the scientist, who died in 1868 at Allerly, near Gattonside, another pretty suburb of Melrose on the other side of the Tweed.

Apart from the 1642 mercat cross, the Abbey is the only antique building in the pleasant town of Melrose, but throughout the town can be detected in its buildings stones that owe their origin to the Abbey and give evidence of the looting in the past.

But Melrose's eastern suburb, the village of Newstead, on the other bank of the Tweed on the road to Earlston, claims to be one of the oldest inhabited places in Scotland, for here in A.D. 80 Agricola is said to have set up his fort. A memorial stone marks the site of the fort. Roman remains found here, including altars, coins of Augustus, Nero and Vespasian, weapons and kitchen implements, can be seen in the National Museum of Antiquities in Edinburgh. Newstead was the home of the masons who built the Abbey, and the local Masonic Lodge is probably the oldest in the Commonwealth.

MERTOUN   *A Bruce Mansion*

Because this parish also holds the glories of **Dryburgh Abbey** and **Bemersyde,** the gentler glory of the fine old mansion house of Mertoun House is sometimes overlooked. It stands on a small Tweed-girt peninsula east of St Boswells, a classic mansion designed by Sir William Bruce of Holyrood and Kinross fame. During alterations by the Earl of Ellesmere in 1913 the foundation-stone was laid bare, plainly stating: FOUNDED THE 10 DAY OF JUNE 1703 YEARS BY SR. WILLIAM SCOTT OF HARDEN AND DAM JEAN NISBET HIS LADY.

At the south end of the flower-garden there is an old conical dovecot, 30 feet high, dated 1576, and the pigeons enter and leave their home by a hole in the middle of the roof. In another part of the garden is Old Mertoun House, two storeys high, dated 1677.

Fragmentary remains of the ancient church of Mertoun stand in an enclosed burial-ground at Magdalenhall, less than half-a-mile from Mertoun House. The present parish church which has one or two old and ornamented stones built into the fabric, seems to have been set here in the middle of a wood in 1658.

MIDDLEBIE *Romans' "Middle Station"*

This little village, traditional home of the Bells of Middlebie— one of whom played his murderous part in the tragedy of Fair Helen of Kirkconnel Lee—lies in that little-visited hinterland just off the main **Gretna–Lockerbie** road.

It is argued that the village and parish takes its name from a Roman Camp, the "middle station" between Netherbie in Cumberland and Overbie in Eskdalemuir. The camp is near the village, on the way to Eaglesfield, and in 1731 important Roman relics were unearthed in the ruins of an ancient temple at Land Farm. These, including two Roman altars and a sculptured figure of the goddess Brigantia, are now in the National Museum of Antiquities in Edinburgh.

On the hills north-east of Middlebie is the isolated and conspicuous hill, Birrenswark or Burnswark, probably the site of a Roman station and probably the site of the 10th-century battle of Brunanburh, where Athelstan defeated the allied Scots under Constantine I and the Dublin Danes under Olaf Guthfruthson.

MINTO *Mystery of The Big House*

Across the Teviot from Denholm, bordering on the Hassendean Lands and backed by the Minto Hills, is the tiny community of Minto—church, manse, mansion-house and a row of cottages.

Dark suspicions were entertained locally when a fine four-storeyed mansion was built in 1814 from designs by Archibald Elliot.

In 1814 the first Earl of Minto—an associate of Burke who took part in the impeachment of Warren Hastings—died on his way home from India, where he had been Governor-General. But years after his death the folk of Minto would not believe he was really dead, despite the fact that he was buried in Westminster Abbey. As late as 1825 Scott writes in his diary:

> They think he had done something in India which he could not answer for—that the house was rebuilt on a scale unusually large to give him a suite of secret apartments, and that he often walks about the woods and crags of Minto at night, with a white nightcap and long white beard. The circumstances of his having died on the road

down to Scotland is the sole foundation of this absurd legend. . . . I have seen people who could read, write and cipher, shrug their shoulders and look mysterious when this subject was mentioned. One very absurd addition was made on the occasion of a great ball at Minto House, which it was said was given to draw all people away from the grounds, that the concealed Earl might have leisure for his exercise.

Behind the house are Minto Hills, "as modest and shapely and smooth as Clytie's shoulders". In sharp contrast to them are Minto Crags in the east, large, jagged masses rising about 700 feet sheer.

On the summit of the crags is the ruin of Fatlips Castle, once a stronghold of the Border family of Turnbull of Barnhill, and that small rocky ledge below the summit "where Barnhill hewed his bed of flint" was most likely a look-out post for the Turnbull retainers.

In Scotland there are two castles called by the strange name of Fatlips. That one is on Minto and the other on Tinto might be cause for rhyme if not for etymological speculation.

The church of Minto is a Gothic building of 1831 designed by William Playfair. The manse, a mile away, was probably unique in that it was originally designed—to the taste of the then minister, a Dr Aitken—as a plausible, if somewhat inappropriate, imitation of a villa in Tuscany. It was destroyed by fire in 1954.

MOFFAT   *The Taste of Stale Eggs*

Rachel Whitford was a knowledgeable young lady, the daughter of a Bishop and widely travelled. She was walking one day in the hills east of the village of Moffat. Hot and tired, she slaked her thirst at a nearby spring. What a taste! The taste of that water was later to be described as like that of "stale eggs whipped up with lucifer matches".

But Rachel was not put off. Far from it. She was excited and delighted. She recognised that sulphurous flavour. It was like the water she had sipped in many spas. Surely, with a taste like that, it must be "good for you".

It was. Rachel Whitford made her discovery in 1633. By the following century Moffat was one of the favourite spas of the fashionable world. Its High Street was thronged with the aristocratic and the wealthy, the learned and the ailing, all resorting to the town high in the valley of the Annan to be cured of their 18th-century ills—of which, it would seem, gout was a common one. David Hume was one of the great men who came down to Moffat to drink water resembling "bilge water, or the scourings of a foul gun".

Time has robbed us of the magnificent and gloriously idle wealth that can support a fashionable spa, and has also almost eliminated gout. History, Josiah Boot, Lloyd George and Aneurin Bevan have given us other ways of getting an intake of sulphur than by "taking the waters". But Moffat still bears handsomely the graciously opulent well-bred air with which it became endowed in its sulphurous 18th and 19th centuries.

To begin with, it is so superbly sited. Coming down to it from the north we are enchanted by its aspect as it lies, neat and tree-embowered in the valley below us, with the smooth hills rolling grassily skywards all around it.

To the north rises Gallow Hill—a name describing its historic purpose. To the south the fertile valley of the Annan ribbons away to the Solway 25 miles distant. Within hailing distance of this luxuriant farmland wild mountain burns plunge down from the highest ground in the south of Scotland—Hart Fell (2,651 feet); Ettrick Pen (2,269 feet); Loch Fell (2,256 feet); Queensberry (2,285 feet).

All this we see in our first glimpse of it from the north. After that the descent to it is as lovely as any we know of.

Unlike many Scottish towns that are likewise beautifully situated, Moffat is not offensive and noisome to its surroundings. Its environs are not spattered with gimcrack shacks and straggling bungalows, and its centre bears, for the most part, the closest inspection.

Its High Street is its outstanding characteristic. It is one of the broadest main streets in Scotland. Indeed, in so small a town, that breadth is quite staggering. Down the centre of the street is a widely spaced double file of lime-trees, and on either side of this shady avenue is still room enough for full-width roadways.

Moffat's Ram

Moffat's High Street was spread out to its present width about 100 years ago—at the expense, we fear, of lots of probably lovely old houses. But the result is good, an attractive oblong *place*, of which the principal feature is, undoubtedly, the Colvin fountain. This is built in the form of a tall cairn of huge boulders, surmounted by a majestic ram with curling horns, sculptured by Brodie. The ram symbolises that occupation of sheep-farming which before Rachel Whitford's day and again in this age was and is the principal livelihood of the surrounding hills.

Moffat is a great sheep-farming district and has produced some of the greatest sheep-dog breeders and trainers in the world, and we join with George Scott-Moncrieff in his commendation of Moffat for wisely erecting in its centre a statue "not to a provost, but to the black-faced sheep".

Near the Moffat ram is the relic of Moffat's other occupation: "the waters". This is the Baths House, built in 1827. This building moved William Black to say:

> If Moffat is to be likened to Baden-Baden, it forms an exceedingly Scotch and respectable Baden-Baden. The building in which the mineral waters are drunk looks somewhat like an educational institution with its prim white railings.

The "Ossian" Story

Nicest building in the High Street is Moffat House, now an hotel. It was designed for the Earl of Hopetoun by James Adam in 1751. It is Moffat's outstanding architectural possession, but has an additional claim to our attention. In 1759 James "Ossian" Macpherson of Kingussie was living at this house as tutor to young Graham of Balgowan when he set in motion that literary imposture which was to convulse the world of letters.

It was all, indirectly, Rachel Whitford's fault. Among the eminent folk then in Moffat to take the waters were John Home and Dr Jupiter Carlyle. Both these men were following the fashionable trend not only in cures but also in literature and were enthusiastically seeking traditional Scottish poetry. To them young Macpherson showed some verses which, he said, he had found in the original Gaelic in the Highlands and translated them. It turned out later Macpherson was not even a good Gaelic scholar: he had written these verses himself—about 4,000 lines—when at college. Home and Carlyle and their literary clique were delighted at Macpherson's discovery, and he enjoyed for a spell that scholarly delight. But the young man must have been taken aback when they suddenly proposed that his "Poems of Ossian" should be published.

Up to that moment, no doubt, Macpherson had merely enjoyed the sense of mingling on equal footing with the great men of letters.

He dare not now confess his lie. He allowed publication. In the bookshops appeared *Fingal* in six books and *Temora* in eight, "translated from the Gaelic of Ossian, the son of Fingal".

When Dr Johnson denounced them as a fraud Macpherson challenged him to a duel. Johnson bought himself a stout stick, declaring, "I will not desist from detecting what I think to be a cheat from any fears of the menaces of a ruffian."

The dispute went on long, long after Macpherson's death, and, cheat or not, his poems were immensely popular and had among their admirers such diverse—or perhaps not so diverse—characters as Napoleon and Goethe.

One of the very few famous men of the day who visited Moffat without apparently taking its waters was Robert Burns. He had an altogether more characteristic way of celebrating his visit. Beside the old churchyard gate in the High Street there was once an ale-house that was always pointed out as the place where Willie (Nicol) brewed a peck o' maut and Rob (Burns) and Allan (Masterton) cam to pree. Three miles out of Moffat on the Selkirk road is the cottage, still called Burns Cottage, where Burns wrote the poem *Willie Brewed a Peck o' Maut.*

Jean Lorimer, the "Chloris" of *The Lassie wi' the Lintwhite Locks*, the subject of some thirty of Burns' lyrics, spent her girlhood at Craigieburn, a farm three miles out of Moffat on the road to St Mary's Loch. Burns wrote to her half in jest as a proxy wooer on behalf of a fellow gauger. Jean married a local farmer, but was ultimately deserted. Burns first met her face to face when she was living with her parents at Kemmies Hall, Dumfries.

On a window at the Black Bull—one of the oldest houses in Moffat —Burns wrote with his diamond his *Epigram on Miss Davies (On Being Asked Why She Had Been Formed So Little and Mrs. A—— So Big).*

> *Ask why God made the gem so small*
> *And why so huge the granite?*
> *Because God meant mankind should set*
> *That higher value on it.*

Before the building of the road along which Glasgow–Carlisle traffic now by-passes Moffat, Black Bull Close was a busy thoroughfare carrying all the traffic from the Border to Glasgow and the north. Modern Annandale House is built on the site of the old Toll

House, at which as many as 200 carts a day once paid to pass the turnpike.

Moffat's square-towered church is a neo-Gothic creation of 1887. It was in an earlier church—in the 18th century—that the Reverend Alexander Brown had reason to rebuke his precentor who, proclaiming the banns of four couples, had given them in the wrong order, reading first the names of the four men and then those of their four brides. "Hout tout, sir!" he retorted to Mr Brown. "Nae fear, nae fear! Every yin will ken their ane."

Even in healthy sulphurous Moffat there had to be, apparently, a graveyard, but even in that repository of the uncured the health-giving properties of Rachel Whitford's spring does not go un-recorded. One stone bears a solemn warning against procrastination.

IN MEMORY

Here is interred the body of Colonel Alex.
Ross of Calrossie, Ross-shire, who died in
Moffat, June, 1793. He came there in hopes,
from the use of the waters, to obtain remission
of long and painful illness but, unhappily for
his friends, he had too long delayed resorting
to them and was cut off by his complaint
before he had opportunity of trying their
efficacy.

Buried in Moffat churchyard is John Loudon Macadam, whose name is now "enshrined in every language" as the inventor of Tar Macadam. He died in 1836 in the mansion of Dumcrieff outside Moffat, where is preserved a stone roller said to be the first he used.

Also at Moffat are the graves, with a monument, of James McGeorge and John Goodfellow, who perished in a snowstorm in 1831 in an attempt to get the mails through from Moffat to Tweedshaws.

When the mail-coach arrived at Moffat from Dumfries on the afternoon of 8th February, 1831, Goodfellow, the driver, and McGeorge, the guard, decided, against every warning, to continue their journey north. Extra horses were harnessed to the coach and two local men joined the party of passengers as guides. The coach stuck in the drifts less than a mile from Moffat. The men rode back to Moffat to get a chaise for the women; the postmen tried to go on by horseback. Even so they could not make it. So, abandoning the horses, they decided to go on foot.

Next day a roadman found the bags hanging on a snowpost not far from Tweedshaws. On 12th February searchers found the bodies of the two men near Tweedshaws Cross.

The Devil's Beef Tub

A century later, in 1931, a cairn was erected at the place where they died. It stands near the road, a mile beyond one of the most famous sights in Scotland, the noted Devil's Beef Tub, so called, it is said, because the cattle-raiders hid their spoils in it. In 1746 the Jacobite landlord of the Crook Inn escaped from his guards by plunging head over heels into the misty cauldron of the Beef Tub, and it was this incident which is so beautifully described by the Laird of Summertrees in *Redgauntlet*.

> Ye ken the place they call the Marquis's Beef-stand because the Annandale loons used to put their stolen cattle in there? Ye must have seen it as ye came this way; it looks as if four hills were laying their heads together, to shut out daylight from the dark, hollow space between them. A deep, black, blackguard-looking abyss of a hole it is, and goes straight down from the roadside as perpendicular as it can do to be a heathery brae. At the bottom there is a small bit of a brook you would think could hardly find its way out from the hills that are so closely jammed round it. . . .

And so it is.

Grey Mare's Tail

Another famous sight is reached from Moffat by way of the lovely road to St Mary's Loch. Ten miles along this road is that magnificent waterfall, one of the highest in Scotland, the Grey Mare's Tail, over 200 feet of dashing spume, "white as a snowy charger's tail", cascading over a precipice. It flows from dark Loch Skene, between White Coomb and Lochcraig Head, which James Skene of Rubislaw visited with Scott and said, "It would be impossible to picture anything more desolately savage than the scene".

Two miles south of Moffat, on a peninsula between the Evan and Garpol burns, are traces of Auchen Castle, which Hogg made the residence of William Wilkin, the Annandale warlock. In pretty Garpol Glen is modern Auchen Castle.

Beattock, on the main road from Glasgow to Carlisle, has little more importance than a kind of back-door to Moffat, the place where the traveller turns off the Glasgow–Carlisle road, and the railway junction for Moffat.

Six miles south of Moffat, Lochwood Tower stands beside the Dumfries road. The tower is in ruins, but was once a fortress of the Johnstone family in the heart of a forest of ancient oaks. It was well and cunningly protected by bogs on all sides. Lochwood was burned in 1592 by the Maxwells.

MONIAIVE   *Friend of Burns*

There is something almost self-conscious about Moniaive. Its bent main street and its grouping of windows and gables give it the appearance of sitting always for its picture-postcard portrait, and it is recognisable immediately as one of those villages favoured by artists. Even on dull winter days its walls and cottage roofs seem to glow with water-colour tints.

It stands, grouped around its 17th-century mercat cross, on the road running westward from **Thornhill** to the wide uplands of Galloway.

Its parish church of Glencairn is two miles east of the village. The fourteenth Earl of Glencairn was the friend and benefactor of Robert Burns, who died five years before the poet and is immortalised by the warm and lovely tribute:

> *Thou found'st me, like the morning sun*
> *That melts the fogs in limpid air,*
> *The friendless bard and rustic song*
> *Became alike thy fostering care.*
>
> *The mother may forget the child*
> *That smiles sae sweetly on her knee;*
> *But I'll remember thee, Glencairn,*
> *And a' that thou has done for me!*

About a mile south-west of Moniaive is the site of a chapel dedicated to St Cuthbert, and so called Kirkcudbright.

Above the village, not far from the house in which he was born in 1662, is a monument to the Rev. James Renwick, the last Covenanter martyr. The monument, 25 feet high, was erected in 1828.

MORDINGTON   *Church Door to England*

No village in all the Borders can claim to be so emphatically a Border village, for the main door of Mordington's church practically opens on to the highway which here is the boundary between England and Scotland.

Mordington parish, which was recently united to Foulden, also embraces, since 1650, the ancient parish of Lamberton—and the Old Toll House at Lamberton on the Border was a less notorious Gretna Green. The parish marches not only with the Border but also with the North Sea, and its tiny hamlet of Ross clings to the very fringe of the coastline.

Witches Knowe, west of Lamberton Church, recalls the gruesome burning of two poor women about 1700. Hardly anything survives of Lamberton Church, where betrothal deeds were signed in 1503 between James IV and Margaret Tudor, sister of Henry VIII. The document gallantly stipulated that the maiden should be handed over to the Scots Commissioners "without any expense to the bridegroom". This was duly done on 1st August, 1503; and in June, 1517, she returned to Lamberton Church, a widow.

The old church of Mordington stood in a plantation 160 yards south of Mordington House. A burial vault which had been built against the east gable still remains, and built into its west wall there is a rudely sculptured panel bearing a representation of the Crucifixion, probably dating from the late 15th or early 16th century.

MOREBATTLE   *An Angler's Village*

Beloved by anglers for sport in the Kale and neighbour streams, the village of Morebattle lies tranquil at the foot of the Cheviots.

It has two relics of Border warfare: Corbet Tower, just outside the village, burnt to the ground by the English in revenge for a Scottish raid into Northumberland; and the ruins of Whitton Tower, two miles south of the village, which was ravaged in the reign of Henry VIII.

MOSSPAUL   *Top of the Road*

On the borders of Dumfriesshire and Roxburghshire, at the top of the road climbing up through the valley from **Langholm,** stands Mosspaul Hill Inn. Dorothy Wordsworth, who stayed here in 1803 with her brother William, wrote:

> The scene, with this single dwelling, was melancholy and wild, but not dreary, though there was no tree nor shrub; the small streamlet glittered, the hills were populous with sheep; but the gentle bending of the valley, and the correspondent softness in the forms of the hills, were of themselves enough to delight the eye.

Mosspaul is the annual meeting-place of the Cornets of Langholm and Hawick. Hawick is 11 miles east, Langholm 10 miles south, and the cavalcades from both towns gallop through the hills to exchange fraternal greetings, a romantic and stirring scene.

The Langholm cavalcade come to their rendezvous through the parish of Ewes, with its scattered farm-houses lying along the floor of the valley carved out of the hills by the Ewes Water. The church, dedicated to St Cuthbert and built in 1867, stands on the right bank, 400 feet above sea-level, and in the lee of Meg's Shank—the quaintly named hill towering 1,537 feet above to the north.

Five miles further up, Ewes Water spreads into a lattice of tributaries among the hills whose summits mark the boundary between Dumfriesshire and Roxburghshire: Faw Side, Frodlaw Height, Wisp Hill to the north-west; Tudhope Hill, Geordie's Hill, Pike Fell and Arkleton Hill to the south-east. All approach the 2,000-foot level.

In Ewesdale, three miles before the boundary, there is a farm called Eweslees, where a burn comes tumbling down from the hill above. The scene between here and the boundary is the most spectacular in all Ewesdale. The gradient is steep, the hills crowd in on all sides.

MOUSWALD   *Grierson's Hook*

An iron hook for the hanging up of prisoners! By this barbaric piece of furniture in the mansion-house of Rockhall, near Mouswald, is remembered Sir Robert Grierson of Lag, the notorious Dumfriesshire persecutor of the Covenanters.

W. S. Crockett describes him as "the most callous, most cruel, most malignant of Charles's persecuting bands". A man who, begged by one of his victims for a moment's prayer before death, could answer, "What the devil have you been doing so many years on those hills? Have you not prayed enough?" And when he refused even a grave to the executed Covenanter and Lord Kenmure remonstrated with him, Grierson said, "Take him if you will, and salt him in your beef barrel."

Most notable Mouswald personality in the last 100 years was the Rev. John Gillespie, minister from 1865 to 1912. An enthusiastic agriculturist, he farmed his own glebe and thus won the nickname "Minister of Agriculture".

NEIDPATH   *Guardian to Peebles*

Although Neidpath is so near to Peebles and could well be included in our account of that town, it deserves a chapter on its own. For it is undoubtedly one of the most handsome of the Border Castles, and perhaps the most beautifully situated.

It stands on the crest of a gentle slope at a bend in the Tweed, reflecting its noble visage in a noble river. It is mellow tinted, like pale honey, and despite its obviously formidable strength looks enchantingly benign. It is, in that, a rare old deceiver. For instance, that green slope on which it stands. The grassy pelt covers the formidable rock which supports the mighty bulk of Neidpath. The walls, so softly tinted and aged, are no less than 11 feet thick and their greywrack stones sealed with a cement almost as hard as themselves.

When Cromwell besieged it, Neidpath resisted longer than any other fortress south of the Forth. At the close of the 18th century it was occupied by the historian, Adam Ferguson, and a frequent visitor was Walter Scott.

Its present appearance with two bold towers is well known to Border travellers, but when it was built it was a single peel tower. Later another part was added at right angles, forming the now familiar shape.

Over the courtyard gateway is a scrap of carving that should enthral the lover of puns. The carving is of strawberries; the name of the original owners was Fraser. Those who remember the Norman heritage of the Borders can see the link.

You approach the Castle along a grassy path where once stretched a fine avenue of the famous Neidpath Yews—known to botanists as Taxus Baccata Neidpathensis—and from which, it is said, bows used in the Crusades were made. A few still remain, but the majority went down in 1795 to pay some of the gambling debts of "Old Q", whose tree-felling here and at Drumlanrig moved Wordsworth to that oft-quoted reproach of which the first two words are famous— and they, at least, are verse.

> *Degenerate Douglas; oh, the unworthy lord!*
> *Whose mean despite of heart could so far please,*
> *And love of havoc (for with such disease*
> *Fame taxes him) that he could send forth word,*
> *To level with the dust a noble horde,*
> *A brotherhood of venerable trees.*

NEWCASTLETON   *Breath of Scotland*

A little road from England—not a main road, but a hill-climbing
wandering road which finds its stealthy way across the ridge of
Hadrian's immemorial boundary between the countries—comes
down to this long straight line of a village on the banks of Liddel
Water. Around us are widespread rolling hills. It is a typical
Border scene, all open and expansive. The air seems crystal clear;
it is the very breath of Scotland.

For evidence of how pure and health-giving a corner of the world it
is there is need to quote only one piece of evidence. One day in 1770
an old woman was reaping in the fields nearby, and she fell to talk-
ing, as women of her age often do, about the past, and how many
times she had reaped these fields. "Yes," she murmured, leaning on
her fork and gazing on the hills, "I first reaped here when I was a girl."

"How long ago was that?" her neighbours asked.

She couldn't tell them how many years ago it was. But she recalled
some of the names of those who had reaped alongside her, and someone who overheard that conversation took the trouble to comb
through parish registers. Then it was discovered that the garrulous
old woman had first reaped the field just a hundred years earlier.

Twenty-two years after that reaping scene Scott rode up here on
one of his ballad-hunting raids. His visit created quite a sensation,
not because anyone knew the young man, but because of the manner
of his coming. He came in a gig! It was the first wheeled vehicle
ever seen in that part of the world. . . . Except, perhaps, the Roman
chariots, but no one—not even a Newcastleton reaper—remembered
those.

A year after Scott's visit, Henry, third Duke of Buccleuch, began
building the main street we now see. Despite additions since his
day, the straight street still bears unmistakably the appearance
of a place built to plan. There is a certain austerity about it,
but that suits well those straight sheer slopes of grassy hills behind
it.

Liddesdale is Dandie Dinmont's country, and also the country
of the Armstrongs and the Elliots. The Elliots alone held some 30
to 40 towers on the banks of Liddel and Hermitage burns, but all
except Hermitage Castle were razed to the ground after the Union.

Just over a mile south of the village are the remains of Mangerton
Tower, home of an Armstrong laird of Mangerton who was killed

by the Lord de Soulis whose life he saved. De Soulis had been caught in the act of abducting a local girl and would have died but for Mangerton's aid. Perhaps Mangerton talked a little too much about it, for later Lord de Soulis invited him to Hermitage, and when he went there, expecting princely reward, he got a de Soulis dagger through his ribs. To avenge the honour of the Armstrongs another of the clan, Jock o' the Syde, later spitted his lordship on the point of his sword. So it went on . . . the endless feuding of a Border vendetta.

NEWLANDS — *The Mysterious Steps*

A mile down the valley of the Lyne from Romanno Bridge is the church of Newlands, and a little further down are the remnants of its ancient predecessor, an ivy-cloaked east window and round-headed doorway.

On the face of the hill above Newlands Church are the mysterious Romanno Terraces. These fourteen broad steps are believed, by some authorities, to be relics of husbandry in early British days.

Further down the Lyne, on a hill, is Drochil Castle, built by the Regent Morton. The ruins are substantial and illustrate the desire of this powerful statesman to have here something more akin to a palace than a castle. He hoped to retire here but, three years after Drochil was built, Morton was executed in Edinburgh "as art and part of the murder of our King Henry, Lord Darnley", ten years earlier.

PEEBLES — *Town Amid the Hills*

To appreciate to the full how beautifully Peebles lies in the ample sweep of the Tweed you must climb the slopes of any of its surrounding wooded hills. We have attempted in this volume to choose a photograph doing justice to one of these views.

The immediate approach to the town is splendid. A five-arched stone bridge over the Tweed—begun in 1467, widened in 1834 and 1900 and now ornate with lamp-standards coiled about with the armorial fishes of Peebles' coat—carries you over the river to the foot of the tall crocketed lantern spire of the 18th-century parish kirk. The street curls round the gable ends of clustered buildings, and then we are in the High Street, a wide High Street and the most handsome in the Borders, dignified by fine hotels, bright painted shops and a commanding mercat cross. And even here, in the heart of the town, the exhilarating sparkle of the surrounding hills seems to illumine it all.

Narrow streets lead us to quaint old closes lined with carved lintels or shoot off down to the ample banks of the shallow-brawling Tweed. There's not a corner where we cannot get some glimpse of the grassy forest-dappled hills.

The mercat cross—its shaft is certainly more than 600 years old and bears the arms of the burgh and of Fraser of Neidpath—was almost utterly lost when, in 1807, it was pulled down, owing to its ruinous condition. But Sir John Hay of Kingsmeadows preserved the shaft. It was later erected in the quadrangle of the Chambers Institute, but in 1895 it was erected in its present position where it now stands on a solid modern base.

Other traces of antique Peebles remain. In the lane leading to the station can be seen part of the old town wall built in 1569. The names of such streets as Eastgate and Northgate perpetuate the memory of the days when Peebles was a walled town defended by bastel houses—three-storeyed dwellings with thatched roofs which in emergency were stripped off, fired and thrown down upon the attacking English soldiery.

Also in the High Street is a memorial fountain and bronze medallion portrait to the memory of Professor John Veitch, the Peebles lad born in Biggiesknowe in the old town, who became a University professor and a distinguished man of letters. A present-day Peebles namesake of his, James Veitch, is well known for his novels with a Scottish setting.

Peebles is rich in literary associations, apart from its inevitable associations with Scott. Beside the parish church is Bank House, where lived John Buchan, first Lord Tweedsmuir, and his sister, Miss Anna Buchan, "O. Douglas". Scores of literary pilgrims, many of them Americans, still come to the house asking to see the room where O. Douglas worked. Miss Anna is remembered in the town as "bright and cheerful, just like a character in one of her own novels". The mother of the two writers is best remembered by her remark, when praised for the scones and cakes she baked, "Well, if I can't work with my head, I must work with my hands."

Lord Tweedsmuir was an occasional visitor here while his parents were alive and when the house was occupied by Mr J. Walter Buchan, Town Clerk for 42 years, and Miss Anna.

It was during the clearing of the site for the building of Bank House that the Peebles Silver Arrow, lost from 1664 to 1786, was discovered. The Arrow was presented to the town by James Williamson, Provost of "Piblis", in 1628 to encourage archery, was hidden away for safe keeping by the Town Treasurer in a building formerly used by the Town Council, and discovered by accident when that building was being demolished.

One of the conditions of the competition was that each winner should attach a silver medal to the Arrow, and the existing medals include excellent examples of Scottish silversmiths' craftsmanship. The Town Council of Peebles provide a "Riddle of Claret" after the "shoot". The Silver Arrow was last shot for in 1956 and won by Brigadier T. Grainger Stewart.

James Hogg and Christopher North knew Peebles well; Stevenson lived here in his youth and Crockett in his later years.

Another Peebles literary association is commemorated by the Chambers Institute in the High Street. This building—near to the war memorial—was presented to the town by William Chambers, the publisher. Chambers, who founded with his brother Robert the famous Edinburgh publishing house, was born in Biggiesknowe in 1800. The Institute was once Queensberry Lodging, and in 1725 it was the birthplace of the fourth Duke of Queensberry; that one who became "Old Q" and the "Degenerate Douglas" of tree-despoiling fame.

A gift of £10,000 from Andrew Carnegie helped to enlarge the Chambers Institute to accommodate reading-rooms, libraries, two museums and an art gallery. Its geological collection is claimed to be among the best in Britain.

Not far from the mercat cross is the 17th-century Cross Keys Hotel, believed on not the strongest evidence to be the original Cleikum Inn of Scott's *St Ronan's Well*. In Scott's day it was the Yett Inn and its landlady, Miss Ritchie, has been identified as the prototype of the termagant landlady Meg Dods.

Another interesting Peebles hotel is the Tontine Inn, built by subscription in 1808 at a cost of just over £4,000. Its name perpetuates the curious agreement attaching to its building: subscribers might be of any age and "the longest liver should have the whole". In the dining-room is a musicians' gallery. Members of the Tweeddale Shooting Club, the oldest sporting club in Britain, meet at the Tontine for their three annual dinners—one for the grouse season, one for the partridge and one for the pheasant.

The Waverley Temperance Hotel recalls yet another famous name in Peebles' history. It stands on the site of the surgery of Mungo Park: his house can still be seen in Northgate. In 1801, after his first historic expedition to the Niger, Park settled as a surgeon in Peebles. But within two years he was planning to leave. He confessed to Scott that he would rather brave Africa and its horrors than wear his life out in toilsome rides amongst the hills for the scanty remuneration of a country surgeon.

In the parish burial-ground—at the other end of the town from the big lantern-spired kirk—stands the centuries-old square tower of the Cross Church. The tower may have belonged to the church dedicated to St Andrew in 1195, but more likely it belongs to a chapel of nearly 200 years later, and there are a few ivy-covered ruins of the conventual church of the Holy Cross, founded in 1267 for 70 Red-Friars.

According to John of Fordun there was unearthed at this spot on 7th May, 1261 "in the presence of honest men, kirkmen, ministers and burgesses, a certain magnificent and venerable cross, enclosed in a box inscribed *The Place of Nicolaus, Bishop*". The story was put about that these were the relics of a Culdean saint and prelate martyred in 296 and the discovery induced the townsfolk to subscribe for the building of a church.

The Beltane Fair is Peebles' contribution to the Border Riding festivals. In the Middle Ages the rural sports on Beltane Day were famous over a large part of Scotland. The verses ascribed to James I make note of them:

> *Wes never in Scotland hard nor sene*
> *Sic dansing nor deray,*
> *Nouther at Falkland on the Grene,*
> *Nor Pebillis at the Play.*

Now the festival takes the form of games and the crowning of the Beltane Queen. A march riding ceremony was resuscitated in 1897 to commemorate Queen Victoria's Diamond Jubilee. Gifts to the festival have come from far away, the Beltane Bell from Peebleans in the United States; the leopard skin on the Queen's throne from South Africa; the casket for the Queen's scroll from Canada; the carpet for the steps of her dais from India; the Cornet's standard from Johannesburg; and the Queen's robes from New Zealand.

PENPONT   *The First Pedal Cycle*

Some two miles from **Thornhill** along the ancient pilgrim way to Whithorn is the village of Penpont. Here are the ruins of Tibbers' Castle. The name is said to be a corruption of "Tiberius", the Caesar who is supposed to have built a fortress here. A votive cross marks one of the resting places of the pilgrims.

From Penpont a road runs southward beside the Keir Hills and the Scaur, to the village of Keir. Here, at Courthill Smithy, the blacksmith Kilpatrick Macmillan evolved in 1839 the first machine which can reasonably be called a bicycle.

Twenty years earlier a French inventor had demonstrated in the Luxembourg Gardens what he called a "celeripide", to which the English gave the name "Dandy" or "hobby-horse". This, the first two-wheeled vehicle, consisted simply of two wheels in line connected by a wooden beam on which the rider sat astride and pushed himself along with his feet. Macmillan improved on this by fitting cranks to the rear wheel and pedals by which the rider could propel the machine without touching the ground.

The original machine, now in the Science Museum at South Kensington, looks, to our modern taste, a big and cumbersome thing, but it is the undisputed first bicycle, great forefather of the millions now manufactured every year, as the smithy, graced in 1946 with a plaque commemorating Macmillan's work, is likewise the forefather of the 118 cycle factories in Britain.

PHILIPHAUGH   *Place of Bloody Memory*

West of **Selkirk,** where the glens of Yarrow and Ettrick meet, is the flat of Philiphaugh. On south and east the meadow-land is enfolded by the Ettrick. North and west are the hills of Yarrow. It is a pleasant stretch of tranquil Border country, but a place of bloody memory.

Here on the morning of 13th September, 1645, the Royalist forces of the Marquis of Montrose were annihilated by the Covenanter troops of General Leslie. It was one of the decisive battles of Scotland's history: it tumbled into final ruin the fading cause of Charles I in Scotland.

But the horror attached to the name of Philiphaugh does not lie in mere facts of defeat and victory in a hard-fought battle. There have been many battles as grim and deadly on Scotland's soil, but

Philiphaugh gains hateful prominence because of an outburst of cruelty which even today, centuries after the event, sickens and shames us.

Montrose and his troops, weary and weakened after a succession of successful encounters with their enemies, reached this spot on the evening of the 12th September. The King's captain-general in Scotland chose the flat of Philiphaugh for his camp, judging it a place of good natural defence, as indeed it was. After but the minimum of defensive trenching his army of 600 settled down, needing a sleep and feeling secure. Montrose retired for the night with his captains to a lodging in the West Port of Selkirk.

Montrose was ill-informed of his enemies' movements. Leslie, now marching swiftly upon him from East Lothian with 6,000 troops, was well informed, and on the night of the 12th he was within three miles of Montrose.

In the thick autumnal mists of the early morning the royalist troops cooked a leisurely breakfast, straggling half-heartedly on to parade when General Leslie's horse burst on them. By the time Montrose arrived on the scene, leading a courageous and momentarily successful counter-attack at the head of 100 troopers, the day was already lost. He would have died on the field had his friends not persuaded him to save himself to fight again in the King's cause. With a party of 30 others he fled to Yarrow vale.

Four hundred Irishmen, driven into Philiphaugh farm, fought to the death. Soon only 50 of Montrose's cavalry were still alive. They surrendered. It was complete victory for Leslie, and at that it might have ended, a sad enough story.

But then the real horror began. John Buchan has told of it in *Montrose*, one of the greatest biographies in the English language.

Now came the harvest of the triumphant Covenanters. It began on the day of the battle, when 300 Irishwomen, with their children, were butchered on the field. The cooks and horseboys also perished to the number of some 200. The remnant of the Irish under Stewart had surrendered on terms, but the ministers who accompanied Leslie remonstrated against the Lord's work being hindered by a foolish clemency. They argued that quarter had been granted to Stewart alone, and not to his men; Leslie professed himself being convinced by this shameless quibble, and the unarmed Irish were cut down as they stood, or shot next morning in the courtyard at Newark castle.

Many had escaped and were slaughtered singly as they wandered among the moors of Tweed and Clyde. One large party of the poor creatures were brought to Leslie's camp at Linlithgow. They were flung over the bridge of Avon, and were either drowned in the river or stabbed with the pikes of the soldiers who lined the banks. The records of the Irish rebellion hold no more horrid cruelties.

On into October the dreadful butchery went. One by one Montrose's friends were dragged out for execution. The ministers of the kirk commented, "The work gangs bonnily on." From synods and presbyteries flowed appeals to Parliament not to be too merciful. They need have no fear: the Estates were hell-bent on a career of devastating slaughter.

Montrose held prisoners in the castle of Blair. A lesser man might have been driven to horrible reprisals. But he restrained his troops. To them he declared, "Never shall our enemies induce us to rival their crimes, or to seek to outdo them except in valour and renown."

East of the modern mansion-house of Philiphaugh is a stone pyramid erected by the late Sir John Murray. "To the memory of the Covenanters who fought and fell on the field of Philiphaugh and won the battle there, 1645." Surely it is one of the least worthy of Scotland's memorials. Those men, had they known what was to be done, would surely have preferred that their victory be not commemorated.

Famous Footba' Match

Across Yarrow Water from Philiphaugh, on a tongue of land between Ettrick and Yarrow, is Carterhaugh, which on a December day in 1815 was the scene of a celebrated game of footba' when the lads of Yarrow matched themselves against the lads of Selkirk. It was no puny eleven-a-side match: the "teams" totalled several hundreds, all lusty young fellows using their brawny limbs to serious purpose in what was described by the *Edinburgh Journal*—and we can well believe it—as "rough and animated" contest.

Heralded by pipers the Yarrow lads came marching down the glen wearing sprigs of heather; the Selkirk lads wore sprigs of fir. The "first game" was won by the Selkirk men "after a severe conflict of an-hour-and-a-half". The "second game, still more severely contested" was won by Yarrow after "a close and stubborn struggle of more than three hours". The Sheriff of Selkirk, Sir Walter Scott, who attended the match with James Hogg, "threw up his hat and in Lord Dalkeith's name and his own, challenged the Yarrow men, on the part of the Souters, to a match to be played upon the first convenient opportunity with *one hundred picked men only* on each side". On the evening of that memorable day the Duke of Buccleuch gave a dance at Bowhill for all the nobility and gentry who had witnessed the day's sport and "the fascination of Gow's violin and band detained them in the dancing-room till the dawn".

The sequel to this event—the Duke's decision to give Selkirk a piece of commemorative plate and the trouble that caused Sir Walter —is described in our Selkirk chapter.

Up Ettrick banks from Carterhaugh is three-storeyed Oakwood Tower, built by Robert Scott in 1602 on the site of the birthplace of the 13th-century wizard Sir Michael Scott.

Here the road from Selkirk begins its climb up the Vale of Ettrick through the moorland hills of the parish of Kirkhope. At Ettrick-bridge End a bridle-path crossing the hills to **Yarrow** passes Kirk-hope Tower, lonely sentinel of this old route through Ettrick Forest.

POLWARTH   *The Best Lasses*

Around the village green of Polwarth trees and cottages are sprinkled in a charmingly casual fashion. In the centre, until recently, was a thorn-tree around which the villagers gaily danced at weddings and kirns.

> *At Polwart on the green,*
> *Our forbears aft were seen,*
> *To dance about the Thorn,*
> *When they gat in their corn.*

A kirn, by the way, is the harvest-home jollification. Originally it was a dance in the open air or in a barn. Now it is more often held in the church-hall or even in a distant hotel; the farm workers go to it in buses or in their own cars.

We have already, in our chapter on Greenlaw, quoted the antique verse about the lasses o' Lauder, and Gordon, and Earlston, which comes to the triumphant conclusion that "The lasses o' Polwart are the best o' them a' ".

At the west end of the village is the remarkable "Black Well". If a stranger drinks of the waters of this well, he will so fall in love with Polwarth that he will never be able to leave it.

But the highlight of Polwarth's romantic charm is centred in its old-fashioned little kirk, embowered in trees and mantled with ivy, and with a Latin inscription above the south door claiming that the parish church has stood here from before 900. In 1703 the Marchmont family added the solid square bell tower and gifted a bell inscribed: *Given to the Kirk of Polwarth by Lady Grizel Kar Countess of Marchmont, 1697. R. M. Fecit Edr. 1717.* So the bell seems to have been presented twenty years before it was made.

At the east end of the church is the vault in which Sir Patrick Hume, afterwards first Earl of Marchmont, lay for a month concealed from Charles II's soldiers, while his brave 12-year-old daughter Grizell risked her life to bring him provisions stealthily from Redbraes Castle, which was their home. Every night for a month she crept out on her dangerous mission, until it was deemed wise to move Sir Patrick to a cellar in Redbraes. There Jamie Winter and his young mistress scraped away the earth with their own hands to make a hiding-hole. Sir Patrick stayed there until he could flee to Holland.

PRESTON AND BUNKLE   *Three Castles*

> *Bunkle, Billie and Blanerne*
> *Three castles strong as airn,*
> *Built when Davy was a bairn;*
> *They'll a' gang doon*
> *Wi' Scotland's croon,*
> *And ilka ane sall be a cairn.*

All three castles are in this parish. All three were destroyed in Hertford's raid in 1544, when so much of the Border was "birnd and owaiertrown".

But Andrew Lang—again, as he did over Abbey St Bathans—waxes more wrath when he tells us how our own Scots 19th-century forbears used the three "cairns" as quarries for their own day-to-day farm building, and in 1820 actually pulled down an 11th-century church at Buncle and used the stones to build the present church.

One arch escaped destruction, a small semi-circular Norman arch which is probably one of the earliest Norman ecclesiastical fragments in Scotland. In the apse behind this arch lies Mrs Margaret Home, Lady Billie, whose murder in 1751 by her butler is still the favourite local "thriller".*

The parishes of Bunkle and Preston were united as early as the 16th century, and the ivy-clad ruin of Preston Church stands high on the

* See chapter on Eyemouth, in which parish the murder was committed.

left bank of the Whitadder, about a mile and a half from Bunkle Castle. The moat round Bunkle Castle can still be traced, but of Bunkle village not a sign is to be seen. This is perhaps just as well if we are to believe the old description of its womenfolk:

> Laird i' the midden up to the knees,
> The clartiest clatches within the four seas,
> Smellin o' peat-reek oot and in,
> Bleared and girnin, yellow and dun
> Beardy and runkled, grisly and grim,
> Fu o' shern up to the chin;
> The Wabsters' Wives o' Bunkle toon
> Wad frichten the Turks or auld Mahoun,
> And Boulie-backed Tam o' the green
> His wife was wi the Deil yestreen
> And gray-faced barkin't sutor Gib
> Wi' a' the wives is unco sib,
> And barmy breeks o' Lintlaw Mill
> Grips deep o' the mooter for his yill
> And Pate o' the Mains, your wife's a witch
> She's fa'en i' the fyre and burnt her mutch.

Part of the old forest which once covered the northern half of the parish can still be seen beside the road from Duns to Grantshouse at the spot known as the White Gate. William Wallace is supposed to have camped for one night in Bunkle Wood in 1296 during his pursuit of Patrick Earl of Dunbar from Spott Moor to Norham.

Edincraw, "where the witches bide a' ", is the modern hamlet of Auchencraw, where hair-raising tales are told not only of fearsome things the witches did—put the evil eye on cattle and crops, called up storms, sank ships—but also of fearsome punishments inflicted on those wretched beings.

The old *mires* or bogs have long since disappeared, though the name remains, as in Drake-mire, now the scene each year of point-to-point races.

In the centre of Preston village is the shaft and base of the old mercat cross, and along the road to Chirnside is an old and interesting jail. It is under the bridge which carries the road and the burn. Half the arch is partitioned off by stone walls, and the chamber thus formed is believed to have been used as a prison by the Lords of the Regality.

Dumfriesshire   **The Lowther Hills**

Lauder   **The Parish Church**

Lauder   **Thirlestane Castle**

St Abb's Head   **Pettycarwick Bay**

Border Riding   **Braw Lad at Abbotsford**

Maxwelton House   **Annie Laurie's Home**

Mellerstain House   **An Adam Mansion**

Mellerstain   **Garden and Lake**

RESTON   *The Railway Village*

This village was built when the railway was built, to be the junction for **Coldingham,** but there is mention in one of the Coldingham charters of "the chapel of St Nicholas, situated in the vill of West Riston".

After that we have to wait until the year 1880 for further mention of religious foundations in Reston: in that year a Free Church was built, which is used as the parish church today.

ROBERTON   *Auld Wat's Home*

Running alongside Borthwick Water on its way to join the Teviot outside Hawick is one stretch of that most enchanting of roads in all the Borders—the road which finds its way across the southern reaches of Ettrick Forest, from **Yarrow** to **Ettrick** and over the border from Selkirkshire to Roxburghshire and down Borthwick Water to the Teviot.

Above Borthwick Water stand the church and manse of Roberton, and nearby, on the banks of Harden Burn, is the old fortress of Harden, home of "Auld Wat of Harden", that famous old rascal. Walter Scott was proud to claim descent "from that ancient chieftain whose name I have made to ring in many a ditty, and from his fair dame, the Flower of Yarrow".

To his fortress overlooking the Beef Tub Auld Wat brought home in 1567 his beautiful bride, Mary Scott, "the Flower of Yarrow". It is claimed that her beauty and gentleness have become known to us through the beautiful boy she saved from Wat's moss-troopers when they had brought him as a prize from a Cumberland raid. The youth grew up under her protection and is said to have composed both words and music of many of the Border songs.

Mary it was who, when the last bullock from England had been consumed, placed on the table a dish containing a pair of clean spurs—a hint to the men that it was time to go foraging for the next dinner. Walter Scott goes on:

> Upon one occasion when the village herd was driving out the cattle to pasture, the old laird heard him call loudly to drive out Harden's cow.
>
> "Harden's cow!" echoed the affronted chief. "Is it come to that pass? By my faith they shall soon say Harden's kye."
>
> Accordingly he sounded his bugle, set out with his followers, and next day returned with *a bow of kye, and a bassen'd bull.*

On his return he passed a very large haystack. It occurred to the provident laird that this would be extremely convenient to fodder his new stock of cattle; but as no means of transporting it were obvious, he was fain to take leave of it with the apostrophe, now become proverbial, "By my soul, had ye but four feet ye should not stand lang there."

So proud was Walter Scott of this ancestor and so in love with the country surrounding Harden that at one time—long before his Abbotsford days—he planned to restore the then ruined Harden and make it his summer residence. It was not restored until 1864 when among the features left intact were the roof of the hall, notable for its curious stucco work; the lobby paved with marble, and a mantelpiece bearing an earl's coronet and the initials W. E. T. for Walter, Earl of Tarras.

ROMANNO BRIDGE — *Ancient Camp*

The Romans, it is said, gave the hamlet of Romanno Bridge its name, for the road they built from their camp at Lyne passed through the village.

At a point where the highway crosses the Lyne Water there is a steep narrow bridge. And round the bridge are grouped the mill, school and the few cottages of the community. Fishermen know this village well, for annually they come from a wide district to tempt the wily trout for which the Lyne is famous.

Although mentioned as long ago as in the reign of David I (1124–53), the most important incident in the history of Romanno seems to be the great and memorable "tulzie" that took place on 1st October, 1677, between two clans of gipsies—the Faws and the Shaws—who were then returning from Haddington Fair.

On the scene of the conflict now stands a dovecote with this inscription on the lintel:

> *The field of gipsie blood, which here you see,*
> *A shelter for the harmless dove shall be.*

The man responsible for the inscription was Dr Alexander Pennycuik of Newhall, the author of an admirable little book *The Description of Tweeddale*, which is still quoted and often referred to. He lived from 1652 to 1722, and in 1676 married Margaret Murray, heiress to the estate of Romanno.

The mansion of Romanno stands five furlongs north-east of the village, and is a plain, two-storeyed building which, as it seems to date from the reign of George I (1714), must have been built by Pennycuik himself. From 1736 it became known as Lamancha.

RUTHWELL   *A World-famous Treasure*

Even the most casual visitor sauntering through the galleries of the Royal Scottish Museum must have been halted by the commanding figure of a tall gracefully proportioned cross, a reproduction of the world-famous Ruthwell Cross. The original Cross stands in the parish church of Ruthwell, the village six miles from Annan on the margin of the raised beach of the Solway.

Ruthwell Cross is one of the rarest treasures of antiquity that Scotland possesses, for it bears the earliest known specimen of written English. Of its four faces the side ones are carved with interlaced vines and animals, and on the margins we see verses that were carved there some 1,300 years ago. The verses are in Runic characters. The great scholars have deciphered these and discovered them to be extracts, in 7th-century Northumbrian dialect, from *The Dream of the Rood*, a devotional poem believed to have been written either by Cynewulf or Caedmon, 7th-century Northumbrian poets. On the principal faces are inscriptions in Latin and carvings of the life of Christ, including the healing of the blind, the Annunciation and the Crucifixion.

The Cross, believed to be the work of Northumbrian invaders, might have been originally set up around A.D. 680 at Prieststide near the sea and brought later to the parish church of Ruthwell. It is almost 18 feet high and is sunk in a well in the church for want of headroom.

We owe the preservation of the Cross first to the stubborn and courageous Rev. M. Gavin Young, minister at Ruthwell from 1617 to 1671 who, when the presbytery came to see him "put down" this idolatrous monument, began to deface it but stopped as soon as they had left and buried the Cross in a trench he had dug in the floor of the church. Then, in 1802, the Rev. Henry Duncan, minister of Ruthwell from 1798—when he was ordained there at the age of 24—until 1843, had the Cross re-erected in the garden of the Manse. In 1887 the Cross was moved into the church to protect it against the weather.

From the moment Mr Duncan set the Cross up it excited the interest of scholars throughout the world, and it is now the subject of countless books and papers. Mr Duncan himself contributed a description of it to the *Transactions of the Scottish Antiquarian Society*.

Mr Duncan was an amazing many-sided man. In this mercenary age there are perhaps people who would think that something else he did at Ruthwell was of greater service to his countrymen. Certainly the present Chancellor would think so, for Mr Duncan established at Ruthwell in 1810 Scotland's first savings bank, and the first savings bank of its kind in Britain, and went on to use his influence to procure the first act of parliament passed to encourage such institutions.

He did many other things. Mr Duncan also discovered in Dumfriesshire something of far greater antiquity than the Ruthwell Cross. On Corncockle Moor, near Lochmaben, he found footprints of reptilian quadrupeds, and these he had inserted into the walls of his summer-house. Mr Duncan sketched, he sculptured, he gardened, he studied architecture and literature, geology and archaeology.

When there was a scarcity of flour in his parish Mr Duncan carried through the necessary transactions to have corn shipped from Liverpool. When Bonaparte threatened invasion Mr Duncan raised a company of volunteers, and Mr Duncan was captain of the troop. When he found ignorance of news in his parish and further afield Mr Duncan started a newspaper, *The Dumfries and Galloway Courier*, and Mr Duncan was editor of it for seven years.

His four-volume work *The Sacred Philosophy of the Seasons* ran through several editions. In 1839 he was Moderator. In 1843 he left his manse and founded a Free Church. He died in the very midst of his work—conducting a service in the cottage of an elder in 1846. Thus ended the beautifully energetic and inspiring life of a man who had rendered many and varied services to his parish, to his country and to mankind.

Near the Free Church he founded—on the boundary of Mouswald parish—a 40 feet-high pyramidal monument is erected to his memory.

Burns' Last Days

A mile west of Ruthwell is the hamlet of Brow, a tiny one-time watering-place on the banks of the Solway, notable as the place where Burns spent the last weeks of his life. At the end of June, 1796, dragged by illness "to the borders of the grave", the poet came to this village in the vain hope that a course of waters at the Brow Well and sea-bathing would restore his strength.

At first it seemed the treatment might do him good and he had occasional bursts of optimism. But when a friend, Mrs Riddell of Glenriddel, called on him his greeting to her was, "Well, madam, have you any commands for the other world?"

On 18th July, in a gig loaned to him by Clark of Lockerwood, he returned to **Dumfries,** so weak that he could scarcely stagger from the gig to his doorway. Three days later he died. The Brow Well is preserved and is a place of pilgrimage for lovers of the poet.

ST ABBS   *Street of Dolls' Houses*

Steep irregular little streets run down to the harbour in the familiar beloved pattern of a fisher town, but St Abbs has one street unlike all others. On one side, facing the sea, is a row of simple fishermen's houses. On the other side is a line of the jolliest dolls' houses it is possible to imagine outside a fairy-tale. Each has a small door, a little lace-curtained window and a little chimney atop its pointed roof.

What could they be? We asked an old woman who was peacefully "haein' a hingie", leaning on her bare arms and watching the world go by. She laughed and explained that each solid house had been built for a fisherman and each doll's-house opposite was where the fisherman kept his gear.

So that was it. We leaned, too, and listened for a full half-hour to the kind sing-song of the Scots voice describing the old busy days when 22 vessels, seven men to a vessel, would go out of the harbour of a morning, where now there would be but three or four.

We looked together at the angled, jutting piers and at the Lifeboat house perched high on its stilts above the water. We agreed that it must indeed be a fine sight to see the boat answer a distress-signal and come charging down that steep incline to meet the water in a mighty curving V of a bow-wave.

We looked, too, at the towering cliffs to the north, rising sheer from the sea, and she told us not to miss the walk by the footpath to Pettico Wick or Pettycurwick Bay, and the lofty Lighthouse on St Abbs Head. We walked over short grass with stunted whin and a bit of bell-heather here and there, till we came to the little deserted pier running out into a bay. That jetty was built so that supplies might be brought by sea in a steamer of the lighthouse service. Now supplies come by road.

The harbour was built by a member of the brewing family of Usher—the same who built the Usher Hall in Edinburgh. He also built St Abbs' church and despite his business he made a stipulation that there should be no public house in St Abbs. There is none to this day.

Two religious foundations stood here in the past. One was on The Nabbs, a small peninsula where St Aebba set her 7th-century church, while her sisters, St Helen and St Bey, put theirs at Old Cambus and at Dunbar.

The other is on the Kirk Hill, some 600 yards south-east of the Lighthouse, where are grass-covered traces of a chancel wider than the narrow nave, and a churchyard wall that once surrounded the church.

ST BOSWELLS   *40-Acre Village Green*

St Boswells looks at first glance like nothing more than a great cropped meadow. Here, at the junction of the **Selkirk** and **Melrose** roads near **Dryburgh** Abbey, is what surely must be the most spacious village green in Scotland, a great open space with the dotted roofs of St Boswells glimpsed beyond its 40 level acres. The village takes its name from St Bossil, a prior of Melrose.

The green was once the scene every July of one of southern Scotland's greatest cattle and wool fairs attracting tribes of no fewer than 300 gipsies who formed a shopping street with their double file of carts and made an "Asiatic camp" of tents for children, horses, asses and dogs.

At St Boswells are the kennels of the Duke of Buccleuch's Foxhounds. The Lauderdale and Jedforest are neighbouring packs in this famous fox-hunting territory.

Just over a mile north-west is Newtown St Boswells, the "new town" which sprang up a century ago on the opening of the branch lines to Reston and Kelso.

South-east of St Boswells is the neighbouring parish of Maxton. The village is on the Kelso road, but the church is beside the Tweed. Here is the burying-place of the Kers of Littledean, whose ruined fortalice stands on the banks of the river. Around Maxton village cross "1,000 men of the barony were wont to assemble for war".

From St Boswells the main road direct to Melrose runs north-west, but by far the lovelier way to Melrose, if you have time to spare, is by that road which, by way of the village of Bowden, makes a complete circuit of the Eildon Hills. At Bowden is one of Scotland's oldest churches, built in 1128 and restored in 1909, and the burial place of the ducal house of the Kers of Roxburgh.

ST MARY'S LOCH   *Two Beloved Monuments*

In the narrow neck of land between St Mary's Loch and her pendant Loch of the Lowes are two beloved Border monuments.

One is a statue, the other is an inn. The statue is that of James Hogg, the Ettrick Shepherd, and the inn is Tibbie Shiel's. Never was a statue more appropriately placed, for the poet—benign and at his ease, his plaid comfortingly around him and Hector his dog at his feet—gazes down on the howff which ranked high in his affections. Indeed he expressed the hope that some day, when he was "cauld in the mools" there would be "a bit monument to his memory in some quiet spot fornent Tibbie's dwelling". In 1824 "Christopher North" promised it should be so.

> My beloved Shepherd, some half century hence your effigy will be seen on some bonny green knowe in the forest, with its honest face looking across St Mary's Loch, and up towards the Grey Mare's Tail; while by moonlight all your own fairies will weave a dance round its pedestal.

Well, here the effigy is. Hogg sits on an oak root, grasping his shepherd's staff and holding a scroll bearing the words "He taught the wandering winds to sing". That is the last line of his *Queen's Wake*; verses from the same work are on the panels of the pedestal, and also the words "James Hogg, The Ettrick Shepherd, born 1770, died 1835".

Tibbie Shiel's is now famous the world over and the name of the widow hostess Tibbie Shiel (Isabella Richardson), synonymous with good cheer and convivial evenings, is immortalised in the writings and gossip of such customers as Hogg himself, William Aytoun, John Wilson ("Christopher North") and Robert Chambers.

When she was a girl Tibbie was in the service of Hogg's mother, and was not one bit impressed with the literary attainments of the guests who flocked to her hostelry in Hogg's company. Indeed, she was wont to say of Hogg that he was a "gey sensible man, for a' the nonsense he wrat". But she knew how to make her guests feel at home, cosy and snug in the inn's shelter when wind and rain beat raucously on roof and pane. She died in 1878, in her 96th year, and now lies in Ettrick Churchyard.

The farm of Altrieve where Hogg spent the latter and most famous period of his life lies in the hills north-east of Tibbie Shiel's, beside the burn known as Altrieve Lake. The Duke of Buccleuch—to whose wife Hogg had sent a plea for financial aid just before her death—let Hogg have it for a nominal rent for which he had, in Allan Cunningham's words, "The finest trout in Yarrow, the finest lambs on its braes, the finest grouse on its hills, and as good as a sma' still besides."

At an exhibition of coins and banknotes at Glasgow in 1951 there was shown a British Linen Company one pound note that had belonged to Hogg. The curious history of this pound is recorded in Will Grant's *Tweeddale*. On "The Twelfth" in 1832 Hogg and a relative, Dr Gray, set out from Altrieve for a day's shooting over the country near St Mary's Loch. Before leaving, Hogg put in his pocket this banknote to cover the expenses when he put up at Birkhill, near the Grey Mare's Tail. At the end of the shoot Hogg discovered that he had lost the note, and Dr Gray had to be called upon to foot the bill. Next year Hogg and Dr Gray proceeded as usual to Birkhill, where again they put up at the shepherd's cottage. In the course of the day they rested by a spring on Loch Skene side, and there to their amazement they found under a heather bush the self-same note, lost the previous year.

The bank-note was presented to the British Linen Bank by the Hogg family in 1946.

St Mary's Loch lies at the head of the Vale of Yarrow, locked in the hills between the heights of Tweedsmuir and the tumbling moorlands of Ettrick. It is the largest loch in the south of Scotland; seven miles long, inexpressibly tranquil, reflecting with almost miraculous constancy its clean austere surroundings. In *Marmion* Scott gives a description of the loch which, though of doubtful merit as verse, is an excellent summary of the scene.

> *Abrupt and sheer the mountains sink*
> *At once upon the level brink;*
> *And just a trace of silver sand*
> *Marks where the water meets the land.*
> *Far in the mirror, bright and blue,*
> *Each hill's huge outline you may view,*

Shaggy with heath, but lonely, bare,
Nor tree, nor bush, nor brake is there,
Save where, of land, yon slender line
Bears thwart the lake the scattered pine.
Nor thicket, dell, nor copse you spy
Where living thing concealed might lie.

At the head of the Loch of the Lowes, is Chapelhope, a farmstead which, as its name indicates, stands on the grounds of an ancient chapel, probably "Rodono Chapel", traces of which can still be seen.

Death of Piers Cockburn

Halfway down the west bank of St Mary's Loch, near the mouth of Megget Water, are vestiges of the old tower of Henderland, where, according to the exquisite ballad *The Border Widow's Lament*, the freebooter Piers Cockburn of Henderland was put to death in 17-year-old James V's 1529 purge of the Borders. Cockburn, the story goes, surprised at dinner by the King and his posse of nobles, was hanged over the gate of his own tower. His wife fled to the fastness of Dow Glen and there, at Lady's Seat, tried to drown, in the roar of the foaming cataract, the sounds of his execution. At Chapel Knowe is a grave with a stone slab on which were cut armorial bearings and the words *Here lyis Perys of Cokburne and hys wyfe Mariory.*

I sew'd his sheet, making my mane;
I watch'd the corpse, myself alane;
I watch'd his body night and day;
No living creature came that way.

I took his body on my back,
And whiles I gaed and whiles I sat
I digged a grave and laid him in,
And happed him with the sod sae green.

From Henderland the avenging posse rode on to Tushielaw on Ettrick Water to execute Adam Scott, "King of the Thieves", and then to Teviothead to dispatch Johnnie Armstrong.

A mile from the foot of St Mary's Loch is Dryhope Tower. The unknown writer of an old Scottish ballad declares he wishes he had never set eyes on this tower that sheltered "Yarrow's fairest flower".

"Happy the love that meets return, but mine meets only slight and scorn", complains this poet. His fair one was Mary Scott, born at Dryhope around 1550. Mary—whose legendary beauty was later lauded by Allan Ramsay—married Walter Scott of Harden. Her marriage was the occasion of a strange contract. Five local barons witnessed it and pledged themselves to see that the bargain was carried out. None of the parties or the witnesses could write, so the notary had to sign for the lot. Under the terms of the contract Mary's father agreed to furnish Wat at Dryhope with "man's and horse meat for a year and a day" in return for the profits of the first Michaelmas moon.

When, by 1592, Wat's depredations had won him a notoriety almost equal to the fame of his wife's beauty, James VI issued a Peebles warrant ordering that Dryhope be demolished in punishment for the treason perpetrated by its owner "Walter Scott of Harden".

The tower commands a superb view of Yarrow and the Loch of the Lowes, and its mossy ruins convince us that it must have been, as it claimed, one of the strongest peel towers in Ettrick Forest.

Between Dryhope and St Mary's Loch is Kirkstead Farm, situated on the former glebe lands of St Mary's Church. This ancient church and graveyard, high on the hillside above the loch, are the scene every year of the famous "Blanket Preaching".

SANQUHAR   *The Terrific Crichtons*

West of the Lowther Hills in the upper reaches of Nithsdale and on the main road from Cumnock to **Thornhill,** stands the royal burgh of Sanquhar. The name Sanquhar looms large in Scotland's history by virtue of the two Sanquhar Declarations, defiant manifestoes nailed to the town's mercat cross by the Covenanters. The first, affixed by Richard Cameron in 1680, disowned and declared war on Charles II; the second, affixed by James Renwick in 1685, witnessed against the usurpation of government by James VII. The mercat cross that displayed these historic documents has gone; and in its place in the street stands a ferociously stark granite obelisk erected to the Covenanters in 1860.

On a steep bank overlooking the Nith is the ruin of Sanquhar Castle, a dour rectangular fortress which William, first Duke of Queensberry, apparently preferred as a home even after he had built lovely Drumlanrig. Before the Drumlanrig Douglases acquired Sanquhar Castle it was the home of the Crichtons, Lords of Sanquhar. Outstanding in this line was Robert, sixth Lord Sanquhar, who hired two ruffians to assassinate a Mr Turner, the fencing master who had put out one of his eyes—seven years before! After Turner's murder a reward of £1,000 was offered for the capture of Lord Robert. He was arrested and tried at Westminster Hall on 27th June, 1612. This Scots holder of a 300-year-old barony was tried as plain Robert Crichton, because he was not a peer of England. But he was accorded the dignity of a nobleman's silken halter when they hanged him in Great Palace Yard.

Further down the valley, on the right bank of the Nith, is Eliock, home of kinsmen of the Lords of Sanquhar and of that most famous Crichton, the one to whose name was added the prefix "Admirable". The Admirable Crichton was James, son of Robert Crichton, Lord Advocate of Scotland in the reigns of Mary and James VI. James, born on 19th August, 1560, and presumably at Eliock, was a fellow pupil of James VI, and in his teens was a master of Latin, Greek, Hebrew, Chaldaean, Italian, Spanish, French, Flemish, German, English and Scots.

At 17, visiting Paris, he issued placards announcing that he would present himself at the College of Navarre in six weeks' time to answer orally, in any one of 12 languages, whatever question might be proposed to him "in any science, liberal art, discipline or faculty whatever, practical or theoretic". He made that appearance and succeeded, and next day won a tilting match at the Louvre; then served for a time as a soldier in France. At 20 he was in Italy addressing the senate at Genoa in Latin and lecturing the Doge and Senate at Venice. At 21 he was disputing Aristotle and mathematics with the professors of Padua.

So much is certain. The few later years left to this prodigy are shrouded in mystery. One story has it that, having killed a famed swordsman in a duel in Mantua, he was given the job of tutor to the ungovernably ill-tempered son of the Duke of Mantua. Coming home one night from a visit to a mistress, the Admirable Crichton was attacked by a band of ruffians. He was about to spit one on his rapier when he recognised his pupil and dutifully surrendered his weapon to his pupil. The boy responded to this courtesy by running the rapier through the Admirable Crichton's heart. This was reported in 1582, but there is evidence that James lived until 1585 before he died in some Mantuan brawl.

Further up the valley of the Nith and near the boundary of

Ayrshire is the village of Kirkconnel. The reputed burial-place of St Conal—on Halfmerk Hill, three miles from the village—is marked with an Iona Cross.

SELKIRK   *The Souters' Town*

On a terrace of hills—overlooking the valleys where Ettrick and Yarrow join company for their journey to meet the Tweed—stands the sturdy little town of Selkirk, built so high that you see its spires and gables and grey steep-pitched roofs miles away. Selkirk is the capital of its county, capital of the land of Ettrick, and traditional home of the shoemakers.

Shoe-making is no longer its industry. The last big order for its wares seems to have been that one sent to it by the magistrates of Edinburgh when the magistrates of that city were faced with Prince Charles Edward's peremptory demand for 6,000 pairs of shoes for his barefooted Highlanders. To Selkirk came a plea to furnish 4,000 of them, followed up with an order for a few hundred more.

The tall chimneys of its busy tweed-mills show how times have changed, but every Selkirk man—and, for that matter, every Selkirk woman and babe—is still a Souter, and still likes to sing on Border holidays.

> *Up wi' the Souters o' Selkirk*
> *And down wi' the Earl of Home!*
> *And here's tae a' the braw laddies*
> *That sew the single-soled shoon!*

The centre of the town is a dignified little "place", a breezy upland triangle surrounded by solid clean-built houses, some with deep roofs and dormer windows. The abiding impression we get in Selkirk —the sense of being "up top", held aloft above the valleys of Yarrow and Ettrick and Tweed—is accentuated by the cloud-piercing spire of the Town Hall. The spire, 110 feet high, is Scottish to its very bones, terrifically and delightfully native. Every night from its belfry the curfew still rings out, reminding the weavers of the days when their ancestors made shoon.

There are many things around and near this "place" to remind Selkirk of its past; within a breath of the market-place are more memorials and plaques and such-like than we would ever expect to find in so small an area.

First, of course, is the commanding statue of "the Shirra". There on a 20-foot-high pedestal, wearing his sheriff's gown, stands Sir Walter Scott, looking out over the county of which he was sheriff from 1799 to 1832. The chair from which he administered justice is still to be seen in the Town Hall, and letters of his are preserved in what is now the Sheriff Court House. And in the County Hotel is the ballroom, with musicians' gallery, where he genially presided at many a Border celebration and where he persuaded his daughter Sophia to sing the Souters' song.

The present mercat cross is not so ancient as it looks. The old one, and the flesh-merchants' booths which clustered beside it, have disappeared, but the new one, on the site of the Old Pant Well, looks fine enough. The balustraded pedestal on which it stands is not just an extravagant ornament: it conceals some of the town's water-plant. High up here, you see, water is a precious commodity. Some parts of Selkirk are no less than 600 feet above sea level, and the town pays for its elevation with the expense and inconvenience of having to pump every drop of its water from two wells deep underground.

At the east end of the High Street is another statue, that of Mungo Park, who was born four miles away at the farmstead of Foulshiels. The explorer bears in his hand a scroll inscribed "Die on the Niger", the closing words of a passage in that remarkable last letter he sent when, after the death of two of his comrades, he made his final preparations for his descent of the unknown river.

> Though all the Europeans who are with me should die, and though I were myself half dead, I would still persevere; and if I could not succeed in the object of my journey, I would at least die on the Niger.

On the corner of the explorer's pedestal are bronze figures representative of his African voyages. The statue faces the house in which Park served as a doctor's apprentice to Dr Anderson; the building is now the Municipal Buildings.

Nearby, on the memorial to the poet, J. B. Selkirk, is a panel with two female figures representing the mourning sisters in his *Selkirk after Flodden*.

In front of the Selkirk Institute is another memorial; this a bronze bust to Selkirk-born artist Tom Scott. The Institute stands on the site of his birthplace.

Flodden Monument

Beyond the Mungo Park statue is yet another statue, one raised in 1913—the 400th anniversary of the battle of Flodden—to commemorate the part played by the souters when William Brydon, the Town Clerk, led some 80 men of Selkirk to fight for their King in that fateful field. There is a legend that of all this company only one returned, carrying with him—to prove the valour of his fallen comrades—an English standard. This Flodden Memorial, with Thomas J. Clapperton's statue of a man-at-arms carrying a standard and halberd, perpetuates the legend. The monument bears the lamenting words "O Flodden Field". When he unveiled the memorial Lord Rosebery took the opportunity of roundly castigating James IV for his "almost insane chivalry" in dismounting and fighting on foot, a valorous but fatal action which lost him his life and the lives of the nobles who followed his royal and reckless example.

Selkirk's Common Riding is one of the great annual Border festivals and is notable for that dramatic and stirring ceremony when the Standard Bearer "casts the Colours" in the market place. He represents that sole survivor of Flodden who rode back alone to the town, and on that spot cast down the Colours in wordless and tragic intimation that all his souter comrades had perished on Flodden's bloody field.

A banner, declared to be the one brought back from Flodden, long preserved by the Selkirk Weavers' Corporation, came into the possession of J. B. Selkirk, and is now preserved in the Public Library. The Library, incidentally, is housed in what was formerly Selkirk's County Jail, acquired by the County's historian, Provost T. Craig-Brown, converted into a library and gifted to the town, and in 1889 opened as such by Andrew Lang, whose Selkirk birthplace is now a hospital.

Opposite St Mary's Church is a memorial to later souters who lost their lives in their country's cause—those ones who died in our 20th-century wars. For this memorial, designed by Sir Robert Lorimer, Clapperton was also the sculptor.

At the West Port end of the town is the memory of another battle almost as decisive in Scotland's history as Flodden and equally tragic. A plaque over a shop doorway marks the site of the house where the Marquis of Montrose was lodged when news came to him of Leslie's dawn advance on the flat of Philiphaugh a mile away.*

At the West Port is also the site of the Forest Inn, where Robert Burns stayed during a visit to the town in 1787 and spent a miserably wet evening excluded, unwittingly, from the social gossip of the civic worthies.

Nearby is the entrance to the beautiful Haining Estate with its Italianate house embowered in woodland. East of the Haining mansion is Peel Hill, site of the old Castle of Selkirk, frequently the residence of William the Lion, who dated many of his charters there. The Haining estate covers part of the former royal hunting grounds around the Castle. The Royal Company of Archers shoot here for the Selkirk Silver Arrow and are later entertained in the town to a riddle—12 bottles and a magnum—of claret.

Of suspect antiquity but nevertheless by now traditional is the Selkirk ceremony of "licking the birse" which any personage must perform on being made a burgess of Selkirk. Three or four boar bristles such as shoemakers use are dipped in wine, passed through the lips of the prospective burgess and then affixed to the seal of his burgess ticket.

Scott—who is half suspected of dreaming this ceremony up in his own romantic brain—decided to incorporate the birse in the decoration of the goblet the Duke of Buccleuch presented to the town after the celebrated footba' match at Carterhaugh.* He found it difficult. He wrote to Bowhill:

> It is a most unmanageable decoration. I tried it upright on the top of the cup: it looked like a shaving-brush, and the goblet might be intended to make the lather. Then I thought I had a brilliant idea. The arms of Selkirk are a female seated on a sarcophagus, decorated with the arms of Scotland, which will make a beautiful top to the cup. So I thought of putting the birse into the lady's other hand; but, alas, it looked so precisely like the rod of chastisement uplifted over the poor child, that I laughed at the drawing for half-an-hour. Next I tried to take off the castigatory appearance, by inserting the bristles in a kind of handle; but then it looked as if the poor woman had been engaged in the capacities of housemaid and child-keeper at once, and, fatigued with her double duty, had sat down on the wine cooler, with the broom in one hand, and the bairn in the other.

But Scott was not beaten. After consultation with an expert he decided to: "have the lady seated in due form on the top of the lid

* See Philiphaugh chapter.

. . . and to have a thistle wreathed around the sarcophagus and rising above her head, and from the top of the thistle shall proceed the birse".

The Arms of Selkirk depict the Virgin and Child with the Royal Arms of Scotland in the foreground and the Kirk of St Mary's in the background. King David, before ascending the throne, founded a monastery in Selkirk; a later charter transferred it to Kelso.

SKIRLING   *A Wrought-iron Garden*

One of the strangest gardens in the world is to be seen at Skirling, on the western frontier of Peeblesshire and close to the Lanarkshire town of Biggar. It is a garden of perpetually blooming wrought-iron. Lord Carmichael of Skirling planted it around the house he fashioned for himself at the fringe of Skirling's village green.

Lord Carmichael, who died in 1926, was Governor of Victoria, then of Madras, and later Governor of Bengal. In addition to being a considerable statesman, he was a connoisseur of art. He had also a whimsical sense of humour, and that expresses itself here at Skirling in a reckless love for wrought-iron.

The outside walls of the garden and the railings around the house prepare us for what lies beyond. At the garden gate a wrought-iron watchdog strains ferociously on its wrought-iron chain. Below the eaves a wrought-iron monkey swings the summoning bell. A wrought-iron lizard curled on a bracket dangles a wrought-iron lamp. The four winds of heaven are plotted by a wrought-iron devil atop a wrought-iron world. Atop every upright of the long line of railing squat wrought-iron beasts and wrought-iron imps and wrought-iron birds. A wrought-iron dragon has its three wrought-iron young at its feet. An elfin grins a wrought-iron grin. A wrought-iron fox glides through the hedge, and a wrought-iron pig does patient duty as a shoe-scraper.

All these pieces are the work of the famous artist in wrought-iron, Thomas Hadden of Edinburgh, and it seems that when once Lord Carmichael had hit upon this idea of ornamentation his invention and his humour knew no pause. Always he was sending Hadden new demands for fresh ingenuities. He began furnishing his garden with wrought-iron; first classic stands for the flower-tubs; then excellently contrived screens with intertwined roses and lizards and birds.

But he went further. He began demanding that the very flowers themselves should be of wrought-iron. And here now they are—tall

Peebles   Amid Tweeddale Hills

St Abbs   **The Harbour**

West Linton   **Mendick Hill**

West Linton   **Ancient stone**

Melrose Abbey

The Crown of Thorns

Fan Vaulting

BORDER MONUMENTS

Coldstream's M.P.

Moffat's Ram

Thornhill's Pegasus

Peebles Cross

irises and tulips and poppies and rose-bushes; their delicately curled thin petals dusted with aged green and shadowed with dark metallic hues. During summer their iron shapes are softened or concealed by the presence of nature's actual foliage, but in winter these strangely still yet uncannily vibrant iron plants stand boldly iron-blooming against grey Scottish skies.

As for the house itself, rarely have we seen a conversion so ingeniously and picturesquely performed. Across what were originally two cottages was laid a timber face, enclosing passage and landing. What was once a barn is graced with a magnificent Italian ceiling wondrously gleaming with gilt. Among the treasures in the house is the cap worn by Charles I at his execution, embroidered in gold thread with device of pelican and young, presented to the James who later became first Lord Carmichael for the services he had rendered his King during the Civil War.

Another relic is a goblet given to John Carmichael, third Earl of Hyndford, by Catherine the Great, wondrously engraved with minute pictures of castles and hunters and bears and hounds and stags and Catherine herself aiming a fowling-piece. Earl John was the notably successful diplomatist who, when he was sent by George II to mediate between Frederick of Prussia and Maria Theresa, earned from Frederick the right to incorporate the arms of Prussia on the Carmichael coat. In 1744 he went to Catherine's court on a special mission. From 1752 to 1764 he was ambassador in Vienna.

Here also are spirited paintings by James Howe, born at the manse of Skirling in 1780. This work by the famous animal painter is of the Skirling Horse Fair, famed through the shire for its jollity and drinking. Another Howe work shows Howe himself, with palette and brushes, surrounded by contemporary characters.

The Carmichael house, like all the houses around the green at Skirling, is embowered in trees. In fact, if you come to Skirling in high summer the thing which will first impress you will be the great slabs of shadow below the heavy trees. The green is large, a delightfully uneven flow of turf tumbling through those shadows towards the sun-dappled faces of the buildings beyond, the cottages and the village shop and the joiner's shop and the smithy "ayont the burn".

Looking down on this scene, from the crest of its own hill, is the village church in a churchyard which still bears the circular shape of the hill-fort it once was. The artist Howe is buried here and also the great churchman and scholar W. P. Paterson, born at Skirling Manse in 1860, and beginning his schooling at Skirling School. Here also is the Carmichael burial enclosure guarded by kneeling stone angels carved by Mrs Meredith Williams, whose work can also be seen at Edinburgh's National War Memorial.

SMAILHOLM   *Scott's Border Nursery*

Six miles from **Kelso** is the village of Smailholm, and south of the village, high on Sandyknowe Crags, "standing stark and upright as a warder, is the stout old Smailholm Tower, seen and seeing all around".

So Dr John Brown described Smailholm Tower. Certainly there is no disputing those words "seen and seeing all around". From its ravaged crest you can gaze over a tremendous sweep of Border country—Lammermuirs and Moorfoots and Eildons and Cheviots all spread magnificently around you. As for being seen, the tower dominates the view for miles as you approach it. In fact so outstanding is it on the landscape that old topographical works described it as "a conspicuous landmark to direct vessels to Berwick".

It is a square and simple fortress, 60 feet high, planted firmly amid the boulders of its rocky eminence almost on the exact frontier of Roxburghshire and Berwickshire. Small windows pierce its nine-foot-thick walls; a turnpike stair climbs narrowly its south-east corner.

It must have been one of the very first Border fortresses that Walter Scott ever knew, for just below it is the farm of Sandyknowe which was his frequent home in his early boyhood when his grandfather, John Scott, farmed it. One speculates on how many times the little boy stared up at the battered old square shape on the hill and just what part it played in kindling the imagination that was to flower so luxuriantly in later life. Certainly he himself claimed that his consciousness of existence dated from Sandyknowe. In the year before his death he paid it a last farewell visit. On that occasion Turner was in his company, and while the painter sketched Scott recalled how the habit of lying on the turf here among the sheep and lambs when he was a lame infant had given him his peculiar tenderness for those animals. Smailholm church, Norman with later alterations, was dedicated in 1253. A modern stained-glass window commemorates the parish's association with St Cuthbert.

SOUTHDEAN   *Place of Border Ballad*

Between **Hawick** and the Cheviots the parish of Southdean straggles over a wide patch of the hilly frontier of Scotland. At Southdean in 1388 James, Earl of Douglas, planned the raid which took him into England as far as Durham. After capturing the pennant of Henry Hotspur, Lord Percy, at Newcastle, he retreated to Otterburn, and in battle there he was killed, and Percy was taken prisoner. The battle is the subject of one of the earliest English ballads, *The Battle of Otterbourne.*

In Southdean parish and close to the Border is the scene of another Border battle, the famous "Raid of Redeswire" in 1575.

The ruins of the pre-Reformation church of Southdean stand beside the main road to England, but the present church is a mile to the north at Chesters. A monument in the churchyard and a window in the church commemorate the poet James Thomson, whose father came to be minister of Southdean a few weeks after the poet's birth.

STOBO   *Three-part Kirk*

East of **Broughton,** beside the Tweed, is Stobo church, a most impressive parish church, famous for a heavy square saddle-roofed tower topped with a tiny belfry. The tower, nave and chancel are all Norman, but later alterations have given them the appearance of buildings of different periods. The church has been restored with reverent regard for its austere and stony dignity.

Within the porch is a round-headed doorway, one of the oldest pieces of ecclesiastical building in Scotland. Every stone of the canopied tomb on the north wall of the chancel has a mason's "W" carved upon it. Here, during the 1863 restoration, were found a skeleton, four German coins and a Scottish, probably James V, coin.

A mile further up the Tweed, on the same bank, is Stobo Castle. This castellated pile, adorned with the battlements and towers of earlier ages, took six years to build—1805 to 1811.

STOBS CASTLE   *"The Gouden Gartins"*

South of **Hawick** on the road that leads into Liddesdale Stobs Castle stands near the right bank of the Slitrig Water, in the company of post office and railway station of the same name.

Stobs was anciently the seat of the Elliotts. In 1666 a Gilbert Elliott of Stobs—whose grandsire rejoiced under the intriguing title of "Gibby wi' the gouden gartins"—received a baronetcy. His great-grandson, George Augustus, was made Lord Heathfield in 1787 for his gallant defence of Gibraltar.

In 1903 Stobs estate was acquired by the Government as a military training ground.

SWINTON *And Its Swine Hunters*

Enclosed on three sides by solid rows of houses is Swinton's village green, with its swings and chutes and football posts: while nearby are to be seen the mercat cross, war memorial, the square clock-tower of the former U.F. Church, and the ancient burying ground round the Auld Kirk.

The church's most noteworthy feature is a full-length effigy in a recess beside the pulpit. The figure holds a book between its hands, and the slab at the back of the recess bears a curiously faulty representation of the Swinton arms, and the words HIC JACET ALANUS SVINTONUS MILES DE EODEM.

The last two words are a Latin translation of that intriguing Scottish title "of that ilk" which so appeals to the foreigner. And indeed this is generally accepted as the tomb of Sir Alan Swinton of that ilk.

In one of the walls near the Laird's Loft, where are many Swinton memorials, is an interesting shelved aumbry. On the pulpit rails are two magnificently carved Swinton boars.

There is a fine bell in the church-tower, whose name is Mary—MARIA EST NOMEN MEUM 1499.

According to the Lyon the Swintons of Swinton hold the oldest authentic charter records of any family in Scotland. They go right back to pre-Norman-Conquest times, when the Edulfings ruled the land between Tyne and Forth, from the great rock fortress of Bamburgh, and the first recorded Scottish knighthood was bestowed upon Ernulf de Swinton by King David about 1140. There is a legend that the family were awarded the Berwickshire lands in return for their services in clearing the countryside of the wild boars or swine that infested it—hence the name Swinton and the heraldic boars. But actually Edulf de Swinton got the lands for helping Malcolm Canmore to the Throne.

Major-General **Sir** Ernest Swinton had much to do with the introduction of the tank in World War One—a story he tells in his autobiography *Over My Shoulder*; he had already gained fame as a story-writer under the pen-name Ole Luk-Oie.

TEVIOTHEAD *The Hanging at Caerlanrig*

Hereabouts Mr Walter Scott had directed us to look about for some old stumps of trees, said to be the place where Johnnie Armstrong was hanged; but we could not find them out.

Dorothy Wordsworth wrote thus in her journal as she described the ride with her brother up Teviotdale from **Hawick** to **Langholm**. Johnnie Armstrong and his followers were hanged on trees at Caerlanrig Chapel, south of the present church of Teviothead, during the 16th-century "purge" of the Border when the young King James V led an expedition against the freebooters of Teviotdale, Annandale and Liddesdale.

It is said that the King camouflaged this expedition to look like a royal hunting party so that the Border brigands should think he was in pursuit of nothing more than deer. This is likely, for he had used the same trick earlier to good effect: when he skipped out of Angus's clutches from Falkland to Stirling he had got away by pretending to be hunting.

But whether it was so on this Border foray or not, it does seem that he caught the Border freebooters napping—found Cockburn at his dinner in his castle near St Mary's Loch; Adam Scott, so called "King of the Thieves", at Tushielaw; and Armstrong at Teviothead.

Armstrong rode up from Langholm to meet the King at Caerlanrig, apparently hoping to gain favour by submission to his sovereign. He came into James' presence with 36 followers magnificently accoutred, and offered to maintain himself and them always at the King's service. He threw in for extra weight an offer to bring any English subject—duke, earl or baron—before the King in a fixed number of days.

But Armstrong's submission was in vain. The young King . . . the drama of the scene is heightened when one remembers a feature often overlooked: James was then only in his teens . . . turned aside, telling his men to take the Border tyrant out of his sight. Armstrong continued his attempt to mollify the King, then seeing his pleas went unregarded, exclaimed with proud anger, "It is folly to seek grace at a graceless face."

According to the old ballad the King's retort to Armstrong ran:

Away, away, thou traytor strang,
Out of my sicht thou mayst sune be.
I grantit never a traytor's lyfe,
And now I'll not begin with thee.

That was the end. Armstrong and his retinue were strung up. A stone in the glebe is said to mark the spot where stood the tree that served as gallows.

Beside the memorial commemorating this event is the grave of the poet author of *Scotland Yet*, the Rev. Henry Scott Riddell. A cairn to his memory overlooks Teviothead Cottage, the house given to Riddell by the Duke of Buccleuch after the poet became incumbent at Caerlanrig Chapel in 1833. In 1841 Riddell showed symptoms of insanity and for three years was confined in an asylum at Dumfries. When he came back he resigned the living, but Buccleuch allowed him to retain his cottage and there he died in 1870.

THORNHILL *The Ducal Tie-pin*

This village has, unmistakably, the ducal imprint. Even if we were not aware of the existence of neighbouring **Drumlanrig**, we would nevertheless recognise Thornhill as a village sited on a noble doorstep. We recognise that particular blend of dignity and humility—the dignity of ducal spaciousness and the humility of well-trained, well-planned obedient streets in which doorways and windows are as regularly spaced as buttons on a flunkey's waistcoat.

Look, for instance, at Thornhill's main street. So small a village never needed one so wide. But ducal dignity demands that it should be so, and most handsomely it sweeps uphill—a rural Champs Elysées, the whole lined with pollarded lime-trees planted by a Duke of Buccleuch in 1861, casting pompous sonorous shadows over the sturdy red-sandstone shops and the residences of doctors, dentists, solicitors and veterinary surgeons. And all that wide street seems to have been planned for the single purpose of attracting our eye and leading our feet towards the ducal column standing in the centre of the village. This monumental piece is situated in the heart of the village, in the very centre of the cruciform plan of Thornhill, pinning the whole lot into place on the lovely bosom of the valley of the Nith, as a highly elegant cravat is pinned. The slender fluted column, put here by a Duke of Queensberry in 1714, has for its jewelled head the winged horse of the Queensberrys—to keep us in mind always of the fact that their magnificent Drumlanrig is near at hand.

Down beside the river, at Nith Bridge, is a much more ancient cross, a 12th-century or earlier Celtic shaft with dragonesque and interlaced ornament, perhaps as a shrine for travellers fording the Nith, though that is only conjecture.

At the end of the Thornhill avenue running east from the Queensberry Cross is the tall-spired church built by the Duke of Buccleuch in 1841. At the west end of the village is another church built later by the people themselves. In the Parish Hall is a bust of Joseph Laing Waugh, author of *Thornhill and its Worthies*.

The village has its own museum, founded by a former Thornhill practitioner, Dr Grierson, an indefatigable collector of memorabilia. The miniature museum has among its exhibits Burns relics, chief of which is the original manuscript of *The Whistle*, written during that convivial evening at Friars Carse down the Nith in Dunscore parish.

In 1946 Thornhill folk formed their own Village Committee with the aim of enhancing communal amenities and welfare. They have done great work already. They have provided seats—nicely placed in sunny quiet reflective spots—for the weary. They have improved the approach to the river at Nith Bridge, a favourite summer bathing-spot. They have produced a useful guide to their own village.

So Thornhill can surely lay claim to have done well for itself in all ages—getting itself well built in the days of ducal despotism and getting itself improved in the days of democratic freedom. It sets an example also to many another place by being able to enjoy industrial prosperity without losing its rural charm. It is the centre for modern grain mills and a sausage-and-bacon factory which has carried its name succulently far beyond its village boundaries. Yet these important money-making concerns have not disturbed by an inch the quiet country spaciousness of the place.

Thornhill is in the parish of Morton, and in addition to the lovely **Drumlanrig** Castle the parish has two antique fortresses—Morton and Closeburn.

Eleventh-century Morton Castle, some three miles north-east of Thornhill, is the most impressive structure of its kind in Nithsdale. Its ragged bulk glowers from the top of a hill above Morton Loch. The eight-to-10-feet-thick wall of its south front, flanked with circular towers, is almost entire. Historians still dispute about the age and ownership of the place, but the story most accepted is that it was held by Thomas Randolph, Earl of Moray, he who captured Edinburgh Castle for Robert the Bruce, and then passed to the Douglases who became Earls of Morton.

Here, ballads tell us, lived the unhappy Lady Morton who fell in love with a castle servant, and when the Earl cast him into the dungeon, carried food to him and planned his escape. The Earl exacted a terrible revenge. He had the youth bound to two wild unbroken colts and:

> *Away, away, the rapid pair*
> *Still flew on wings of fear*
> *Along the wild and rugged road*
> *That leads to Durisdeer.*

The head of the victim was found near **Durisdeer** and an upright stone marks a spot grimly known as The Heads.

At Closeburn is another castle beside a loch, this one modernised and occupied. Its square tower is 56 feet high, has walls from five to 12 feet thick and is said to have Norman mouldings hidden away below the plasterwork of later builders. It was the home of that Kirkpatrick who helped Bruce in the slaying of the Red Comyn at Dumfries.

TORTHORWALD   *Parish in the Moss*

Across the flat green landscape of Lochar Moss east of Dumfries Lochar Water ambles and trickles towards the Solway. The road to **Lochmaben** crosses the Moss through the parish of Torthorwald, with its villages of Torthorwald, Collin and Racks.

From the age of five to 12, John Gibson Paton, later to become the great South Seas missionary, attended Torthorwald parish school before he became, like his father, a stocking-maker.

South of Torthorwald village is the curious ruin of Torthorwald Tower, whose immensely thick walls are bound together with a mortar as hard as their stone. It was inhabited by the Carlyles and the Kirkpatricks, as well as by a natural son of the Regent Morton who was created Lord Torthorwald by James VI.

TRAQUAIR   *Scotland's Loveliest Big House*

Of the "big houses" of Scotland Traquair is undoubtedly the lovliest and most appealing. It is not grand in the style of **Meller-**

stain or Hopetoun, nor sumptuous like **Drumlanrig** and Culzean. But it is everything a great house should be, and no other home in Scotland has so much the aspect of being monumental yet lived in, dignified yet domestic.

It wears the air of an old château; yet it is Scottish to its bones, with grey harled walls and corbelled turrets, all topped with a steeply pitched roof along which a row of peaked dormer windows perch and gossip in the sun. Visit it, if you can, on an autumn afternoon, when the sun is low, throwing the shadows of peaked roofs across the courtyard, and the light is golden, making mellow the walls and striking soft repetitive notes of light from the rows of little windows in the shadowy façade.

One of the less pleasant mysteries of the last century is that Scottish builders could commit the extravagant vulgarity of Balmoral and other baronial monsters in a land where a Traquair shone as exquisite example of what a great residence could be.

It claims—as other Scottish houses claim—to be the oldest inhabited house in Scotland. Certainly there was a royal hunting lodge here in the days when Alexander I hunted Ettrick Forest, and at Traquair William the Lion signed the charter which gave Glasgow its abbey lands and its being. But at that time Traquair was only one tall tower beside which the Tweed flowed—so conveniently near that the laird could fish for salmon from his bedroom window—and so inconveniently near that his cellar was often flooded.

Now Traquair stands nearly a quarter of a mile from the Tweed. It is not the house but the Tweed that has moved. When James Stuart, 17th-century first Earl of Traquair began building the château we see nowadays, he diverted the Tweed along a new bed. The old simple tower of Traquair is enfolded in the north-east corner of the house he built.

A strange mysterious character, this first Earl of Traquair. He played a doubtful role in Scotland's history during and after Charles I's Civil War; and his enemies declared he was a traitor. But he disputed the charges and won a pardon from Charles I. The blackest story told against him is his alleged betrayal of Montrose when he kept the Marquis ignorant of Leslie's advance and left him helpless to face the disaster of **Philiphaugh**. In the hall at Traquair is preserved a door-knocker claimed to be the one Montrose pounded in vain when he sought shelter on his flight from the battle. Though it is hard to believe that fleeing captains-general, however hard-pressed, bang door-knockers, or, having failed to get an answer, run on like disregarded errand lads.

However, forgetting Earl James's politics, we must give him his due for Traquair. Somehow, amid all the bustle of feverish intrigue, he found time to build this Stuart mansion beside the Tweed, pushing the river back a quarter of a mile to give the big house elbow room and space to spread terrace gardens—and keep water out of the cellars. His son carried on the work, adding these wings which complete the picture of the Traquair we see now—a high central block from the sides of which flow the two long wings enclosing the courtyard. On the northern façade the château-like motif is repeated with ogee-capped pavilions at each end of the garden terraces.

The "Steekit Yetts"

Traquair's most spoken-of feature is undoubtedly the locked gateway. Between high posts surmounted by stone bears which clasp the family's coat, are the famous "Steekit Yetts" with the long grassy never-used drive stretching sad beyond them.

One story says that Charles, seventh Earl of Traquair, closed and locked the gates in 1796 on the cortege taking his young wife to burial, and that the sorrowing nobleman declared they would never again be opened until another Countess of Traquair sought entry. There was never another Countess: his son, the eighth and last Earl, died unmarried. The sister of the eighth Earl, Lady Louisa Stuart of Traquair, died in 1875, in her 100th year, the last of her line.

The more popular theory of the closed gates is, of course, the story chosen and nourished by Scott. This says that they were locked when Prince Charles Edward had departed after a '45 visit, the Earl of that day declaring they would never be unlocked until a Stuart sat crowned again in London. Less hope of that happening than that there should be some day another Countess of Traquair.

Because this main entrance is closed against us we must, as Waverley had to do when he came to Tully-Veolan, find some other entrance to Traquair, so we reach the house by way of what is still described, despite all the years that have passed since the main gates were steekit, as "the temporary entrance".

Within the house all is mellow and gracious, an 18th-century elegance charmed to fragrant domesticity; an atmosphere where the crackle of new-baked bread or the rustle of new silk are alike expected, where the day's barking of dogs and scrubbing in the yard will give way to the evening melody of the harpsichord and the soft murmurs of love.

In the oldest part of the house—in the peel tower—is the King's Room. In this room Mary stayed with Darnley not long before she kissed him goodbye on the eve of his blowing up, and here is a quilt in which she and her four Marys embroidered stitches. Traquair possesses other relics of that sinister and beautiful sovereign. Perhaps the most touching are the cradle of her James and a little picture she fashioned from cut paper when herself a child. Of later Stuart memory is an Amen glass, one of the very few left in the world, bearing engraved upon it the toast: *God Bless the Prince of Wales, the true born Prince of Wales, sent us by Thee. Send him soon over to kick out Hanover, and then we'll recover our old liberty. Amen.*

The Priest's Room on the top floor of the tower has a secret stair. On this floor also is the library, with an interesting frieze of classical faces painted by some prentice hand. In the High Drawing-Room are oak beams, beautifully decorated with Biblical quotations, discovered recently during repairs to the ceiling.

Beyond Traquair House is the *Bush aboon Traquair*, scene of Dr John Campbell Shairp's tender and haunting poem, and further up Traquair Water is Traquair village. The church has a quaint outside stair to the gallery, and in a vault adjoining is the burial place of the Stuarts of Traquair.

Nearby is the burial-place of the Tennants, and further up the burn is The Glen, residence of Lord Glenconner and early home of Margot, Countess of Oxford and Asquith. The Glen was the scene of *Lucy's Flittin'*, the only poem of note written by William Laidlaw, who was tenant of the farm of Traquair Knowe, before he became Scott's amanuensis.

TWEEDSMUIR   *Birthplace of the Tweed*

It is always an exciting experience to seek out the birthplace of a big river. There, standing astride the infant spring, we conjure up the map of the river's whole life, a burn growing into a river, flowing on to its wide destiny in the towns and its ending in the sea. Perhaps we even set paper boats or barks of twig asail in the new-born trickle and, doing so, imagine them carrying us along the historic course. Particularly exciting is it for us to visit the birthplace of the Tweed. For that river is the brilliant thread woven throughout all our Border volume, and after all much of our visiting in this Border land has been to memorials of the past and monuments of dead forgotten causes, whereas here we can see something beginning, see a sparkling gushing birth, full of sunny optimism.

Tweed's Well is Tweed's acknowledged birthplace. It lies to the right of the road as we come north from **Moffat,** just after we have left the Devil's Beef Tub behind us and crossed into Peeblesshire and begin the seven-mile descent to Tweedsmuir village. There are, inevitably, other claimants to the dignity of being the birthplace, one of them being a little rivulet which joins the spring of Tweed's Well a few yards below its source. This streamlet is known as Cross Burn by reason of an old traveller's cross which stood beside the former road over Corse Dod. But Tweed's Well, by name and tradition, is the true beginning of Tweed's 97-mile journey to the sea. Ninety-five miles of that journey are in Scotland and the first 36 miles are in Peeblesshire, which is why that country was once named, far more descriptively, Tweeddale. To describe those first 36 miles we steal the description quoted by Francis Groome. It has never been better done.

> Here and there its banks have an abrupt picturesqueness, but as a rule its flow is a rippling rapid movement spreading out in silvery sheen by the foot of the confining hill, or amid the narrow haughs by the way. Occasionally a knowe or rock juts out from the bank, and then the river swings round the obstruction into a restful pool, again to pass into the rapid ripple of its falling soft-sounding stream; still bare of tree and bush until at Polmood it becomes scantily fringed with alders and birches. Ever and anon a burn from its mountain glen joins and enriches the river; and thus is suggested the reserve of beauty and solitude in the valley of the Tweed, for the glen leads the eye upwards, between hills meeting hills in a wonderful harmony and symmetry of fold, to the half-seen, dim, massive heights which form the broad and lofty background of the valley. Those long, rounded, far-spreading heights, seldom visited, spaces of dreamy solitude and soul-subduing pathos, are never at any season of the year without their charm.
>
> Early June decks them with a tender green, in which are set the yellow violet and the rock rose, and even the cloudberry lifts its snow-white blossom from the heart of the black peat-moss. Midsummer deepens and enriches the bloom, and brings the bracken. In early August the braes and moors are touched and brightened with the two kinds of the heatherbell ere they gradually flush deep in large breaks of the common purple heather. Autumn, late autumn, throws the fading beauty of tender colour over the heather bloom; and the bent of the Moorland, "the bent sae brown" of the old ballads, that knew and felt many a blood-stain in long gone foray and feud,

throws in October days its tresses free to the wind with a waesome grace, touching the heart as with the hushed life of the old story. And in winter the snow wraps those hills in a robe so meet, that their statuesque outlines are seen and followed in their entireness and in their minute details, as at no other time; standing against the heavens in the clear relief of forms, new, as it were from the sculptor's hand.

Just below Tweed's Well is Tweedshaws, where Merlin, last of the Druids, met St Kentigern when Arthur annihilated Druidism in the battle of the Liddel Valley. At Tweedhopefoot dwelt the Covenanter James Welsh.

Amid such surroundings, seven miles down the valley from Tweed's Well, the little village of Tweedsmuir clusters around Tweedsmuir Kirk, an 1874 building in Romanesque style, built on a green hill. In the porch is a war memorial made from an oak tree planted by Scott at Abbotsford.

In the churchyard an old stone records:

> Here lyes John Hunter, martyr, who was cruelly murdered at Corehead by Col. James Douglas and his party for his adherence to the word of God and Scotland's covenanted work of Reformation, 1685.

Near the village, above Cadger's Acre and sheltered by the twin peaks of Upper Oliver Dod and Nether Oliver Dod, are the mansion-house of Oliver and the site of Oliver Castle, probably built by Oliver Fraser in the reign of David I.

At the village a road crosses the chasm of the Tweed by an old single-arch bridge and straggles upwards into the hills to St Mary's Loch. It skirts the long, narrow, artificially formed Talla Loch that supplies the distant housewives of Edinburgh with water for their kitchen taps. This reservoir was completed in 1905 at a cost of £1,250,000. Traces of the long railway built between the village of Broughton and Talla during its construction can still be seen along-side the main road.

At the head of Talla Loch, at the end of the winding cart-track that is a masterpiece of primitive road-building, is Gameshope, a shepherd's cottage, 1,450 feet above sea level. One of the last occupiers was a Mr John Thomson, who ran sheep in wild Talla Hill canyons before the reservoir flooded them. Three centuries ago Covenanters hid beside Gameshope Loch, and in June 1682 a great Conventicle was held beside the then powerful falls of Talla Linns.

Northward along the road to Edinburgh from Tweedsmuir we reach Crook Inn, a hostelry dating from the days of the stage coaches. A Jacobite landlord of the Crook Inn was taken prisoner at Culloden, and the route from there to his trial at Carlisle lay past his very door. He it was, who, further down the road, eluded his captors by rolling into the Devil's Beef Tub ravine. He returned to the Crook, where he was hidden until the hue and cry died down.

Robert Burns passed this way in the mail coach on his way from Dumfries to Edinburgh and a little past the Crook Inn he came to the now famous spot where

> Willie Wastle dwelt on Tweed,
>   The spot they ca'ed it Lincumdoddie,
> Willie was a wabster guid,
>   Could stown a clew wi' ony bodie.

WAMPHRAY   *Horse Thief's Tower*

The village is tucked away in the hills of Upper Annandale, some six miles south-east of **Moffat**. Its three cascades—The Pot, The Washing Pan and Dubbs Caldron—were favourite haunts for those who took the waters in Moffat's spa and sought the picturesque in the remoter corners of Dumfriesshire.

A clump of trees not far from the church marks the site of Wamphray Tower, held in the 16th century by William Johnstone, the Galliard, whose horse-stealing raid and his death form the theme of the ballad *The Lads of Wamphray*.

WANLOCKHEAD   *Highest Village in Scotland*

If for no other reason than to say you have visited the highest village in Scotland, you will come to Wanlockhead, which straggles beside the road climbing over the Lowther Hills from Lanarkshire to Dumfriesshire. You might also come in search of gold. Gold was mined here 400 years ago and, the geologists tell us, can still be found. But the opening of lead mines late in the 17th century is the real reason for there being any village up here, 1,350 feet above sea level, and its neighbouring village bears the descriptive name of Leadhills.*

There is a tumble-down air about Wanlockhead, an impression of disorder which might have persisted since gold-rush days. Certainly

* See *Glasgow, Kyle and Galloway* volume of *Queen's Scotland*.

the village looks as though the folks who came rushing up here with their bits and pieces dumped them down on any handsbreadth of land which they had reached when their breath gave out. There are cottages at all levels and all angles, many of them stuck bleakly on a bald landscape, but some clustering together in what could be called, for want of a better term, the village street. But the breezy hills are all around, and any little hillock beyond the village will reward us, after a moment's scrambling, with staggering views of Scotland's southern uplands.

In high summer this high landscape glows with colour; the fields are flecked with violets and the cottage plots bloom with the violas for which the village gardeners are famous. The road from Wanlockhead to Mennock and **Sanquhar** in Nithsdale cuts through the defile of the Mennock Pass and this alone is worth the climb to Wanlockhead, for the descent is one of the most impressive in Scotland.

WESTERKIRK   *The Shepherd Boy's Library*

The main road through Eskdale climbs from **Langholm** to **Eskdalemuir** along the right bank of the Esk. But on the other side of the river is another road, one which curls round the foot of the hills from Sorbie to the village of Penpath, in the parish of Westerkirk.

This remote Dumfriesshire village became the owner of the finest library possessed by a rural community. It owed it all to the boy who was born in a Westerkirk shepherd's cottage in 1757 and now rests in Westminster Abbey.

The boy was Thomas Telford. Westerkirk knew him as a cheery youngster. "Laughing Tam" they called him in the days when he helped his widowed mother in these fields. When he was in his teens and apprenticed to a stonemason, a Langholm woman gave him the run of her library, and there, it must be, was born the love of literature that was to stay with Thomas Telford throughout all the years of his great and inspired work as an engineer.

Even when he was an eighteenpence-a-day mason Telford was writing verses for the *Edinburgh Magazine*. His later poem on his native valley, Eskdale, won him Southey's praise; and after the death of Robert Burns there was discovered among the poet's papers a letter from Telford begging Burns, in verse, to write more poems in the vein of the *Cotter's Saturday Night*.

Telford was 23 when he left his native hills to work as a mason in the New Town of Edinburgh. Two years later he was hewing stone for the new Somerset House in London. By now "Laughing Tam" had grown up, but still he was of a notably happy friendly disposition, and all who met him fell in love with him. Sir William Pulteney, owner of Westerhall, the mansion near Penpath, and husband of the great heiress, niece of the Earl of Bath, gave Telford his first big job, the alteration of Shrewsbury Castle. This led him eventually to his appointment as architect of the Ellesmere Canal, whose two great aqueducts have been acknowledged as "among the boldest efforts of human invention in modern times".

From then on it was triumph after triumph for Telford—the 18-year project of the "Caledonian Canal", which changed the face and life of the Highlands; harbours at Wick, Aberdeen, Peterhead, Banff and Leith; the Gotha Canal, linking the Baltic and the North Sea, which won him a Swedish knighthood; and famous bridges, including Edinburgh's Dean Bridge.

We seem, in our glance at the peaks of a brilliant man's career, to have come a far way from the Border parish of Westerkirk. But "Laughing Tam" never forgot his native heath, and after his death in 1834 it was found that he had made a bequest "to the minister of Westerkirk in trust for the parish library". Within twenty-six years the annual income from the Telford bequest had provided so many books that the folk of Westerkirk subscribed to build a library to hold them.

WEST LINTON   *Pride in Stone*

The village sits, like its neighbour **Carlops,** in the shadow of the Pentland Hills. Some of it lies on the main road to Edinburgh, but the centre of it is down a hill out of sight of that highway. There West Linton's short main street curves on to a grassy stretch beside the amber waters of the Lyne, and there, islanded in its area of crisp green turf, stands the church.

West Linton is a tranquil genteel place, much favoured as a residential area for well-to-do Edinburgh folk, and it immediately impresses us as stout and cleanly built. Building, and indeed everything to do with the mason's craft, has in fact been West Linton's speciality for centuries. Pride in such things is still evident. Way up on the road climbing to the Pentland heights through the woodlands beside the Lyne we find this pride demonstrated on a wall beside the road. There a carved stone declares: "This dyke was the work of

Traquair   The Stuart Mansion

Traquair   A Farm Scene

The Tweed   **Near Bemersyde**

James Fleming of West Linton—1948". It is delightful in this day and age to find such pride in local craftsmanship.

The village's communal pride in its work is witnessed by the preservation of West Linton carved stones in the walls of the main street. West Linton stonecutters, using stone from Deepsykehead quarries, were famous as carvers of gravestones. In the 17th century there was a notable West Linton stone carver, James Gifford. He it was who carved a statue of his wife to put upon the village pump.

In the West Linton churchyard was once a marble slab to the memory of James Oswald of Spittals which bore this invitation:

> This marble table, sitting at which I have often cultivated good living, I have desired to be placed over me when dead. Stop, traveller, whoever thou art; here thou mayest recline, and, if the means are at hand, mayest enjoy this table as I formerly did. If thou doest so in the right and proper way, thou wilt neither desecrate the monument nor offend my manes. Farewell.

Unfortunately this hospitable tombstone was carried off and sold 100 years ago.

Even the women of West Linton, it seems, devoted themselves to carving, for the galleries and windows and pulpit of the parish church were carved by them; one of those so busying herself being daughter of Sir William Fergusson, surgeon to Queen Victoria.

In the southern reaches of the parish is lovely Mendick Hill, a hill which, because of its isolation, looks much higher than its 1,450 feet, and, seen from the west, by Dunsyre, well deserves its description of "miniature Matterhorn".

WESTRUTHER *Country of the Last Wolf*

A colourful derivation suggested for the name of this parish is "wolf-struther", "marshland infested with wolves", and natives talk of the last wolf in all Scotland, roaming this very parish, and perhaps killing among its victims the Lady of Gamelshiel Tower, a dozen miles to the north, in the wild moor country around Cranshaws. The end of this last wolf in Scotland came in no epic struggle, no Twilight of the Wolves, no lupine Gotterdammerung: it was dispatched on the narrow bridge across the Blakeha' Burn by an old wifie wielding a frying-pan.

The more prosaic derive the parish name simply from West-struther, "marshland to the west", in relation to Dogden Moss, a stretch of swamp to the east. You may take your choice. But it seems certain that all this countryside was at one time peopled with every kind of creature: witness other place-names in the parish, Raecleugh, Hindside, Hartlaw, Harelaw.

> *There's hart and hind and daw and raw,*
> *And of a wilde bestis grete plentie,*

says the *Sang of the Outlaw Murray*.

At Harelaw the wretched Sir John Cope and his defeated dragoons were seen in full flight for the south after the Battle of Prestonpans. That flight will never be forgotten as long as there are pipes and drums to keep it alive by beating out the mocking ballad *Hey, Johnnie Cope, are ye wauken yet?* When Sir John reached Berwick, he was received by Lord Mark Ker, of the Lothian family, with the well-known sarcasm "that he believed he was the first General in Europe to bring the first tidings of his own defeat".

> *Says the Berwickers unto Sir John;*
> *"O what's become o' all your men?"*
> *"In faith", says he, "I dinna ken,*
> *I left them a' this morning!"*

On this same Harelaw Moor there is a lovely spot marked on the map as *Well* (*chalybeate*), but round and about among the country people—who like lovely names for lovely places—it is known as The Virtue Well, and even in the height of summer it runs cold and clear. It has never been exploited. No pump-rooms are there. No winter gardens. No gouty irritable old gentlemen or bulgy-eyed lap-dogs. But wise, quiet people come and drink its mineral wholesomeness, and go away the better for it.

Every year for long there came to it one of the best-loved ladies in the whole of Berwickshire, the Lady John Scott, who has been dead now for more than half a century, but whose memory is as fresh as the waters of the Virtue Well. She grew up in Spottiswoode House (now demolished), and married Lord John Scott, second son of the fourth Duke of Buccleuch. She was interested in all country things, fond of old times and old ways and old folk. She is often called the authoress of *Annie Laurie*, but it was the tune she wrote, and put it to the verses written by Douglas of Fingland to Anne, daughter of Sir Robert Laurie of Maxwelton. Lady Scott, an eager antiquarian, excavated the Mutiny Stones on Byrecleugh Ridge in Longformacus parish, though without finding the treasure said to be there. She dug into Clacharie Cairn in Lauder parish, discovering six cists and a rudely ornamented clay urn containing burnt bones.

Twinlaw Cairns in Westruther she excavated, too, but found little to settle the vexed question of their origin. These two circular cairns, of rough whinstones and some five feet high, are conspicuous landmarks on the summit of Twinlaw, 1,466 feet above the sea, near the Watch Water, which we saw in the parish of Longformacus being harnessed to Berwick's water supply. They are said to commemorate a battle in which two brothers were leaders of the opposing armies and fought to the death before the tragic fratricide was revealed. Then soldiers of both armies formed lines to the Watch Water from the summit of the hill, and passed up one by one the stones which went to form the Twinlaw Cairns. Edgar, tradition says, was the name of the two brothers: Wedderlie House belonged to the family of Edgar from the 14th to the 18th century, and the Edgar Burn still flows between Twinlaw and lonely ruined Evelaw Tower.

Wedderlie House, still inhabited, is a fine small three-storeyed mansion-house, part of it being an early 17th-century keep, with later additions to the east. Of Spottiswoode House the two lodges survive, an arresting sight along the road with high crenellated walls holding clocks above their gables.

Bassendean House has for long been a seat of the Homes, and the old church of Bassendean is still used as the Homes' burial-place. There were once chapels at Bassendean, Spottiswoode and Wedderlie. The walls of Bassendean chapel still stand, roofless and crumbling, 300 yards south-east of Bassendean House, but nothing remains of the other two. Lady John Scott excavated the remains of a fort just north of Spottiswoode House and also a Crannog at Whiteburn Moss, but with little result. She was buried on 16th March, 1900, beneath the floor of the old church at Westruther, a picturesque and much overgrown ruin a few yards from the present-day church of Westruther, built about 1850.

Detached, irrelevant note: In the year 1800 tea was such a rarity in these parts that there existed only three tea-kettles in the whole parish, one at Spottiswoode, one at Wedderlie, and one at the Manse.

Maggie's June Snowball

It was, finally, a Westruther girl, Margaret Lylestone, who married Thomas Hardie of Tollishill, a farm in **Lauder,** and so became the heroine of the famous story of *Midside Maggie* or *The Bannock of Tollishill.* When Hardie, tenant of the notorious Duke of Lauderdale (1616–82), could not pay his rent, Maggie betook herself to Thirlestane Castle, and so winsomely did she plead her case that the Duke agreed to waive the year's rent if she promised to bring him a snowball in June. In a deep cave in Tollishill she buried her ball of snow, hid it far down under stones and tended it daily. When June came round, the Hardies took their snowball to the Duke, who kept his word and let them off their rent. Little did he know how handsomely his generosity was to be repaid. Not long after, at the Battle of Worcester, he was taken prisoner, and lay for years in a London gaol.

Meanwhile the farm back home at Tollishill prospers and Maggie lays by a store of golden coins. At last she bakes a bannock, and making her way to London, sings *Leader Haughs and Yarrow* ever and anon in her sweet country voice until she gains admittance to the prisoner in his cell. With beating heart and air serene, she cries: "Come, pree the bannock!" The scone reveals its value, and ere long the Lauderdale release is purchased.

In 1660, when the Duke returned to Thirlestane, he brought to Maggie at Tollishill a silver girdle, a lovely and precious thing, which was handed down from one generation to the next, until in 1897 it was gifted to the Scottish National Museum of Antiquities in Queen Street, Edinburgh. And there it can be seen today.

WHITSOME   *The Eager Congregation*

Whitsome is made up of two ancient parishes, Whitsome and Hilton, united in 1735. Nothing remains of the old church of Whitsome where such crowds flocked to hear the preaching of the well-loved Thomas Boston that the little church could not contain them, and some zealous ones climbed on to the thatched roof and tore strips off it that they might see the great preacher as well as hear him.

Hilton's old church has left some low green mounds to indicate its site and size. A rhyme still exists which uses Hilton church as a kind of gauge of measurement.

> *This is like Hilton kirk—*
> *It's baith narrow and mirk,*
> *And can only haud its ain parish folk.*

YARROW

Wilson's *Tales of the Borders* includes *The Whitsome Tragedy*, in which a father and son, unknown to each other, meet in mortal combat at Whitsome Fair. Because of that bloodshed the Fair has been prohibited ever since.

YARROW   *River of Mystery*

There is a mystery about the Vale of Yarrow. From Yarrow's source at **St Mary's Loch** to its meeting with Ettrick Water near Selkirk it is only 14 miles. Yet no 14 miles in all Scotland is richer in memories, legends and romance. There's the mystery.

Wordsworth tried to shrug it off. He tried to see Yarrow as just another stream flowing between bare Ettrick hills.

> *What's Yarrow but a river bare,*
> *That glides the dark hills under?*
> *There are a thousand such elsewhere*
> *As worthy of your wonder.*

But there are not a thousand such elsewhere. Wordsworth, who wrote those lines on his first visit, found that out later; as countless others have found it out since. He visited Yarrow again, following its whole course with James Hogg as his guide. And yet again, this time with Scott. And there happened to Wordsworth what happens to all of us, to people far less sensitive and less imaginative than a poet: the sweet mystery of Yarrow won him over. Walk down this vale—or, if you travel on wheels, for glory's sake forget your haste and come down slowly—and all the way from its beginnings up there within "the inner sanctuary of the whole Scottish Border" to Ettrick you will be under the spell of Yarrow.

The valley is so rich in features of outstanding interest that in this volume we have had to isolate them into chapters on their own, and we beg you to seek out those chapters—on **Bowhill** and its neighbouring Newark Castle; on **Philiphaugh** for the account of that cruel slaughter and the jolly footba' match at Carterhaugh; and on **St Mary's Loch** for the story of James Hogg, shepherd of Yarrow's hills.

The upper half of the valley is the Yarrow of the ballads. The oldest surviving ballad, *The Dowie Dens o' Yarrow*, recounts the murder of Walter Scott, third son of Robert of Thirlestane, by his brother-in-law, John Scott of Tushielaw. The scene of the combat might have been at Deuchar beyond Yarrow Kirk on a stretch of land known as Annan Street, where massive stones are pointed out as the monuments to the dead, but are actually much older.

> But in the glen strove armed men;
> They've wrought me dule and sorrow;
> They've slain—the comeliest knight they've slain—
> He bleeding lies on Yarrow.

> She kissed his cheek, she kaimed his hair,
> She searched his wounds all through;
> She kissed them, till her lips grew red,
> On the dowie houms of Yarrow.

The 16th-century *Willie's rare, and Willie's fair*; Hamilton of Bangour's *Busk ye, busk ye, my bonny, bonny bride*; John Logan's *Braes of Yarrow*; Wordsworth, Scott, Hogg, "Christopher North", Riddell and J. B. Selkirk, all sing of Yarrow.

Yarrow's 17th-century church, destroyed by fire in 1922, has been finely restored. Nearby is the Broken Bridge, beloved by artists, and the old Deuchar Bridge; above the burn are traces of Deuchar Tower. From Yarrow Kirk a bridle-path climbs through a dip in the hills over to Ettrick Valley by way of the Witchie Knowe and Kirkhope Tower.* At Whitefield, above Yarrow Kirk, is the ancient Liberalis stone, commemorating the two sons of Liberalis who died in the battle of Yarrow, A.D. 592

Down the valley from Yarrow village is Foulshiels, birthplace of Mungo Park. Here is Yarrow's deep pool, where Scott found Park plunging one stone after another into the water and anxiously watching the bubbles.

"This appears," said Scott, "but an idle amusement for one who has seen so much adventure."

"Not so idle, perhaps, as you suppose," answered Mungo. "This was the way I used to ascertain the depth of a river in Africa." He was then planning his second and last journey.

YETHOLM   *"Old Meg she was a Gipsy"*

The alphabet decides that we end our Border volume here at Yetholm. We could not have chosen better. For here we are, back on the very frontier, and from the pastoral country around Kirk

* See Philiphaugh chapter.

Yetholm and Town Yetholm we can gaze over the Border to England's lovely Cheviots.

The two Yetholms are pretty tranquil villages. They do not seem to mourn very much the many things they have lost. So many things! Eighty years ago Francis Groome made a list of their losses. The Yetholms, he recorded, had lost their busy weekly market. They had lost the celebrity of their Fastern E'en games. They had lost the profitable smuggling of Scots whisky, which once kept a fifth of their inhabitants employed in deals valued at up to £20,000 a year.

And they had even lost their gipsies. Yes, even the gipsies have gone, though we can still see the home of Esther Faa Blythe, last Queen of the Gipsies. The cottage is still known as the "Palace". The great crowd that gathered here in 1883 to see Esther buried witnessed the end of the gipsy dynasty. Queen Esther had lived to see the disappearance of her kingdom, and she left on record her tart impressions of Yetholm: "Sae mingle-mangle that ane micht think it was either built on a dark nicht or sawn on a windy ane." And she described the inhabitants as "maistly Irish, and nane o' my seed, breed and generation".

No one knows when the gipsies first came into Scotland and settled in Yetholm, but as long ago as the 15th century official papers mention bands of strange vagrants infiltrating from over the Border, and in 1505 James IV signed a letter of commendation to the King of Denmark on behalf of one "Anthonius Gagino, Count of Little Egypt". A writ of James V in 1540 refers to "Johnne Faw, lord and erle of Litill Egypt". He was one of the gipsy "royal house" of Faa who held court at Yetholm, and lorded it over these tribes who wandered through the Border country, bewildering the natives with their tribal customs and dignities and titles of "lords and erles".

The most illustrious gipsy of all, Jean Gordon, who was to become the Meg Merrilies of Scott and Keats, was born in Yetholm. Throughout his life Scott was fascinated by the gipsies and their romantic tribal life. He was kind to them even when sitting in udgment on them as a Sheriff. Around Earlston and Mellerstain as a boy he saw them often encamped, and one day he met Jean Gordon's grand-daughter, Madge—six foot of tanned Amazonian gipsy lass wearing her bonnet of straw and "dressed in a long red cloak, who commenced acquaintance by giving me an apple, but whom, nevertheless, I looked on with much awe."

"Meg Merrilies" married into the royal house, becoming wife of Patrick Faa. By him she had four sons. Three of them, and their wives, were all hanged for sheep-stealing at Jedburgh in 1730. Meg's other son was murdered by a gipsy. Meg's husband was transported for fire-raising.

And she herself came to a bitter but valiant end when she went begging into Carlisle soon after the 1745 Rebellion. She was an old woman then, but the sight of Jacobite heads spiked on the top of Scotchgate fired her to outspoken contempt for the House of Hanover. In that ever-fascinating book on Scott's characters, *The Scott Originals*, W. S. Crockett tells what happened then.

> Rascaldom gathered thick about her, and the poor old gipsy, without a friend either to support or rescue her, was mercilessly pelted with mud and stones. Those who came within her grasp, indeed, paid for their forwardness, for Jean was a stout woman still, and not easily "dauntered". But her assailants succeeded in dragging her down the street and plunged her headlong into the river. As often as she got her head above water, she shouted, "Up wi Charlie yet!" and as long as she had voice left, she continued to exclaim, "Charlie yet! Charlie yet!" till she was left to her fate. Strange to say, she managed to crawl to the side and take shelter under a hedge, where next morning she was found dead, exhaustion and exposure having brought about her end.

Surely more tragic than the execution of Jacobite nobility and lairds is that drowning of a poor old gipsy woman moved to courageous crazy defiance in the face of death by nothing more than a blind loyalty to a Prince? If that story—and the stories of other humble folk who suffered in his name—ever reached Prince Charles Edward, how surprising it is that a warrior Prince could slacken off into futility and drift disreputably to so sickly an end.

Well, with Yetholm's gipsies and Crockett's story of the death of Meg Merrilies we have come, it seems, to Carlisle, and a fitting close to our volume will be the song Meg sang as she defied the English crowd:

> *To wanton me, to wanton me,*
> *Ken ye what maist wad wanton me?*
> *To see King George hung up at Rome,*
> *To see King Jamie croon'd at Scone,*
> *To see England taxed and Scotland free:*
> *This is what maist wad wanton me.*

YETHOLM

But to daunton me, to daunton me,
This is what sair does daunton me:
To see an ill-faur'd German loon
Keep wrangfu' haud o' Scotland's croon,
And a' laid low that high should be:
This is what sair doth daunton me.

THE END

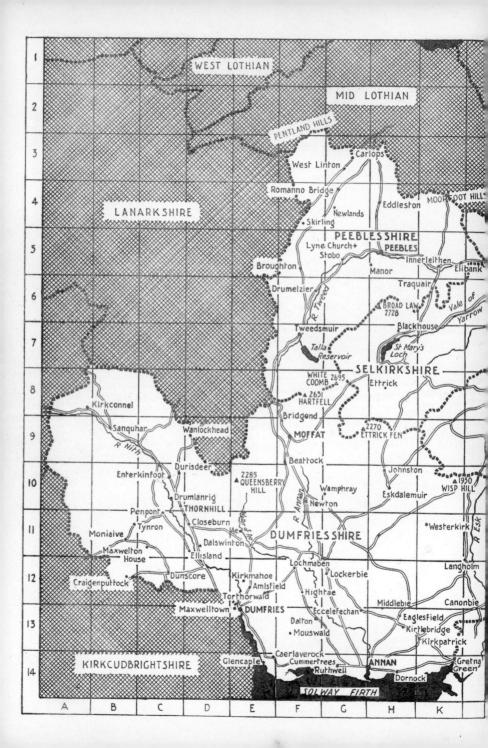

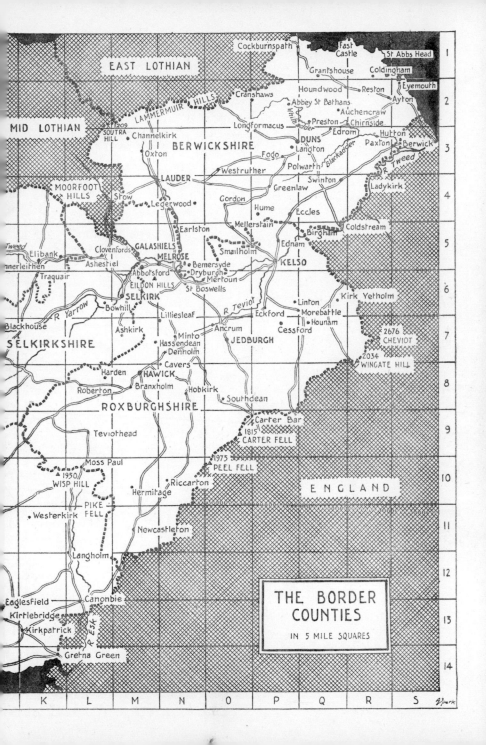

THE BORDER
COUNTIES

IN 5 MILE SQUARES

INDEX

NOTE: This is a master-index to all the places, people and items of interest written about in this book.

PLACE-NAMES—Names of places in the area covered by the volume are printed in **heavier type**. When such names are printed in CAPITALS it indicates that a separate article is devoted to that place, in which case the page-number first given is the number of the page on which that article begins. The other page-numbers (after the map-reference) indicate mention of that place in other articles in this volume.

MAP-REFERENCES—These, printed in parentheses, refer to the maps on preceding pages.

A

ABBEY ST BATHANS, 5, (P-2) 68, 179

ABBOTSFORD, 6, (M-5) 3, 21, 24, 27, 49, 97, 99, 209

Abide with me (Lyte), 82

Adams, architects, 3, 63, 116, 136, 154–5, 162

Admirable Crichton, 191

AE, Forest of, River of, 14, 15 (E-11)

Aikieside, Cockburnspath, 39

Aikman, William, artist, 155

Ainslie, Rachel and Robert, 66, 67

Aird, Thomas, poet, journalist, 63

Aitken, Margaret (Mrs Carlyle), 79

Aitken, Rev. Dr, Minto, 160

Albany, Duke of, 30, 135

Ale, Water of, 16, 22, 91, 146

Alexander I, 205

Alexander II, 132, 157

Alexander III, 15, 76, 123, 132

Allanbank, Allanton, 83, 84

Allerly, Gattonside, 158

Alloway, Ayrshire, 12

Alnwick, Northumberland, 55

Altrieve, Yarrow, 188

AMISFIELD, 15, (E-12)

ANCRUM, 16, (O-7)

Anderson, Sir Rowand, 120

Angus, Earls of, 16, 141

ANNAN, 17, (H-14) 46, 50, 66, 183

Annan, River, 47, 150, 160, 161

Annandale, 2, 147–9, 165, 201, 210

Anne, Queen, 16, 26

Applin Cross, Coldingham, 41

Aquinas, Thomas, 68

Archers, Royal Company of, 173, 195

Argyll, Duke of, 88

Arkleton Hill, 168

Armstrong, Johnnie, freebooter, 31, 89, 138, 189, 201

Armstrongs, 89, 138, 170, 171

Arnott, Dr Archibald, 80

Arran, Earl of, 47

ASHIESTIEL, 20, (L-5) 7

ASHKIRK, 22, (M-7)

Athole, Duke of, 88

Auchen Castle, 165

AUCHENCRAW (Edincraw), **22** (Q-2) 180

Auldgirth, Dunscore, 72

Auld Quay, The—see Glencaple

Austen, Jane, 154

Australia, 48, 110

AYTON, 22, (R-2) 41, 90

Aytoun, William, writer, 187

B

Bachup, Tobias, builder, 63

Badenoch, Lord of ("The Red Comyn"), 61

Ballantynes, James and John, 129

Balliol, John, 59, 63

Balmaclellan, Galloway, 30

Balmoral, 10, 205

Bankend, Caerlaverock, 30

Bannockburn, 62, 121

Barnhill, 160

Barrie, Sir James M., 60, 61

Barry, Sir Charles, 26

du Barry, Mme, 26

INDEX

INDEX

Deloraine Burn, 33
DENHOLM, 49, (N-7) 34, 104, 108, 159
Derby, 54, 64
Deuchar, Yarrow, 218
Devil's Reef Tub, 165, 181, 208, 210
Devorgilla, Lady, 59, 61
Dogden Moss, 213
Don Quixote, 71
DORNOCK, 50, (H-14)
Douglases, 16, 18, 25–6, 34, 47, 52–4, 63, 74–6, 104, 106, 107, 112, 135, 141, 149, 157, 169, 173, 190, 196, 199, 202–4, 209
Douglas, William, of Fingland, 154, 214
Douglas Burn, 25
Douglas Tragedy, The, 25
Dowie Dens of Yarrow, The, 217
Drakemire, 180
Dream of the Rood (Caedmon), 183
Drochil Castle, 171
DRUMELZIER, 51, (F-6) 33
DRUMLANRIG, 52, (C-10) 3, 12, 76, 94, 169, 190, 202, 205
Drumlanrig, Lord, 74
DRYBURGH, 54, (N-6) 2, 3, 24, 85, 119, 158, 186
Dryfe, River, Sands, 150
Drygrange, 77
DRYHOPE TOWER, 57, 189, 190
Dumbarton Castle, 111
Dumcrieff, Moffat, 164
DUMFRIES, 58, (E-13) 2, 3, 4, 15, 17, 28, 89, 99, 104, 133, 148, 149, 163, 164, 166, 185, 202, 204, 210
Dunbar, 5, 40, 114, 139, 151, 186
Dunbar, Earls and Countess of, 5, 43, 80, 180
Duncan, Rev. Henry, Ruthwell, 183
Dunglas, 67
DUNS, 66, (P-3) 22, 84, 85, 95, 101, 139, 180
Duns Scotus, John, 68
DUNSCORE, 69, (C-12) 4, 154, 203
Dunsyre, Lanarkshire, 213
Durham Cathedral, 35
DURISDEER, 74, (C-10) 204
Dye Water, 45, 151

E

Eaglesfield, (H-13) 159
EARLSTON, 76, (N-5) 102, 158, 178, 219

East Nisbet, Edrom, 83
ECCLEFECHAN, 78, (S-13) 47, 134, 135
ECCLES, 80, (P-4)
ECKFORD, 81, (P-6)
EDDLESTON, 81, (H-4)
Eden Water, 82
Edgar, King of Scots, 40
Edgars of Wedderlie, 215
Edgeworth, Maria, 13
Edie Ochiltree (*The Antiquary*)—see Gemmels, Andrew
Edinburgh, 13, 28, 31, 35, 36, 58, 101, 102, 114, 125, 154–5, 212—
 Blacklock, Dr Thomas, 18
 Bonar, Horatius, 128
 Borderers' Association, 76
 Canongate, 52
 Castle, 149, 204
 Castle Street, 88
 Constables' Bookshop, 49
 Corstorphine Parish Church, 136
 Dean Bridge, 212
 Grassmarket, 144
 Greyfriars, 143
 Heriot's Hospital, 143
 High Court, 124
 Hogg, James, 88
 Holyroodhouse, 143, 158
 James V, 88
 Mary Queen of Scots, 78
 National Museum of Antiquities, 85, 114, 158, 159, 216
 National Portrait Gallery, 143
 National War Memorial, 198
 Netherbow, 143
 Queensberry House, 52, 74
 Royal Burgh, 132
 Royal High School, 71, 128
 Royal Science Museum, 183
 Scott, Adam, 89
 Scott, Sir Walter, 9, 98
 Souters o' Selkirk, 192
 Talla Reservoir, 209
Edincraw—see Auchencraw
Edington Castle, 37
Edinshall Broch, 68
EDNAM, 82, (P-5)
EDROM, 83, (Q-3), 139
Edward I, 29, 62, 148
Edward II, 55, 157
Edward, Prince of Wales, 25
Eildon, Lord, 44
EILDON HILLS, 85, (M-6) 1, 6, 124, 198

INDEX

INDEX

INDEX

Home, Mrs Margaret, Lady Billie, 92, 179
"Hotspur", Harry Percy, Earl of Northumberland, 34, 199
HOUNAM, 113, (Q-7)
HOUNDWOOD, 113, (Q-2)
Howburn Farm, Houndwood, 114
Howe, James, artist, 197
HUME, 114, (P-4) 100, 116
Hume, David, philosopher, 37, 161
Hume, Grizell, 145, 155, 179
Hume, Sir Patrick, 1st Earl of Marchmont, 145, 155, 179
Hundalee Mill, 124
Hunter, John, Covenanter, 209
Hunter, William, of Cockrune, 72
Huntly Burn, 6, 49, 76
HUTTON, 115, (R-3)
Hutton, John, 30

I

Inchcape, Earl of, 38
INNERLEITHEN, 117, (K-5)
Irving, Edward, 18
Irving, Washington, 8, 13
Irvings of Bonshaw, 135
Isle Tower, 73

J

James I, 30, 57, 174
James II, 57, 127, 132
James III, 127, 132, 141
James IV, 44, 68, 78, 96, 136, 142, 149, 167, 194, 219
James V, 15, 17, 51, 88, 189, 199, 201, 219
James VI, 39, 45, 47, 51, 58, 65, 68, 92, 93, 112, 166, 190, 191, 204, 207
James VII, 190
"James VIII", the Old Pretender, 127, 220
Janssen, artist, 143
Jardines, 18, 150
JEDBURGH, 117 (O-7) 2, 3, 16, 32, 49, 55, 56, 78, 85, 89, 93, 103, 112, 220
Jed, Forest of, 124
Jed Water, 32, 93, 118, 123
Jock o' Hazeldean, 105
Jock's Shoulder, 86
Johnson, Dr Samuel, 163
Johnstones, 150, 166, 210
Jones, Paul, 65

K

Kale Water, 167
Kames, 80
Kames, Lord (Henry Home), 80, 89
Katie's Pool, Enterkin Pass, 86
Keats, John, 219
Keir Hills, 65, 175
Kell Water, 45
KELSO, 124, (P-5) 2, 3, 43, 55, 67, 85, 94, 95, 113, 119, 146, 151, 154, 186, 198
Kelso Chronicle, 127
Kelte's Linn, 85–6
Kemp, George Meikle, architect, 82
Kenmure, Viscount, 66, 168
Kent, the late Duke of, 121–2
Kers, 6, 34, 35, 84, 93, 119, 120, 121, 124, 144, 145, 186, 187, 214
Kilbucho, 28
Killmade Water, 45
Kilmarnock edition (Burns), 19
King's Pool, Eskdalemuir, 86
Kinmount, 47
Kinmount Willie, 31
Kinnel, River, 14, 15
Kinross House, Fife, 143, 158
Kipford, 31
Kirkbank, Eckford, 81
Kirkbride, 85
Kirkconnel, 135, (A-8) 159, 192
Kirkcudbright, Moniaive, 166
Kirkhope, 33, 178, 218
KIRKMAHOE, 133, (E-12)
KIRKPATRICK-FLEMING, 134
Kirkpatrick, Sir Roger, 62, 204
Kirkton in Ewes, 89
Kirkwood, E. H., artist, 144
KIRTLEBRIDGE, 135, (H-13)
Kirtle Water, 134, 135
Knox, John, 126, 158

L

LADYKIRK, 136, (R-4)
Lag, Tower of, 71
Laggan Burn, 71–3
Laidlaw, William, 11, 26, 207
Lamancha (Romanno), 183
Lamberton, 167
Lamb Hill, Lockerbie, 149
Lammermoors, (N-2) 1, 5, 39, 45, 85, 151, 198
Landheads, 20
Lang, Andrew, poet, romancer, 5, 179, 194

232

INDEX

LANGHOLM, 137, (K-11) 31, 89, 102, 110, 167, 168, 201, 211
Langlee, 99
LANGTON, 139, (P-3) 68
Langton Burn, 85
Lasswade, Midlothian, 38
LAUDER, 140, (M-4) 35, 102, 146, 178, 215
Lauderdale, 35, 78, 140, 144
Lauderdales (Maitland), 52, 142, 143, 216
Laurie, Annie, 3, 73, 154, 214
Laurie, Sir Robert, of Maxwelton, 72–3, 214
Leadervale, 77
Leader Water, 35, 76, 77, 146
Leadhills, Lanarkshire, 210
Learmont, Sir Thomas—see Thomas the Rhymer
Lees Haugh, Coldstream, 43
Leet, River, 43, 80
LEGERWOOD, 144, (N-4)
Leithen Water, 117
Leitholm Peel, 80
Lely, Sir Peter, 143
Lennel, 44–5
Lennoxes, 30, 56
Leslie, General Sir David, 67, 175, 176, 194, 205
Leyden, John, 34, 38, 49, 111
Liddel Water, 31, 170
Liddesdale, 33, 85, 110–12, 170, 199, 201
Lilliard's Edge, 16
LILLIESLEAF, 146, (N-7) 108
Lincluden Abbey, Galloway, 65
Lincumdoddie, 210
Lindean, 196
Lindisfarne, Bishop of, 94
Linglie Hill, 33
Linlithgow, West Lothian, 10, 30, 176
Linnaeus, Carolus, botanist, 51
Lintalee, 124
Linthill, 91
LINTON, 146, (P-6)
Littledean, Maxton, 186
Lloyd George, Earl, 161
Locharbriggs, Lochar Moss, Water, 15, 29, 168, 204
Loch Fell, 161
Loch Leven Castle, Fife, 10
LOCHMABEN, 147, 184, 204, (F-12)
Lochwood Tower, 166
LOCKERBIE, 149 (G-12), 79, 159

Lockerwood, 185
Lockhart, John Gibson, 8, 11, 12, 14, 21, 27, 34, 87, 88
Logan, John, of Restalrig, 92
London—
    Bridge, 59
    Great Palace Yard, 191
    Kenwood, Hampstead, 155
    Queensberry, Duchess of, 75
    Science Museum, 134, 174
    Somerset House, 212
    Thames, 128
    Waterloo Bridge, 128
    Westminster Abbey, 159, 211
    Westminster Hall, 191
LONGFORMACUS, 151, (P-3) 214
Lorimer, Sir Robert, 97, 194
Lowes, Loch o' the, 58, 187, 189, 190
Lowther Hills, 15, 86, 190, 210
Lukup, William, Drumlanrig, 76
Lundie, Mary, hymnwriter, 128
Lyne, River, 171, 182, 212
Lyte, Henry Francis, hymn-writer, 82

M

Macadam, John Louden, 164
MacDiarmid, Hugh (C. M. Grieve), poet, 4, 137
Macdonald, Flora, 10
McGall's Brig, Edrom, 84
MacKenzie, William Forbes, 81
Mackenzies of Newbie, 18
Mackie, R. L., historian, 141
McMichael, Daniel, Covenanter, 75
Macmillan, Kilpatrick, 65, 175
McMurdo, John, 53
Macpherson, James, "Ossian", 162
Magdalenhall, Mertoun, 158
Maid of Norway—see Margaret, Princess
Mair, Rev. Dr William, Earlston, 77
Maitland—see Lauderdales
Maitlands of Lethington, 146
Malcolm II, 24
Malcolm IV, 117
Malcolms of Burnfoot, 137
Mangerton, 171
MANOR, 152, (H-5)
Manuel, Mary, Allanton, 84
Marchmont, 1st Earl of, 145, 155, 179
Marchmont, last Earl of, 114
Marcus, canon of Dryburgh, 57
Margaret, Princess of Scotland (Maid of Norway), 25

INDEX

Northumberland, 1, 27, 32, 34, 44, 55, 115, 167, 183, 199
Northumberland, Earls of (Percy), 27, 34, 199
Norwegians in Dumfries, 64
Novodamus, Charter of, 17
Nuns' Walk, Coldstream, 43

O

Oakwood Tower, 178
Ochiltree, 145
Old Cambus (Auldcambus), 39, 40, 186
Old Mortality (Robert Paterson), 30, 48, 65, 99, 110
"Old Q", William Douglas, 4th Duke of Queensberry ("Degenerate Douglas"), 169, 173
Oliver Castle, Dod, House, 209
Orange, Mary, Princess of, 30
Orange, William, Prince of, 30
Original Secession Church, 36
"Ossian"—see Macpherson, James
Otterburn, 34, 106, 199
Overbie, 86, 159
Oxford and Asquith, Margot (Tennant), Countess of, 207
Oxton, Channelkirk, (M-3) 35

P

Pappert-law, 88
Park, Mungo, explorer, 153, 174, 193, 218
Partanhall, 23
Paterson, J. Wilson, architect, 120
Paterson, Robert (Old Mortality), 30, 48, 65, 99, 110
Paterson, William, founder, Bank of England, 16
Paterson, Very Rev. Dr W. P., 198
Patino, Isabel, 103
Paton, John Gibson, missionary, 204
Paxton, (S-3) 91, 115–16
"Pearlin Jean", Edrom, 83
Pease Bay, 38
Peden, William, Covenanter, 50
PEEBLES, 171, (H-5) 2, 33, 58, 81, 152, 153, 168
Peel, John, 104
Peel, The, 22
Penmanshiel, 39
Pennycuik, Dr Alexander, 182
PENPONT, 175, (C-11) 75

Pentland Hills, 32, 81, 198, 212
Penton Linns, 31
Peter Pan (Barrie), 61
Pettycurwick, St Abbs, 185
PHILIPHAUGH, 175, 33, 194, 205, 217
Picts, 16, 32, 86, 151
Picts' Work Ditch—see Catrail
Pike Fell, (L-11) 168
Pink Boy (Reynolds), 26
Pitscottie, Lindsay of, 88
Playfair, W. H., architect, 95, 160
Polmood, 208
POLWARTH, 178, (P-3) 102, 145, 155
Pope, Alexander, poet, 75
Portmore, 81
Posso, 152
Powfoot, Pow Water, 46
Powsail Burn, 51
PRESTON AND BUNKLE, 179, (Q-2)
Prestonpans, East Lothian, 214
Pringle, Walter, Covenanter, 100, 143
Printonan Hill, 80
Pulteney, Sir William, Westerhall, 212
Purdie, Charles, Boldside, 13
Purdie, Thomas, 21

Q

Queensberry, William Douglas, 1st Duke of, 52, 76, 190
Queensberry, William Douglas, 4th Duke of ("Old Q", "Degenerate Douglas"), 169, 173
Queensberry, Dukes and Earls of, 18, 47, 52, 63, 74–6, 104, 169, 173, 190, 202, 203
Queensbury (Hill), 14, (E-10) 15, 161

R

Racks, 204
Raeburn, Sir Henry, 26
Raecleugh, Westruther, 214
Ramsay, Sir Alexander of Dalhousie, 107, 112
Ramsay, Allan, poet, 28, 32, 58, 153, 190
Ramsays of Dalhousie, 83, 96, 107, 112
Randolph, Thomas, Earl of Moray, 67, 149, 204
Rankin, Rev. William, Legerwood, 144

INDEX

INDEX

Scott, John, botanist, 50
Scott, Lady John, of Spottiswoode, 152, 154, 214
Scott, Mary, "Flower of Yarrow", 57–8, 110, 181, 188–90
Scott, Michael, wizard, 85, 157, 178
Scott, Tom, R.S.A., artist, 106, 193
Scott, Sir Walter—
  Abbotsford, 3, 6–14, 27, 49, 99, 182
  Anne, daughter, 12
  Ashiestiel, 20
  Bailie Nicol Jarvie, 142
  Ballantynes, 129
  "Beardie", great-grandfather, 129
  Black Dwarf, 152–4
  Branxholm, 27
  Bride of Lammermoor, 93
  Broadmeadows, 27
  Buccleuch, Duke of, 26, 54, 178, 195
  Caddonfoot, 38
  Caerlaverock, 30
  Carterhaugh, 177, 195
  Catrail, 33
  Charlotte, wife, 12, 33, 88
  Clovenfords, 38
  Dalkeith, 27, 115, 177
  Dandie Dinmont, 170
  Darnick, 49
  Dogs, 21, 128
  Drumlanrig, 54
  Dryburgh, 56–7
  Earlston, 77
  Eildon Hills, 85
  Ettrick, 38, 87
  Eve of St John, 198
  Ferguson, Adam, 169
  Gemmels, Andrew, 132
  Guy Mannering, 30
  Harden, 58, 181
  Hawick, 106
  Hogg, James, 13, 21, 87, 89, 177
  Jedburgh, 122
  Kelso, 2, 124, 128–9
  Kemp, George Meikle, 82
  Laidlaw, William, 26, 207
  Lasswade, 20, 38
  Lay of the Last Minstrel, 27, 122, 156
  Lennel, 45
  Leyden, John, 38, 50
  Lockhart, J. G., 12, 14, 21, 27, 34
  Marmion, 22, 45, 198
  Matheson, Peter, coachman, 158
  Meg Merrilies, 219
  Melrose Abbey, 156

Scott, Sir Walter—*cont.*
  Merlin, wizard, 33
  Minto, 1st Earl, 159
  Napoleonic invasion, 115
  Neidpath, 169
  Newark Castle, 27
  Newcastleton, 170
  Old Mortality, 30, 48
  Park, Mungo, 218
  Peebles, 173
  Purdie, Charles, 13
  Purdie, Tom, 158
  Raeburn portrait, 26
  Redgauntlet, 165
  Rhymer's Glen, 49
  St Ronan's Well, 117, 173
  Sandyknowe, Smailholm, 198
  "Scott's View", Bemersyde, 24
  Selkirk, 20, 38, 98, 177, 192, 195
  Skene of Rubislaw, 21, 165
  Sophia, daughter, 11, 193
  Southey, Robert, 98
  Teviothead, 201
  Traquair, 206
  Turner, J. M. W., 198
  Tweedsmuir, 209
  Waverley, 206
  Whale, Lancelot, 128
  Wordsworths, 13, 106, 122, 201, 217
  Yarrow, 27, 38, 58, 181, 217, 218
Scott-Moncrieff, George, 162
Scotts, 2, 3, 6, 10–12, 16, 22, 26–7, 33–4, 57–8, 85, 89, 100, 105, 110, 128–9, 152, 154, 157–8, 178, 181, 188–90, 193, 198, 201, 214, 217–18
Scotts of Harden, 22, 57–8, 110, 158, 181, 188–90
SELKIRK, 192, (M-6) 2, 20, 22, 26, 38, 53, 89, 97, 98, 133, 163, 175–7, 186, 195, 217
Selkirk, J. B., poet, 193, 194
Seton, Christopher, 62
Shairp, John Campbell, 207
Shaw, The (Broughton), 28
Shaws, gipsy clan, 182
Sheridan, R. B., playwright, 104
Shirra's Knowe, 22
"Siller Gun", 64
Simprin, Swinton, 68
Sitwell, Sacheverell, 155
Skene, James, of Rubislaw, 21, 165
Skene, Loch 165, 188
Skipmire (Amisfield), 16
SKIRLING, 196, (F-4)
Slitrig Water, 199

237